The Political Economy of Violence against Women

Oxford Studies in Gender and International Relations

Series editors: J. Ann Tickner, University of Southern California, and
Laura Sjoberg, University of Florida

The Political Economy of
Violence against Women

JACQUI TRUE

OXFORD
UNIVERSITY PRESS

OXFORD
UNIVERSITY PRESS

Oxford University Press is a department of the University of Oxford.
It furthers the University's objective of excellence in research,
scholarship, and education by publishing worldwide.

Oxford   New York
Auckland   Cape Town   Dar es Salaam   Hong Kong   Karachi
Kuala Lumpur   Madrid   Melbourne   Mexico City   Nairobi
New Delhi   Shanghai   Taipei   Toronto

With offices in
Argentina   Austria   Brazil   Chile   Czech Republic   France   Greece
Guatemala   Hungary   Italy   Japan   Poland   Portugal   Singapore
South Korea   Switzerland   Thailand   Turkey   Ukraine   Vietnam

Oxford is a registered trade mark of Oxford University Press in the UK and certain other countries.

Published in the United States of America by Oxford University Press
198 Madison Avenue, New York, NY 10016

© Oxford University Press 2012

Library of Congress Cataloging-in-Publication Data
True, Jacqui.
The political economy of violence against women / Jacqui True.
p.   cm.—(Oxford studies in gender and international relations)
ISBN 978-0-19-975592-9 (hardcover : alk. paper)—ISBN 978-0-19-975591-2 (pbk. : alk. paper)
1. Women—Violence against. 2. Sex discrimination against women.
3. Sex crimes. 4. Women and war. 5. Women—Social conditions. I. Title.
HV6250.4.W65T78   2012
362.82'92—dc23   2012001769

Printed in the United States of America
on acid-free paper

To past, present, and future women's human rights defenders in every place—for their bravery and courage, and for never giving up on the aspiration of a dignified life for all women.

CONTENTS

ACKNOWLEDGMENTS

THIS BOOK HAS BEEN a long time in the making. I began research on it while I worked with Yakin Ertürk, the United Nations Special Rapporteur on Violence Against Women, on her report to the Human Rights Council on the political economy of women's human rights in 2008. This was a challenging experience conceptually and empirically. I am indebted to Yakin for her wisdom and vision of bridging political economy and human rights frameworks and for inspiring me to write this book. During that time I surveyed UN member-state parties, scholars, and activists worldwide to see how far and in what ways there was recognition in policy and practice of the political economy roots of violence against women. I learned a lot from the responses to that survey and much appreciated the help I received from many fellow researchers. They opened the door for me to the rich, interdisciplinary body of research, often underappreciated, from all parts of the world on women's economic and social status and their vulnerability to violence. I was also able to see just how far states and other nonstate actors have to go in fulfilling their obligations to end violence against women.

I wish to thank the University of Auckland, New Zealand, for providing the research support that allowed me the time and assistance to write this book, and particularly Professor Barry Reay for encouraging this research agenda while chair of the Faculty of Arts Research Committee. I also want to thank Phillipa Norman, my research assistant in the final stages of writing this book. It was a great joy to work with her and share both some of the troubling findings of this research and its purpose. Phillipa's professionalism and enthusiasm for the project greatly helped me complete it in the context of my imminent move to Australia and Monash University. I presented aspects of this book and its argument at numerous national and international conferences and meetings with scholars, activists, and policymakers, including at expert meetings held at the Office for the High Commissioner for Human Rights (OHCHR) in Geneva. I would like to thank in particular for their feedback, encouragement, and wealth of knowledge Megan Mackenzie; Bina DaCosta; Brooke Ackerly; Ann Tickner; Lisa Prugl; Ann Orford; Hilary Charlesworth; Madeleine Rees; Francoise Roth; Lois Herbert of the Battered Women's Trust, Christchurch; Debbie Hagar; Janet Fanslow of the New Zealand Family Violence Clearinghouse; Jessica Trask, now leading the "Its not OK" campaign at the New Zealand Ministry of Social Development; Don Clark at UNESCAP-Bangkok for sharing research and information on the United Nations' work in the Asia-Pacific; and staff in the International Development Group of the New Zealand Ministry of Foreign Affairs and Trade.

For four years now I have been reading the news daily about incidences of violence against women around the world and wanting to be part of the solution to ending that violence. It is hugely motivating to work on such life-and-death issues from a feminist perspective, which is deeply committed to social and political change. I thank my editor, Angela Chnapko, for believing in this project from the outset, and the team at Oxford University Press for making the publishing process incredibly straightforward and supportive.

Jacqui True
Melbourne

The Political Economy of Violence against Women

CHAPTER 1

From Domestic Violence
to War Crimes

*The Political Economy of Violence
against Women*

Introduction

Eliminating violence against women globally is one of the key struggles and wishes of our age.[1] Just when we thought that things were getting better for women, that gender equality was on the horizon—we have the vote, civil and political rights in most countries, access to higher education, and increasing paid economic opportunities—in many parts of the world, violence against women appears to be becoming both more common and more egregious. Violence against women is a major problem in all countries and worldwide, affecting women in every socioeconomic group and at every life stage. However, poor women belonging to groups such as indigenous peoples, migrants, refugees, human rights defenders, ethnic or racial minorities, those with disabilities, or those living in conflict situations are generally more vulnerable to violence. Although sexual and gender-based violence are defining characteristics of contemporary conflict,[2] violence against women is not limited to wartime or conflict zones; it is highly prevalent in peaceful settings as well. This violence is endemic in locations of apparent economic prosperity and political empowerment such as free trade or special economic areas and new democracies, as well as in conditions of impoverishment and political repression. Why is this? What fuels this violence against women? How can we understand its causes in order to stop the violence and its far-reaching consequences for all our societies? These are the questions that this book seeks to answer.

For women, and for all communities, how to prevent violence against women is literally a life-or-death challenge. In their book *Half the Sky*, Nicholas

Kristof and Sheryl WuDunn (2009, 1) consider the global movement to bring about gender equality to be the key struggle of the twenty-first century: "In the nineteenth century, the central moral challenge was slavery. In the twentieth century, it was the battle against totalitarianism. We believe that in this century the paramount moral challenge will be the struggle for gender equality around the world." That the book reached number eight on the *New York Times* best-seller list suggests that many others, including this author, agree with them.

Some of the apparent uptake in the violence against women largely perpetrated by men has to do with the raised consciousness of the issue. As a child, I thought it strange that the best thing my mother could say of my father was that he didn't hit her! Violence against women in the society I grew up in was largely invisible—hidden inside homes, behind the muffled screams and the daily grind of women's lives. In the context of what I now know about the pervasive and egregious violence against women, this comment no longer seems strange at all. As a result of broader societal awareness and antiviolence campaigns, women today have been increasingly reporting men's violence against them to police and social agencies. They have been naming the patterns of abuse and control that they experience *as violence*. The statistical evidence that shows increasing violence against women is affected by improved reporting systems within countries, and at the international level, improved ways of measuring the prevalence of violence. Some of these systems count incidents of violence as if they are discrete. They do not assess whether or not these incidents add up to a systematic pattern of violence against individual women and women collectively who live in fear of imminent violence. However, this new reporting and measurement have brought into public view a pandemic of violence that has been masked by both women's silence and men's institutional power.

This chapter introduces the reader to the problem of violence against women identified by women's movements, states, and international organizations. It explores prevailing definitions of violence against women, including the increasingly common term *gender-based violence*, and introduces the political economy approach of this book, which seeks to understand the broader context of violence and insecurity experienced by many women. The chapter also reviews the available assessments and data on the prevalence of violence against women and the many methodological and political challenges with measuring this violence globally (Watts and Zimmerman 2002; Geneva Centre 2005). As Ann Tickner (1992) argues in her path-breaking book *Gender in International Relations*, when we see the world from the perspective of women's experiences of insecurity rather than the security agendas of states, we can begin to appreciate the multidimensional continuum of violence. That continuum extends from violence in the home, to the structural violence of poverty, to the ecological violence associated with the depletion of our planetary resources and natural disasters, to the violence of war and its aftermath, which has conventionally been the exclusive focus of "security studies."

With this gender perspective on violence, it is possible to see that even though most violence against women is perpetrated by men, it is the gendered social and economic inequalities between women and men that make women most vulnerable to violence and abuse in whatever context. That is to say, it is not just poverty that heightens women's vulnerability to violence; it is women's impoverished situation relative to men that is at the root of violence. Thus, much of the violence against women is gender based, and "gender inequalities are a form of violence that contributes to the insecurity of all individuals" (Tickner 1995, 48). However, this book goes further than this. It argues that the gendered inequalities that fuel the violence against women are rooted in structures and processes of political economy that are increasingly globalized.

What Is the Problem?

very interesting

Nowhere in the world do women share equal social and economic rights with men or have the same access as men to productive resources.[3] Economic globalization and development are creating new challenges for women's rights, as well as some new opportunities for advancing women's economic independence and gender equality. The proliferation of armed conflicts, often caused by struggles to control power and productive resources, has also set back efforts to protect and prevent violence against women. Furthermore, postconflict and posthumanitarian crises and natural disaster processes have tended to deepen gender inequalities in economic and political participation, negatively affecting women's vulnerability to violence. Yet despite these glaring realities, the current global political economic order is often neglected in analyses of violence against women (True 2010).

The United Nations secretary-general's (2006) in-depth study on violence against women stressed the lack of a comprehensive and integrated approach to violence against women.[4] Yet official UN approaches make no linkages between the effects of financial crises, macroeconomic policies, and trade liberalization and the prevalence of violence against women in particularly affected regions. This is evident, for example, in the Millennium Development Goals, which do not explicitly identify violence against women as a distinct goal. Similarly, the UN secretary-general's UNITE campaign launched in 2008, with the original aim of ending gender-based violence by 2015, mentions the structural, underlying causes and consequences of violence. But the campaign does not explore the linkages between the achievement of women's rights to political participation, their degree of social and economic equality, and the prevalence of violence against women.[5] Nor do the available UN Development Program indexes include indicators of violence against women when tracking the progress of women and analyzing the patterns of gender inequality.[6] Instead, the data and analysis of women's political representation, women's economic opportunities, and violence against women are treated separately (see UNIFEM 2005). Proposed indicators and databases on violence against women are primarily aimed at measuring the prevalence of violence and the extent of state responses to prosecute and protect against violence. They do not identify the causal factors for this violence or target specific predictors of violence in order to prevent it.

Likewise, UN Security Council resolutions on women, peace, and security since 2000 single out sexual violence in conflict-affected settings from ongoing forms of violence against women. They do not contextualize this violence within the gendered structures of economic impoverishment and lack of opportunity that are not addressed typically by political settlements or by peacekeeping missions (the subject of further discussion in Chapters 7 and 8). Not dissimilarly, feminist security studies within international relations that discuss gender and security only in the context of war or armed conflict or examine the sexual exploitation of women only in terms of trafficking across borders mobilize a gender bias (Sjoberg 2010; Sjoberg and Lobasz 2012). Such an approach tends to perpetuate the invisibility of violence against women in peacetime and within national borders. It also makes it difficult to comprehend and explain its systemic causes. Violence against women becomes, rather, epiphenomenal, derivative of another, more major social process at work such as war or capitalism, albeit one given increasing public attention and media coverage.

On a positive note, the UN Committee on the Elimination of All Forms of Discrimination Against Women (CEDAW) has recognized the linkages between forms of violence against women such as trafficking, domestic violence, and exploitation and women's lack of enjoyment of economic and social rights when commenting on state reports complying with the CEDAW treaty (see also SRVAW 2000). For instance, in 2009, they expressed concern about the effects of the current international financial and economic crisis upon the full realization of the human rights of women and girls worldwide, including the potential increase in societal and domestic violence against women.[7] However, a systematic gender analysis of the socio-economic conditions that may produce or increase violence against women has not been conducted by any international body or by scholars, and the national legal and policy provisions to address violence against women have not, for the most part, extended to the economic sphere or explored the political-economic causes and impact of violence against women. In short, both scholarship and policy lack any thoroughgoing analysis of the gendered social, political, and economic inequalities that shape women's vulnerability to violence in whatever setting. This book seeks to rectify the neglect of the contemporary global political economy and its effect on the prevalence of various forms of violence against women, in scholarship and policymaking. It highlights the patterns of material power and relationships that profoundly affect both the prevalence of violence and insecurity and the efforts to eliminate them.

The Political Economy Approach of This Book

A feminist political economy approach attends to the local and global contexts in which violence against women occurs. As a method, it broadens both the explanation and the solutions to violence against women. In contrast to conventional economics, political economy makes explicit the linkages between the economic and the social and political. It reveals the workings of power not only through visible coercion that is direct in its effects but also in the material basis of relationships that govern the distribution and use of resources, benefits, privileges, and authority within the home and society at large. These material relationships shape the institutional and ideological formations of society where gender identities and status are constructed and the boundaries of rights and freedoms determined (UNFPA 2008, 3).

Numerous observations and calls for action from women's advocacy groups, development NGOs, and UN agencies suggest the need to widen the violence against women framework to take account of the structural causes and consequences of violence evident in women's poverty and labor exploitation, socioeconomic inequality with men, and lack of political representation. Yet because violence against women occurs in all socioeconomic groupings, on the face of it, a political economy analysis is often dismissed. By developing a political economy approach to violence against women, this book aims to fill a major gap in thinking and policy. Such an approach avoids the compartmentalization and selective treatment of violence against women that disconnects the problem from its underlying causes. It provides a framework for individuals, communities, states, and other actors to realize more fully their obligations to prevent violence and to uphold women's human rights whether in good or bad times. The political economy method deployed in the chapters of this book aims to show the ways increasingly globalized economic power and structures reinforce gender inequalities, making women more vulnerable to violence, especially some groups of women. The core elements of the feminist political economy method applied to a wide range of forms of violence against women in each of the chapters of this book are explained in detail in Chapter 2.

A key aim of this book, therefore, is to inspire new interdisciplinary discussion and research. Nancy Fraser (2009, 115) has argued that the emancipatory promise of feminism depends on our "reconnecting struggles against personalized subjection to the critique of a capitalist system." She encourages feminists to "think big" by bringing back and integrating feminist political economy with cultural critique (Fraser 2009, 117). This book's political economy argument about the significance of material inequalities in perpetuating violence against women complements feminist scholarship that is attentive to the local sociocultural contexts of violence and to the need for culturally sensitive interventions to eliminate this violence (Merry 2006, 2009). Both cultural discourses and neoliberal economic globalization constitute major challenges to the achievement of gender equality and the elimination of violence against women (SRVAW 2000, 2001, 2006d, 2007). However, this book rejects any "cultural" arguments that condone practices judged by women's movements and human rights defenders to be abusive or violent to women. Strategies for addressing culture defenses of violence against women must include a political economy perspective that lays bare the material foundation and underlying vested interests of many cultural norms and practices. This book responds to that need.

How Do We Define Violence Against Women?

What is violence against women? What does it consist of? What are its various forms? Violence against women is a violation of human rights as established in international law. The term is a political, as well as a legal, framework constructed by women's human rights activists from around the world to forge solidarity and recognition of the specific exclusions and wrongs experienced by women in many different contexts globally. The most widely used definition of violence against women is provided by the United Nations' legal framework set out in the General Assembly's Declaration of the Elimination of Violence Against Women (resolution 48/104 of December 1993). Articles 1 and 2 of this resolution define violence against women as:

> [a]ny act of gender-based violence that results in, or is likely to result in, physical, sexual or psychological harm or suffering to women, including threats of such acts, coercion or arbitrary deprivation of liberty, whether occurring in public or in private life.

The UN definition embraces, but is not limited to, physical, sexual, psychological/emotional, and, most recently, economic violence or exploitation occurring in the family or community and/or perpetrated or condoned by the state.[8] The forms of violence against women and girls mentioned in the definition are multiple and wide-ranging, including battering, (marital) rape and sexual abuse, forced trafficking, intimate partner violence, maternal death, femicide, female genital mutilation, dowry deaths, honor killings, female infanticide, sexual harassment, forced and early marriage, and violence related to exploitation. Violation of the right to life, liberty, and security of the person shapes the enjoyment and fulfilment of all other human rights, including economic and social rights such as the rights to work, health, social security, education, food, housing, water, and land.

As well as a violation of human rights, violence against women is considered to be a form of systemic discrimination. Women are typically victims of violence precisely because they are women. Gender constructions of women as inferior or subordinate to men within and across societies have made violence against women both acceptable, in many places at many times, and invisible. As the CEDAW committee has stated, violence against women is that "directed against a woman because she is a woman or that affects women disproportionately."[9] Some women are also subject to violence as a result of multiple vulnerabilities including membership in a racial or ethnic minority or migrant, refugee, and other marginalized groups that intersect with gender. Thus, women and girls' experiences and risks of violence are not the same, although they may be attributed to similar causes testifying to the universalism of human rights within a world of difference (Ackerly 2008).

Violence Against Women or Gender-Based Violence?

Violence against women (VAW) occurs in a context of unequal gender relations. The concept of "gender-based violence" (GBV) captures women's experience of violence due to unequal gender power relations but not exclusively, since men are also victims of violence due to gender stereotyping and denigration when they fail to live up to dominant forms of masculinity. Thus, GBV affects both men and women, whereas VAW embraces those violent acts that are primarily directed toward women by virtue of their gender and affect women disproportionately. Although not synonymous, violence against women and gender-based violence are similar and used interchangeably within this book with a qualification that explains my strong preference for retaining the term *violence against women*. Many governments have chosen to adopt "gender neutral" language to discuss domestic violence against women occurring in the family or home. Unfortunately, this language tends to mask the reality that women and girls are more likely to be killed or injured by male partners than by any other class of individuals—a finding consistent across every study in every national context (see Bureau of Justice Statistics 2007; Tjaden and Thoennes 2000). There is also far greater prevalence of sexual violence against women and girls from intimate partners (Tjaden and Thoennes 2000). Large numbers of women and girls seek care in emergency departments for injuries due to violence from a male partner (Biroscak et al. 2006; Schafer et al. 2008); however, few documented cases exist of partner violence from female partners as the source of a significant portion of emergency department visits by men or boys (Reed et al. 2010, 350). Having said this, the book is strongly of the view that violence against women is a men's issue (which is the focus of Chapter 3), not least of all because some men's violence gives all men a bad name (Flood 2010, 9).

Measuring the Scope and Magnitude of Violence Against Women

Recognizing that gender-based violence affects women disproportionately, what is the prevalence of this violence and how can we measure it? Can we ascertain the scope and magnitude of violence against women globally?

Cross-National Evidence/Data on Violence Against Women

Worldwide, gender-based violence is the leading cause of death of women between the ages of 19 and 44—more than malaria and car accidents combined, and causing as many deaths and disabilities for women as cancer (Johnson et al. 2008, 1). Of all crimes, "sexual assault and intimate partner violence are the most under-reported" (Johnson et al. 2008, 3; Lievore 2003, 2005). A US government nationally representative survey reveals that nearly one in five women reported experiencing rape or attempted rape; one in four women described being beaten by an intimate partner; and one in three women said they had been victims of rape, beating, or stalking or a combination thereof (Rabin 2011). This study, among others, exposes the underestimated incidence of violence against women in the United States (Rabin, 2011). But when violence against women is reported as pervasive, it is often relegated to the inevitable biological characteristics of men (Cockburn and

Oakley 2011). Yet cross-cultural studies show significant variation in the degrees of violence against women, suggesting that it is not inevitable but rather is linked with certain social, cultural, and economic factors that can be identified and addressed (see Levinson 1989; Sanday 1981; Johnson et al. 2008).

Our increasing knowledge and awareness of gender-based violence leads us to want to understand the phenomenon better and to instigate policy change. However, there are significant challenges in studying all of the forms of gender-based violence comprehensively and cross-nationally. We must be able to measure or count the violence to mobilize the action and resources to end it. Several factors that are inherent in multicountry studies of VAW can impact the meaning and accuracy of results. These include the lack of comparable data and reporting on the prevalence and incidence of violence against women across countries; cultural considerations that affect the degree and robustness of reporting behaviors; the subjectivity of violent experiences; translation; differences in interviewing style and technique; and the fallibility of women's and men's memories (Johnson et al. 2008). In places of marked gender inequality, violence against women is underreported by women—it may not even be a crime—and negligently dealt with by authorities or recorded as "accidents" (Krug et al. 2002). Other challenges include defining "violence," defining the lifetime measure of a study, and defining the population (age range, partnership status). These methodological issues are important because they set parameters around what we can find from a study and determine the comparability of the results. For example, the US National Survey commissioned by the National Center for Injury Prevention and Control at the Centers for Disease Control and Prevention used a broad definition of domestic violence and sexual violence, and the results were far greater than expected. In another study (International Violence Against Women Study), conservative definitions of violence probably mean that the results underestimate the actual incidence of violence and we cannot compare across the data produced by these two different surveys. A "violent event" is recorded as one incident of violence. But the experience of violence is ongoing, beyond the actual battery—the hit, punch, rape, and so on—and may involve a succession or pattern of incidents. For instance, most women in the US study reported suffering from posttraumatic stress disorder. The violent event intersects with other factors that compose women's lives, such as their lack of education, employment status, or poverty. Hence, even studies that show the incidence and prevalence of violence against women tell us little of the important contexts that compose the whole experience of violence.

Despite the challenges of studying violence against women, the two most rigorous international surveys of domestic and sexual violence only (not including other forms listed in the 1993 UN definition of violence against women) illustrate unambiguous global patterns. The World Health Organization (WHO) study consisted of standardized population-based household surveys across ten countries involving urban and rural settings. Asking questions about respondents' specific experience of intimate partner physical violence, the study measured the prevalence and the incidence of violence.[10] The results indicated that physical violence by a male intimate partner is widespread in all of the countries included in the study, affecting between 13 and 61 percent of women and girls and, on average, between 23 and 49 percent (Garcia-Moreno et al. 2005, xii). However, sexual violence was more frequent than (generic) physical violence in most settings, although the two often coincided (Garcia-Moreno et al. 2005, 31, 41). The greatest amount of overall violence was reported mostly in rural settings in developing countries. The fact that there was a great deal of variation between countries and in different settings again indicates that violence is not inevitable (Garcia-Moreno et al. 2005, xii). Like the US survey, the WHO study reveals that younger women are at increased risk of violence (Garcia-Moreno et al. 2005, 33). The study also revealed that commonly mentioned perpetrators were people known to the victim—and this was more true the younger the girl was (Garcia-Moreno et al. 2005, 41). Another study, the cross-national International Violence Against Women Study (IVAWS), reveals an average victimization rate of over 35 percent of the 16 years and above female population (Johnson et al. 2008). The number of women who experienced at least one incident of physical or sexual violence since age sixteen was between 20 and 60 percent (Johnson et al. 2008). Rates of violence by intimate partners ranged from 9 to 40 percent. Again, the study revealed that violence by intimate partners or known men is much higher than violence perpetrated by strangers (Johnson et al. 2008). Across all countries, the trends of violence committed by intimate partners were astonishingly consistent. Where countries varied most was in the trend of violence committed by nonintimates, or strangers (Johnson et al. 2008).

Looking at current international research of domestic and sexual violence is helpful, although we still need to strive for universal indicators of violence and greater coverage and comparability across countries in these surveys. Yet even the best aggregate survey will be limited, since it cannot capture the broader, often global processes of which violence against women is a part. This book does not generate any new statistical data of its own. Rather, it seeks to understand the global patterns of violence against women in a range of contexts by marshaling together the existing empirical research from several disciplines and fields of research.

Redistribution

Calculating the Economic Costs

Another way to "measure" violence against women is to calculate the economic costs. These costs include direct costs, as well as opportunity costs, of the failure to prevent violence for individual women; for governments, business, and society; and for children or future generations. These costs have been quantified as monetary estimates in many country-specific studies and in the UN secretary-general's in-depth study (see section "Economic Costs of Violence Against Women"). They include direct costs to criminal justice, health, employment, and social welfare systems, as well as opportunity costs of the failure to prevent violence.

In terms of the costs to individual women, gender-based violence in public and private spheres prevents women from being able to access economic opportunities, livelihoods, and welfare benefits. Studies have shown that women who are victims of domestic violence typically earn less income across their lifetime than women who have not been victims of violence. For instance, one such study in Managua, Nicaragua, found that women victims of domestic violence earned just 57 percent of the income of their unaffected colleagues. A Bolivian rural women's organization found that it could not equally distribute agricultural land for farming to women and men unless they addressed the problem of domestic violence as part of their development work—the absences of women participants due to injuries suffered from domestic violence were too frequent (Hombrecher 2007, 40).

The economic costs of violence against women to business and government are considerable. Health care, employment, productivity, and criminal justice costs have now been calculated in many states, in order to raise awareness of the problem of violence and the need to collectively address it (see Day 1995). For instance, in 2009, the Australian government estimated that violence against women costs the government $13.6 billion per annum (National Council to Reduce Violence Against Women and Their Children 2009). In another study, it was assessed that the cost of violence against women in the United Kingdom is equivalent to more than 550 euros per resident annually (Walby and Allen 2004). In Fiji, the cost of domestic violence has been calculated at $300 million per annum, or about 7 percent of gross national product (Fiji Law Reform Commission 2004). Estimates of lost wages due to family violence amounted to 1.6 and 2.0 percent of gross domestic product in Nicaragua and Chile, respectively (Morrison and Orlando 1999). In the United States, preventive measures in the Violence

Against Women Act are considered to have saved the country $16.4 billion (Clark, Biddle, and Martin 2002). In 2003, the Columbian national government spent approximately $73.7 million (0.6 percent of their national budget) to prevent, detect, and offer services to survivors of family violence.

It is considerably more difficult to quantify the costs of violence against women to a whole society and its development, as well as to future generations. However, some studies have documented the impact of this violence on the children of women victims. Researchers in Nicaragua found that children of women who were physically and sexually abused by their partners were six times more likely than other children to die before the age of five, with one-third of all child deaths in this setting being attributed to partner violence (Bott, Morrison, and Ellsberg 2005). Violence against women hinders mothers from being able to take care of their families, trapping generations in a cycle of poverty. Wife abuse in South India has been linked to decreased nutritional status in children due to women's decreased chances of controlling income (Rao and Bloch 1993). This creates a range of challenges for the health and education of future generations.[11] Similarly, the health of women who have suffered violence and HIV/AIDS has a negative effect on their children, as well as their economic activity, thus creating a cycle of poverty, poor health, and vulnerability to more violence (Remenyi 2007, 13).

While these economic rationales for ending violence against women have been very successful at increasing awareness and government funding for antiviolence programs, especially in developed countries, they will likely not help the most vulnerable women in the world in the short to medium term. The realization of social and economic rights for these women is an immediate and essential condition for eliminating the prolonged and systemic violence they experience.

Overview of the Book

This book gives you an overview of the troubling "big picture" of violence against women globally. I am not the first to try to do this. The UN secretary-general, UN Women, the World Health Organization, and a whole range of advocacy campaigns in many different contexts have attempted to do the same. The difference here is that I seek to examine the structural causes of this violence in the material processes linked to globalization. Until we have a good understanding of what causes the various different forms of violence against women, we cannot know what strategies will be most effective in ending it. While there are a huge number of small-scale studies from different parts of the globe analyzing the drivers of certain types of violence against women, there are few compelling global studies of the causes of different forms of violence against women taken together. Maybe this is simply impossible. Efforts to conduct such studies are plagued by methodological difficulties in collecting and analyzing data on violence against women, including problems with the measurement and reporting of this violence as discussed previously. However, given the enormity and urgency of the problem, I think it is worth trying to comprehend violence against women in terms of global structures and processes, common to many settings.

Having introduced the political economy approach of this book, I flesh out this approach further and suggest a framework for understanding and ending violence against women in the next chapter, building on multidisciplinary approaches. Violence against women is often not addressed adequately or completely precisely because with our disciplinary or sector lenses, we often see only a part of the problem or the problem from just one perspective. In Chapter 3, I consider the construction of masculinities in the context of competitive globalization to be a key cause of violence against women. In particular, the chapter examines the material and identity-based losses many men experience with the restructuring of economic and social relations that globalization is bringing about. In Chapter 4, I examine gendered forms of labor exploitation in the global political economy to which women are especially susceptible. They include transnational domestic labor and trafficking for sex, prostitution, and other indentured labor. Chapter 5 explores new spaces of gender violence at work in free trade zones, special economic areas, and transition countries as a result of the liberalization and deregulation of markets. Chapter 6 follows logically from this chapter, analyzing the policies of international financial institutions that perpetuate gender-based violence by increasing economic and social austerity. The chapter also examines the deleterious impact of financial liberalization and crises on violence against women, especially domestic violence, as a consequence of extreme financial stress and insecurity in households. In Chapter 7, I investigate the proliferation of armed conflict fueled by the global competition over resources and power and the scourge of sexual violence in these wars. Whether strategic or not, sexual violence is not simply a spoil of war; it is integrally linked to the material basis of power in societies in conflict. Chapter 8 then turns to the postconflict context and considers why gender-based violence spikes after the formal negotiation of peace. It shows how this continued violence further compounds gendered economic and social inequalities, excluding women from key roles and decisions in the peace-building and reconstruction period. Chapter 9 also focuses on postcrisis material contexts but in the aftermath of natural disasters rather than war. We learn that women are far more likely than men to die during or after a disaster, and that gender-based violence is also pervasive and perpetuated by international humanitarian responses. Finally, in Chapter 10, I conclude by considering what it will practically take to end violence against women given the political economy framework of the book, and how we might revise our efforts to gain some traction on the struggle and wishes of our age and of many women to live without violence. I map out the many research questions and agendas that are bursting from the pages of this book that I hope other students and researchers will take up with me. There are hundreds of papers, theses, and PhD dissertations to be written on each and every topic traversed in the chapters of this book. My greatest wish is that this book will inspire that important and ongoing work.

| # What Has Poverty Got to Do With It?

Feminist Frameworks for Analyzing
Violence against Women

[We] *recogn[ize]* that women's poverty and lack of empowerment, as well
as their exclusion from social policies and from the benefits of sustainable development, can place them at increased risk of violence, and that
violence against women impedes the social and economic development
of societies and States, as well as the achievement of the internationally
agreed development goals, including the Millennium Development Goals.

—UN Economic and Social Council (2010)

Violence is not only a human rights violation but also a key factor in
obstructing the realization of women's and girl's rights to security,
adequate housing, health, food, education and participation. Millions
of women find themselves locked in cycles of poverty and violence,
cycles which fuel and perpetuate one another.

—IRENE KHAN, Executive Director, Amnesty International (2008)

Introduction

What has poverty—or wealth for that matter—got to do with pervasive and
egregious violence against women globally? As one women's international
NGO has stated, "when one thinks of women's human rights issues, one
usually thinks about violence against women and not about poverty, housing,
unemployment, education, water, food security, trade and other related economic and social rights issues" (Programme on Women's Economic, Social
and Cultural Rights [PWSCR] 2010, 1). But is there a relationship between
women's poor access to productive resources, such as land, property, income,

employment, technology, credit, and education, and their likelihood of experiencing gender-based violence and abuse? Indeed there is.

Poor women are more vulnerable to violence than women in high-income groups, even though women of all groups and different economic statuses experience violence. However, it is the material gender inequalities between women and men with respect to income, property, employment, and so on that best explain the high prevalence of violence against women, and these gender inequalities are not necessarily correlated with the poorest quintiles of populations or even the poorest countries. Data from the World Health Organization (WHO 2005) study on the prevalence of sexual violence perpetrated by a partner during a woman's lifetime across ten countries reveal a statistical correlation between countries scoring high on the gender development index (GDI) and those countries with lower rates of violence against women. Conversely, the lower the levels of human and gender-equal development, the higher are the levels of violence against women (Remenyi 2007). So women are more likely to enjoy better economic and social status and an environment enabling them to prevent or be protected from at least some forms of violence in countries with greater gender equity. According to the Social Watch Gender Equity Index, which ranks 157 countries on their progress on gender equity in education, economic participation, and political empowerment, income alone is no guarantee for gender equity. Countries with very high per capita incomes, such as Luxembourg and Switzerland, have the same equity level as Mozambique, a country with a much lower income level.[1] Among the countries with the highest achievement of gender equity is Rwanda, one of the poorest countries.

The upshot of these findings is that violence against women is linked to women's relative poverty and economic status but not in a straightforward way (Bott, Morrison, and Ellsberg 2005). One study found that all women except the wealthiest quintile experienced domestic violence in the Dominican Republic; in Haiti, women in the third quintile were most likely to experience domestic violence; and in Cambodia, those in the poorest quintile were most likely to experience violence (Kishor and Johnson 2004, 299). However, studies also suggest that violence against women, domestic and other forms, may actually rise as women gain greater access to social and economic opportunities and resources, and in some settings, women in the poorest households may be somewhat protected from violence (Jewkes 2002). Women's increasing economic activity and independence is often viewed as a direct threat to male dominance, which may lead to increased male violence against women when they begin working outside the home, including when they migrate transnationally to work. "Where women have a very low status, violence is not 'needed' to enforce male authority. . . . Partner violence is thus usually highest at the point where women begin to assume non-traditional roles or enter the workforce" (Heise and Garcia-Moreno 2002, 99). A disturbing example of this trend is the apparent increase in acid attacks in Bangladesh and Pakistan, despite increases in the proportion of women obtaining higher education and more paid employment in those countries. This case is discussed in more detail in Chapter 3 with respect to masculinity and men's responses to globalization and changing gender relations.

This chapter sets out the elements of a feminist political economy method that stresses the linkages between poverty, material gender inequalities, and violence, building on a range of approaches from several disciplines to understanding and ending violence against women. This political economy method is new only insofar as it has rarely been employed to analyze different forms of violence against women, as well as their causes and consequences. The method builds on the scholarship and activism of many feminists, but especially those in the interdisciplinary fields of international and development studies. In particular, the method is consistent with Ann Tickner's (1992) feminist approach to global security and Cynthia Cockburn's (2010, 2012) and Cynthia Enloe's (1989, 2004, 2010) feminist analyses of war and (anti)militarism that emphasize the continuum of war and peace given women's experiences of violence. Disaggregating sexual violence in "war" from women's structural subordination in "peace," for instance, is not helpful in understanding or ending that violence. "The violence and the inequalities that women face in crises do not exist in a vacuum but are the direct results and reflections of the violence, discrimination and marginalization that women face in times of relative peace."[2] These feminist international relations approaches define security in broad, multidimensional terms and include the elimination of all social hierarchies leading to political and economic injustice. In this book I claim that a sustained feminist political economy approach needs to inform scholarly and NGO research and government and international policies and programs if we are to make any progress in addressing the root causes of violence against women and responding to its global scale and brutality rather than remaining content with saving one woman at a time.

Subsequent chapters in this book illustrate how this method can be employed to analyze the intersection of local norms and global processes affecting violence against women (cf. Merry 2006). They explore strategic sites where structural political-economic forces can be seen to be heightening the conditions for and increasing the extent of violence against women. These sites include economic restructuring and men's reaction to the loss of secure employment (Chapter 3), the abusive exploitation associated with the transnational migration of women workers (Chapter 4), the growth of a sex trade around the creation of free trade zones (Chapter 5), the spike in violence against women in financial liberalization and crises (Chapter 6), the scourge of sexual violence in armed conflict (Chapter 7) and postcrisis reconstruction efforts (Chapter 8), and the deleterious gendered impacts of natural disasters (Chapter 9).

Multidisciplinary Approaches to Violence Against Women

Psychologists, epidemiologists, criminologists and criminal justice professionals, human rights lawyers and advocates, and more recently UN agencies and security sector experts have all sought to understand violence against women in diverse settings: at the individual, interpersonal, and family levels; at work and in the broader community; and in conflict or postconflict and other crisis contexts. But all these experts overlook or neglect to research one or more of the political-economic structures that underpin gender inequality and women's vulnerability to violence, especially at the global level. Here I explore various multidisciplinary approaches that seek to explain and address violence against women, highlighting their strengths and weaknesses from a political economy perspective. The use of a political economy analytical framework suggests a change in the way we understand and respond to violence against women. I then flesh out three elements of a feminist political economy method that should be central in any analysis of—and proposed strategies to end—violence against women:

1. The gender division of labor within the family and household economy
2. The contemporary global, macro-economy in which capitalist competition fuels the quest for cheap sources of labor, often women's labor, and for deregulated investment conditions
3. The masculine protector and feminine-protected identities associated with war and militarism, and division of war front/home front associated with armed conflict and its aftermath

Psychology and the Roots of Individual Behavior

The field of psychology, including feminist psychology, has made major contributions to our understanding of violence against women. Carol Jordan's (2009) review of the research on violence against women reveals that the biomedical and psychological bibliometric databases have experienced the greatest growth in literature volume during the past decades, whereas the sociological, social work, and legal literatures have leveled off or declined.

Psychological studies typically treat the individual as the unit of analysis. Thus, these studies, even though they often involve large populations and rigorous statistical analysis, tend to have less to say about the structural contexts of violence against women. There are some exceptions to this within feminist psychology. But despite the strengths of feminist studies in highlighting the political economy contexts for men's violent behavior and women's acceptance of violence, they nonetheless seek to explain individual behavior by studying individual-level factors, such as drug/alcohol abuse, personal attitudes, and personal characteristics including gender socialization, rather than broader changes in economic and political conditions, whether through experimental, social survey, focus group, or interview methods.

Moreover, psychological research on violence against women is often aimed at treating the symptoms more than the causes of violence. The research is tasked with informing the provision and design of social services and psychological support for perpetrators, as well as traumatized victims of violence. To the extent that it addresses prevention of violence, it is in terms of changeable individual behaviors and factors, rather than government interventions designed to alter political and economic structures that in turn shape individual behaviors. Social psychological approaches to the problem of violence against women can thus be readily accommodated within existing national and international frameworks and policies, since they focus on the individual determinants of behavior rather than the societal or structural causes such as poverty, economic deprivation, income levels, gender inequalities in employment, and access to property rights, health care, education, and political participation. They put the onus back on individuals rather than collective institutions to drive behavioral change rather than institutional change.

Studying Whole Populations and Health Outcomes

Epidemiology is the study of the population-based determinants of health. The health and freedom of girls and women are affected at the population level (Amnesty International 2004; Garcia-Moreno et al. 2006; Bernard et al. 2008; Ellsberg and Heise 2005). Freedom from violence is considered a fundamental indicator of good health, whereas violence, in particular against women, is strongly associated with a range of poor health outcomes including death, disability, maternal and infant mortality, infertility, and mental illness. Violence against women, especially intimate partner violence, is thus a major global public health issue (Ellsberg and Heise 2005). Population health studies involve social surveys of key demographic and social characteristics of a population, and gender inequalities are strongly highlighted in these studies. For instance, intimate partner violence affects the health and well-being of individual women and girls far more than individual men and boys, as well as at the population level. Further, the determinants and nature of violent behavior are found to be different depending on the gender of the perpetrator (Reed et al. 2010, 348).

Epidemiologists seek to identify the risk factors—and conversely, the preventative factors—for violence across a larger population within an ecological model of the causes of violence that extends from the individual level to the community, neighborhood, and society (see Figure 2.1).

However, in reality, most research in the population health field analyzes the individual and family characteristics rather than the neighborhood and society factors influencing violence, even though its purpose is to inform population-based interventions. Moreover, the ecological model for analyzing the determinants of violence, while frequently cited by epidemiologists, is diagrammatic at best. The model fails to analyze the mechanisms connecting individual/community factors and neighborhood/social factors or how the interaction of these factors leads to violence. It merely notices the

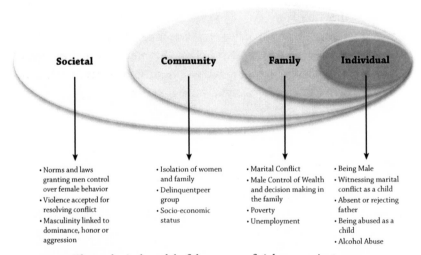

FIGURE 2.1. The ecological model of the causes of violence against women.

SOURCE: Ellsberg, Mary, and Lori Heise. 2005. *Researching Violence Against Women: A Practical Guide for Researchers and Activists*. Geneva: World Health Organization and PATH.

multiple contexts and layers of factors affecting the incidence and prevalence of violent behavior or victimization. It is also unclear within the ecological nesting which factors/levels are causal and/or most important in determining the forms of violence against women. The World Health Organization (2010, 26) simply states that we "need more research to identify modifiable factors to influence violence against women at community/society levels."

They note that "policies to stop violence against women are based on little evidence-based information/knowledge" (WHO 2010, 62). Most studies of violence against women concentrate on risk factors rather than preventative factors, just as most funding is focused on protection and prosecution, not prevention of violence against women (WHO 2010, 3). And of those that focus on prevention, the research investigates behavioral/family-level factors, not community/societal and economic structural factors, causing or correlated with violence (WHO 2010, 20). Looking at the two-by-two table in Figure 2.2, we can summarize the body of knowledge to date. We know most about sector 1, something about sectors 2 and 3, and virtually nothing about sector 4.

Despite the advent of the social science of population health, there is a systematic neglect of the societal/structural causes of violence within epidemiology. This neglect is due, in part, to the historical disciplinary and professional bias of health researchers oriented toward treating individuals or targeted groups of individuals and changing individual behavior directly, rather than analyzing the social relations and structures and changing individual behavior indirectly through societal interventions to affect the structural causes of this behavior. Moreover, because population health studies on violence against women are designed to obtain information from the victims, it is difficult to analyze the factors that contribute to or cause men to inflict violence against women—including political economy factors (Johnson et al. 2008, 79). This hampers our efforts to design policies to address the problem.

	Risk Factors	Preventative Factors
Ecological Level	1. *Individual/Interpersonal*	2. *Individual/Interpersonal*
	3. *Economic/Society/Political*	4. *Economic/Society/Political*

FIGURE 2.2. The state of current knowledge on the determinants of violence against women.

Making Violence Against Women a Crime

Criminal justice approaches to violence against women aim to identify and prosecute the perpetrators of violence while providing victims with some protection and redress through the legal and justice systems. Getting the police and the court system to recognize violence against women—particularly that perpetrated by intimate partners—as a crime has been a major struggle and a major success of women's movements worldwide (Reinelt 1995). Similarly, at the international level, activists for women's rights, such as the Women's Caucus for Gender Justice, have fought hard to have rape, forced pregnancy, and other sexual violence during conflict recognized as war crimes—and indeed, crimes against humanity—able to be prosecuted in the International Criminal Court (Chappell 2008). Yet, criminal justice research and responses to violence against women have often been separated from other forms of violence on the basis that it has distinctive social and political features due to its context in the private sphere of intimate relationships (Kruttschnitt, McLaughlin, and Petrie 2002, 2). There is still the belief in the criminal justice sector if not the criminology discipline that true crimes are perpetrated by strangers, not intimate partners.

The obvious weakness of the criminal justice approach to violence against women is that it deals with the consequences rather than the causes of this violence. Police and legal responses attend to two of the three Ps in efforts to address violence against women: prosecution and protection rather than prevention. In the United States, violence against women is discussed mainly in terms of the legal responses to physical and sexual violence since welfare-based social and economic policies, such as access to social housing and public and child benefits, which might provide options to leave violent partners, are rarely on the political agenda (Stanko 2006, 551; Weissman 2007).

The criminal justice system is based on the assumption that prosecution of crime prevents future crime and ends the culture of impunity for violence against women perpetrated by men. But the World Health Organization (2010) finds that there is little evidence of a deterrent effect in the criminal justice response to various forms of violence against women. Rather than just uphold protection orders or incarcerate male perpetrators, the legal and criminal justice systems need to reinforce nonviolent social norms and challenge the risk factors for violence against women, such as the gendered construction of masculinity and femininity that is predicated on the control of women (Basile 2009, 428). The structural factors supporting these gender inequalities that fuel violence by some men and at the same time make some women more vulnerable than others to that violence are significant. But only a feminist political economy method that compels us to reveal silences and analyze structural factors at all levels can identify and confront those deep-rooted causes of violence against women. A feminist approach to violence against women also compels us to find ways to change this disturbing global pattern. The implication is clear: we need a gender-sensitive political economy method to be able to adequately understand what causes violence against women and what solutions are most likely to end it.

Human Rights—Problem or Panacea?

The international human rights framework has been slow to address women's human rights, including violence against women, a most egregious abrogation of those rights. While it clearly identifies human wrongs and supports the struggles of all those seeking freedom from violence and freedom to live a dignified life, as an approach to understanding and eliminating violence against women, human rights has had some important limitations. The historical bias toward violations of human rights in the public sphere rather than those perpetrated in private is premised on a male-as-norm construct of the individual and, as such, has privileged male over female victims. This individualism fails to challenge the public-private division that is one of the root causes of women's human rights violations (Romany 1994;). Until recently, therefore, most women have been excluded from redress under international human rights law, and the fundamental principle of nondiscrimination in the enjoyment and protection of human rights failed to be upheld (Charlesworth and Chinkin).

Further compounding the negative effects of the public-private division within conceptions of human rights, violations of rights have often been subject to both relativist and essentialist cultural discourses that treat women's rights as expendable and nonuniversal, subject to the rule of particular national, cultural, or religious authorities. These discourses that prioritize cultural autonomy or group "minority" rights over individual, in this case, women's rights not only wrongly characterize cultures and/or tradition as fixed or predetermined but also overlook the unequal and potentially exploitative hierarchical systems within those cultures, as well as the perspectives of those within cultures who have no political voice or representation (Rao 1995).

Preventing violence against women in a neoliberal global environment requires a holistic approach to women's human rights. Advancing women's economic and social rights in the context of global change and crisis situations is crucial not only to women's enjoyment of civil and political rights but also for protecting women and girls from the risks of violence and exploitation. As this book argues, compared with men, women have far less enjoyment of—and access to—particular economic and social rights, such as the right to land, housing, and food. Yet a persistent problem in the human rights system is the dichotomous separation of rights into civil and political on the one hand, and economic and social on the other, along with the simultaneous prioritization of civil and political rights. The prevailing conception of economic, social, and cultural rights as "aspirational" rights to be progressively realized depending on the resources available to the state stands in contrast to civil and political rights, which have been traditionally conceived as "obligatory" rights to be immediately guaranteed.[3] As a result, state parties to human rights treaties have traditionally focused more on reforming judicial and governance structures to address human rights violations and less on preventive initiatives that may require fundamental alterations in economic and social structures. At the same time, nonstate actors such as corporations and international organizations have not been parties to human rights treaties and have therefore not been accountable for human rights abuses. By contrast, grassroots mobilizations of human rights by activists, including women's movements, have focused on the positive duties of states and nonstate actors to meet the basic needs that are implied by economic and social human rights. Activists understand that unless women can achieve economic independence or be empowered socially and politically, the human rights they hear about will remain abstract concepts (Ackerly 2008). The political economy approach of this book thus problematizes the all too familiar nexus between international human rights remedies and violence against women while pushing for the greater integration of the human rights framework and its application to the systemic violence that women experience.

Given the way human rights have been institutionalized, existing human rights mechanisms are not yet adequate to bring about redress to violence against women. A political economy approach is an important modifier to the rights-based framework because it compels us to rethink the dichotomization of human rights and the implicit individualism that, in effect, perpetuate violence against women. Attentive to the material aspects of social relations, such an approach prompts us to search for concrete ways to conceptually and practically realize the universal indivisibility of human rights on the ground, especially to defend the rights of those most marginalized in societies.

Anthropology and the Culture Question

Contrary to discourses of international human rights, an anthropological perspective considers violence against women to be widespread rather than universal (Merry 2006). Given that ethnography is their method,[4] it is not surprising that anthropologists stress local differences rather than the global similarities across the incidences of violence against women and attitudes to it. Anthropologists explore the different meanings of violence, including the causes of and justifications for violence against women, reflected in the narrative of both victims and perpetrators. Merry (2006, 22) states that "violence is part of the performance of gendered identities," of what it means to be a man or a woman in a particular sociocultural context. For example, in Kimberly Theidon's (2004) telling of the sexual violence experienced by Peruvian women raped by Shining Path militia, the violence does not merely engender forced pregnancies but is perpetuated by cultural rumors that the women's suffering is passed to their progeny through their breast milk.

Yet anthropologists recognize that the social, cultural, and legal meanings of a violent incident cannot be separated from their wider social, political, and economic contexts. Scheper-Hughes and Bourgois (2004, 4) argue that it is the "social and cultural dimensions of violence" that give violence its power and meaning, making it both an everyday occurrence and embedded in structures "of poverty, hunger, social exclusion and humiliation." The latter "structural violence" is rendered invisible by the hegemony of "ordinariness." As Elizabeth Stanko (2006, 543) writes: "People understand the impact of violence, the way they are treated, as 'just a part of their daily lives.' They also understand whether those in a position of power to mediate or to minimize the violence will do so or will stay silent." Much violence against women is legitimized within wider community and social relations. Here the cultural anthropological perspective highlights the normalization of inequalities and injustices in everyday life as a key cause perpetuating violence but does not usually extend to analysis of the power and reinforcement of harmful global structures stressed by a political economy approach.

However, the two approaches are complementary. Like the political economy method developed in this book, cultural anthropology sees violence as a fundamentally social, not sociobiological or psychological, phenomenon that is inherent to human beings. Anthropologists do not deploy "culture" or particular cultural meanings in an apolitical way to avoid ethical obligations to end violence in all contexts (Merry 2009 7 passim). Instead, their appreciation for dynamic and complex cultures, as well as human agency, suggests that initiatives to stop violence need to be both sensitive to and tailored for local contexts: in effect, "diminishing violence against women requires cultural transformation" (Merry 2009 25). Anthropologists do not stop their analysis of violence against women at the borders of the local; rather, they track the connections between macro social, political, and economic exclusions and violent behavior in the family, the public sphere, and the international realm. For example, Phillipe Bourgois's study of crack dealers in New

York City makes such connections between brutal domestic violence, violence at work and on the streets, and US inner-city apartheid. Sally Merry (2006) also draws linkages between living in an occupied state and beating up wives, between racial violence and spousal abuse, and between nationalism as a political ideology and male aggression.

Although anthropological studies emphasize the wider context of power and meaning of violence by communities, states, and international institutions, they typically focus on the social life of small groups, one case or one story at a time (Merry 2009, 29). Similar to psychological approaches and epidemiology, which take the individual as the unit of analysis, ethnography is probably not the best method for generating insights into the factors that create global patterns in multiple acts of individual and institutional violence against women. As Nancy Scheper-Hughes (1995) herself recognized in an address to her field, ethnographic knowledge may generate powerful understandings of particular instances of violence, but it may just be "too slow and too local" to have an impact on efforts to stop this violence. For that, we need an unambiguous political-economic, globally—as well as locally—informed analysis.

Securitizing Violence Against Women

Violence against women, especially rape and sexual violence, has recently become the subject of international security and international relations. Physical violence against women perpetrated by enemy states or groups fits well within the remit of security studies, which largely focuses on physical security and threats to it within interstate contexts. Concepts of human and gender security, which are potentially broader and focus on preventing—as well as protecting individuals from—a range of military and nonmilitary threats, are also increasingly part of the security studies approach. But the concept of security, even with modifications, tends to emphasize fatalities in a war or armed conflict rather than everyday violence in peace or on the home front. It is thus limited as an approach to understanding the structural causes and consequences of violence against women.

Rather than illuminate the political-economic dimensions of sexual violence against women, security approaches tend to obscure them. They do not consider how sexual and gender-based violence against women might be prevented in the long term, although the UN Security Council's Resolution 1889 is the first to include language that encourages member states to address the socioeconomic needs of women. The causes of conflict and of violence against women are not well understood by security approaches, nor are they connected to structural inequalities in local household and global political economies that persist and may be exacerbated after conflict. Moreover, actions to end violence against women are framed as instrumental means to the ends of security, peace, and democracy, and gender equality within these goals is not necessarily seen as an aspiration in its own right (Hudson 2009, 53).

Feminist security studies are an important corrective to the masculine bias that informs states and international institutions. They have challenged the gendered stereotypes in security approaches that assume women are either victims or peacemakers and that men are both perpetrators of and protectors from violence. But most feminist studies of security do not analyze the political and economic structures that shape and perpetuate gender-based violence and insecurity (see Sjoberg 2010; Sjoberg and Lobasz 2012).[5] Recent scholarship on gender and security largely ignores the political economy dimension of conflict and fails to highlight the connections and continuum between violence against women in conflict and in civilian life, in postconflict, and/or in development settings. Such a conceptualization runs contrary to Tickner's (1992) and Enloe's (1989) feminist perspectives on global security, drawn from women's experiences of direct and structural violence in peacetime and in war.

Although putting violence against women on the international security agenda has been a hard-won achievement, the "securitization" of this violence has tended to remove the systemic feminist political economy analysis that could address its root causes. By contrast, feminist international political economy (IPE) has made it possible for us to reconsider informal economic activity, feminized economies such as the sex and domestic workers trade, and unpaid work in the home as composing major parts of the globalization story (Marchand and Runyan 2009; Peterson 2003; Whitworth 2004). It is this body of scholarship that could shed significant light on the local and global causes of sexual and gender-based violence.

Political Economy Method Explained

A feminist political economy method comprehends the global, political-economic structures that both condition and heighten women's vulnerability to violence. It addresses the lack of structural and causal analysis in social psychology and population health approaches to violence against women, criminal justice and human rights perspectives, and cultural anthropology and security studies. This method can be employed in the study of any number of questions. It analyzes political and economic power as part of the same transnational authority structure, highlighting the masculine nature of the integrated political-economic authority structure extending from the household to the global realm.

All forms of power—including the use of violence—are understood as having a material basis, often founded on material relations of inequality within and across societies and cultures. The method directs us to investigate the interconnections between the economic, social, and political realms. Such investigations reveal that power operates not only through direct coercion but also through the structured relations of production and reproduction that govern the distribution and use of resources, benefits, privileges, and authority within the home and transnational society at large (Whyte 2009). Thus, for example, direct physical violence may not be necessary to control women who are economically dependent on a male breadwinner and whose attributes and skills as a housewife in the private sphere are not sufficiently valued in the public sphere to ensure an adequate livelihood, but that does not mean that psychological and economic violence is not present. Political-economic processes interact with and reconfigure the institutional and ideological formations of society where, for instance, these gender identities and relations are shaped. As Bina Agarwal (1994, 1459) states, "those who own and/or control wealth-generating property can directly or indirectly control the principal institutions that shape ideology, such as educational and religious establishments and the media. . . . These can shape views in either gender-progressive or gender-retrogressive directions."

The three elements of a feminist political economy method mentioned previously can be employed to analyze the likelihood and prevalence of different forms of violence against women in wide-ranging global contexts. In particular, the method highlights the material situation of women and men with respect to their unequal access to productive resources as part of a more comprehensive explanation of the causes and consequences of violence against women. These three structures are explored concretely in the subsequent chapters of this book.

Gendered Household Divisions of Labor

The first element is the gendered public-private sphere division of labor, which is supported by gender ideologies that hold women primarily responsible for unremunerated, and often invisible, unpaid work in the family or "private" sphere, thus creating inequalities in household bargaining power between men and women. Caring professions in the "public" labor market akin to the unpaid care work women traditionally do in the home are devalued as a result of this prior gender structure (Okin 1989). The internationalization of reproductive work has extended this division of labor to the transnational realm as women from poorer, developing regions and countries migrate to provide care services for families in wealthier regions and countries (Parrenas 2001). In a mutually constitutive way, the strict division of roles in the domestic sphere constrains women's public participation and their access to education and economic opportunities in the market, in turn creating hierarchical structures that entrap many women into potentially violent environments at home and at work. Some women, especially those in developed regions and countries, avoid patriarchal, and potentially violent, situations in the family/private sphere by contracting out care work to poor women, including migrant women from the global South.

Contemporary Neoliberal Globalization

The second element highlighted by a feminist political economy method is the contemporary global, macroeconomic environment. Capitalist competition encourages firms to seek cheap sources of labor and deregulated investment conditions that maximize profits locally and transnationally. In this context, the relocation of industries has disrupted local economies and dramatically changed labor markets, increasing a poorly regulated economy of low pay and insecure jobs, and attracting women from both developed and developing societies into wage employment on a scale unseen before. *The Economist* (2006) states that the increase in women's labor market participation has contributed more to global growth in the last two decades than growth in China, growth in India, and the rise of the Internet combined!

While the neoliberal policy environment has led to the expansion of women's employment, it has also led to the intensification of their workload in the market and at home and to the "feminization of poverty," especially among unskilled and marginalized poor women in developing countries who lack access to productive resources or public services. Such poverty, marginalization, and lack of protective mechanisms make women easy targets for abuse and undermine the prospects for their political and economic empowerment (Elson 2002, 78). These conditions also disempower many men, who may react to the loss of employment and economic opportunities as a result of global competition by reasserting their power over women through violence.

At the same time, neoliberal policies have reduced the state's capacity to regulate and tax capital, resulting in an enforcement problem and difficulties in generating expenditure for social provisioning that could alleviate women's poverty and vulnerability. Indeed, the reduced enforcement and social security role of the state has also been accompanied by communal/"tribalizing" tendencies whereby nonstate actors have gained power and influence in public discourse. These actors, often purporting religious fundamentalism, provide alternatives for education, health, housing, and social support services for impoverished groups; at the same time, they often also resist and undermine the universality of human rights, and in particular, women's rights and their claims to freedom from violence and want.[6]

War, Militarism, and Globalized Conflict

The third element of a feminist political economy method relates to the gendered dimensions of war and peace, which are intertwined with both private patriarchy and the gendered structures of the global political economy. Violent conflict, which often results from struggles to control power and productive resources, normalizes violence and spreads it throughout the societies involved. State- and group-sanctioned violence frequently celebrate masculine aggression and perpetuate impunity with regard to men's violence against women, viewing this violence, inter alia, as the "spoils of war." Conflict, war, and the security agenda impoverish societies as states make trade-offs between military spending and spending for social and economic development and human rights protection, thus creating the conditions for severe violence against women (Balakrishnan 2005, 34).

A feminist political economy approach contests the gendered structure of war and peace by arguing that stability without justice is not possible. The prioritization of national security and electoral machinery by governments over the social and economic security of citizens after war or armed conflict is usually destabilizing in the long run. Insofar as women are unable to gain access to physical security, social services, justice, and economic opportunities due, in part, to the military buildup and privileging of militarized masculinities, their particular vulnerability to violence continues in peace time.

Conclusion

Violence against women is not a "domestic" or a private sphere matter (if it ever was), but part of the broader structure of global power relations. Patterns of violence against women, their causes, and their consequences are integrally linked to patterns of global transformation instigated by economic, political, military, and natural environmental forces. Women's survival strategies and mechanisms for coping within gendered households in the context of economic austerity and competitive globalization have increased their vulnerability to violence.

Globalization has brought about a significant movement in the geographical location, occupation, and social position of women. It has expanded women's formal economic participation, while leaving unchanged the underlying patriarchal structures that perpetuate women's inequality with men and their susceptibility to violence. Women's labor has become part of the competitive dynamic of globalization, yet a large number of women workers in the informal economy, care sector and in unpaid work often fall outside of recognized labor standards and the human rights system. The erosion of state social security systems and the lack of economic security across many parts of the world have led to the feminization of poverty. The following chapters investigate the inextricably connected local and global contexts of displacement, trafficking, home-based production, restrictive immigration, special economic zones, and large developments, among others, that fuel and perpetuate violence against women.

| Losing Entitlement, Regaining Control
Masculinities and Competitive Globalization

Violence against women is a men's issue.

—FLOOD (2010, 9)

Global society is an arena for masculinity formation.

—CONNELL (1998, 16)

Introduction

This book is about violence against women, and central to the understanding of this violence is the political economy of gender relations between women and men. Thus, the focus of this chapter—and much of the discussion in the following chapters—is on masculinities, that is, how the social construction and experience of being a man within the contemporary global political economy leads some men to act out violently toward women. Here masculinities refer to men's individual and collective sense of identity and entitlement within material relations that are grounded in household/family relations but increasingly globalized. The chapter asks: to what extent do men's reactions to economic globalization processes in conflict, postconflict, or peaceful contexts, and to the loss of secure entitlements to employment and status they often bring about, affect the prevalence of violence against women?

As the epigraph by Connell suggests, masculinities today are constructed at the global level, or at least in relation to global processes and changes (see also Hooper 1998). In reality, there are multiple masculinities lived locally and globally. Yet a hegemonic form of masculinity is typically promoted as the masculine model to aspire to. Men and boys are encouraged and rewarded for their achievement of this model, which may change over time while retaining its dominance over femininity. The hegemonic western brand of masculinity today increasingly takes the form of a "transnational business masculinity" and is associated with autonomy, the capacity for reason and control, mobility, and power, whereas the hegemonic notion of femininity is associated with the absence or lack of these characteristics. The rigid, control-oriented masculinity of the military rivals the hegemonic business masculinity, but its influence is waning in many societies due, in part, to the effects of global economic competition. Nonetheless, the construction of masculinity against feminine identities, activities, and institutions supports violent, aggressive behavior by men, often directly targeting or affecting women. If we are to stop violence against women, and violence across societies more generally, we need to change the construction of masculinities, particularly their hegemonic expressions, and celebrate multiple, nonviolent forms of masculinity. One way to do that is to alter the structures and processes of political economy that shape the formation of masculinities and femininities.

This chapter consists of four parts. The first part considers the cost of violent masculinities to global society, setting the agenda for why we should examine the social construction of globalizing masculinities more closely. The second part examines why some men and not others beat, rape, abuse, and kill women, by analyzing different types of masculinities (including the global economic context) and risk factors for being perpetrators of violence against women. Men's backlash against women's rising economic and social status is observed in some regions of the world, leading to an increase in violence, rather than a decrease as we might expect. The third part of the chapter shows the linkages between masculinity and violence against women to be crucial in addressing another major global problem, HIV/AIDS. The final part of the chapter argues that changing men goes in tandem with transforming women's economic and social situation as the most important approaches to preventing violence.

Globalizing Masculinities

International relations, trade, and global markets are inherently an arena of gender formation and gender politics (Connell 1998, 7). Hegemonic masculinity progressively has the attributes and interests of a male entrepreneur, de-emphasizing welfare and generally weakening the position of women, while accentuating "the unregulated power of transnational corporations" and placing "strategic power in the hands of particular groups of men" (Connell 1998, 15). This transnational business masculinity is "marked by increasing egocentrism, very conditional loyalties (even to the corporation), and a declining sense of responsibility for others (except for the purposes of image making)" (Connell 1998, 16).

Parallel to the rise of transnational business masculinity is the "growing tendency to commodify relations with women" (Connell 1998, 16). Although the business masculine identity does not always require physical force to maintain its dominance, it is directly implicated in the structural violence experienced by women. Neoliberal policies that facilitate the expansion of liberal trade and finance by minimizing state-based regulation and public sector costs serve to reinforce this hegemonic masculinity, undermining social welfare and citizenship agendas and other masculine identities. Connell (1998, 17) argues that they ensure that the "patriarchal dividend" in the form of better pay, positions in decision making, and ownership and property rights, as well as sexual privilege for men, is defended, even though it clearly doesn't extend to all men—hence the use of violence (as the chapter explores further). States have "systematically begun campaigns to make their citizens less secure and more vulnerable, both psychologically and economically," which has disproportionately negative impacts on women and their vulnerability to violence (Snider 1998, 18).

This dominance of globalizing masculinities over women and feminized or alternate masculinities occurs in much more subtle ways than other violent masculinities in the context of war, postconflict, extraction, and recession economies. Capitalist systems are structural and therefore do not have intentional behavioral consequences or ideological dictates. But macroeconomic forces reinforce certain gender identities, structures, and ways of knowing and doing as if they were part of the natural order of things (Snider 1998, 4). Importantly, this gendering occurs without explicit masculinity politics in the form of a mobilization of men (Connell 1998, 17). It is in this context—of globalized material relations in which some men fail to achieve the hegemonic business masculinity—that violence against women becomes the norm. Violence against women is increasing, despite apparent societal change in attitudes toward gender equality and women's status. Feminist sociologists Cynthia Cockburn and Ann Oakley highlight the cost of violent masculinities to government, business, and society in the United Kingdom in Box 3.1. In that country, despite the costs that men's violent behavior incurs to the public purse, recovery from the global financial recession, demanding cuts to public spending has largely been paid by women in the loss of their jobs and livelihoods.

Box 3.1 THE COST OF VIOLENT MASCULINITIES

Cockburn and Oakley (2011) canvas the linkages between masculinities and crime, illustrating the culpability and cost of masculinity. After the August 2011 London riots, suspects were analyzed in terms of age, ethnicity, neighborhood, and employment status. Gender was the greatest distinction and yet it went unremarked: 92 percent of the first 466 defendants were male, and all of the 124 individuals charged with offenses involving violence were male. The British Crime Survey reveals that in 2009–10, men were perpetrators in 91 percent of all violent incidents in England and Wales: 81 percent for domestic violence, 86 percent for assault, 94 percent for wounding, 96 percent for mugging, and 98 percent for robbery. Ministry of Justice 2009 statistics reveal that men were responsible for 98 percent of sexual offenses, 92 percent of drug offenses, 89 percent of criminal damage, and 99 percent of child sex offenses. Men commit 87 percent of all traffic offenses and 81 percent of speeding offenses. Home Office data reveal that men are responsible for 97 percent of dangerous driving offenses and 94 percent of motoring offenses causing death or bodily harm. Female offenses were highest in fraud and forgery (30 percent), and theft and handling stolen goods (21 percent).

The authors locate the higher incidence of crime, especially violent crime, in masculine identity. They cite the 2002 *World Health Organization Report on Gender and Road Traffic Injuries*. It states that masculinity "may be" hazardous to health. The overall cost of crime in the United Kingdom, including lost productivity, service costs, and impact on victims, was calculated to be £78 billion a year in 2009. Cockburn and Oakley point out that if men committed as few crimes as women, incidents would fall by 54 percent and the exchequer would save £3.4 billion a year from fewer incarcerations (which cost £45,000 per prisoner per year, 95 percent of whom are male). The authors similarly note that the most masculine crimes are the most expensive: homicide, a sexual offense, and a serious wounding cost £1.4 million, £31,438, and £21,422, respectively (2003 figures). The most feminine crime, theft, is the cheapest, at £844 per incident.

By identifying criminal behavior as a manifestation of socially constructed gender identity, Cockburn and Oakley suggest that solutions must address violent (and costly) masculinities. A business-as-usual prosecutorial approach to crime does nothing to challenge the dominant masculinities that perpetuate most violent crime, especially gender-based violence—arguably the crime that most reinforces violent masculinities. By putting a price on crime attributable to violent masculine identities, Cockburn and Oakley provoke public discussion about social policies that could challenge masculine identities and, in doing so, change male behavior.

Why Do Some Men Perpetrate Violence? The Risks of Being a Perpetrator of Violence against Women

Not all men commit violence against women, but as suggested earlier, particular groups of men, especially those who fail to achieve the hegemonic model of masculinity, are vulnerable to becoming perpetrators of violence. In order to end violence against women, we must understand perpetrators and victims of violence, as well as their relationships and material contexts.

Breadwinner Masculinities

Men's reactions to economic globalization processes, and the loss of male entitlement to privileged employment positions and income they often bring about, can lead them to act out violently against women. Global competition seeks to lower the costs of production, and to the extent that women's labor is cheaper (because of the devaluation of women in the private sphere), firms may prefer to hire women over men especially in competitive, export-oriented industries as is discussed in Chapter 5. Thus, where neoliberal reforms and restructuring open up economies to global competition, there may be greater opportunities for women than men to enter the labor market and gain economic independence.

Yet masculine identities have traditionally been constructed as breadwinner identities, assuming control over income and resources, as well as women. Joachim Kersten (1996, 383) agrees that provision—men's identity as breadwinners legitimating the exclusion of women from formal work—is an essential property of "maleness" along with procreation (normative heterosexuality) and protection (women as property to be protected against "other" enemy men). These breadwinner identities are challenged at home and in the workplace by women's newly valued economic roles. Where globalization processes undermine these masculine identities, we have seen increased levels of violence. For instance, some studies suggest that violence against women may actually rise as women assume nontraditional roles and gain greater access to these socioeconomic opportunities and resources (Heise and Garcia-Moreno 2002, 99; Jewkes 2002); this is despite the association between women's employment and empowerment in indicators such as the UN Gender Development, Empowerment, and Inequality Indexes. Here, globalization and gender equality are linked, albeit as a process of "equalizing down," where gender equality is achieved not by women attaining the same status as men but, in part, by the demotion of men's previous entitlements and status. In this context women's increasing economic activity and independence become a threat to masculine identity and sense of entitlement. This is particularly true when the male partner is unemployed and feels his power undermined in the household (UNICEF 2000). With neoliberal restructuring and economic crises in many states, men may be unable to find alternative employment to provide incomes that fulfill their visions of themselves as breadwinners. They may react violently against women and children in the home and in public spaces, compensating for the loss of economic control.

The case of acid attacks in South Asia discussed in Box 3.2 is an extreme form of male reaction against the perceived loss of status and identity that some men experience when gender relations are changing. Progress toward gender equality is two steps forward and one step backward as men react against women's newfound gains in employment and public life by experiencing women's gains as their losses, and lashing out against them to sustain their social status and economic entitlements.

On December 12, 2011, after years of lobbying by women's groups, the Pakistani Senate unanimously passed two historical bills upholding the rights of women, the Acid Control and Acid Crime Prevention Bill of 2010 and the Prevention of Anti-Women Practices (Criminal Law Amendment) Bill of 2008 (Khan 2011). The Acid Control law establishes fourteen-year to lifetime imprisonment sentences and levies fines up to one million rupees for the perpetrators of the crime (Khan 2011). Although the legislation is a major step forward, prosecution of perpetrators must be accompanied by efforts to confront the gender inequalities reproduced by hegemonic masculinities. Nayyar Shabana Kiyani of the Aurat Foundation, a women's organization in Islamabad, identifies the need for social change: "laws are very good, but unless and until you change the mindset of the people, things won't change" (Toosi 2010).

Box 3.2 ACID THROWING IN PAKISTAN

Acid throwing, or acid attacks, has increased in South Asia since the 1980s (Bollineni 2010). Industrial-strength hydrochloric or sulfuric acid is used in textile manufacturing, a prevalent industry in South Asia. Acid burns through eyes, skin, flesh, and bone (Women Without Borders 2010). It restricts breathing due to toxic fumes and esophageal damage (Bollineni 2010). As a method of committing violence against women, acid is an efficient tool. Crucially, women have absolutely no way to protect themselves from acid. It is as easy to buy as a bar of soap, cheap—around twenty-three cents per liter (Ebrahim 2010)—and reliably destructive (Bollineni 2010). Because it can exact such damage with minimal effort—in Pakistan three sisters had acid thrown on them by two men passing on a motorcycle—the psychological effects for women of the threat of acid throwing are profound (Women Without Borders

Box 3.2 (*continued*)

2010). Women are overwhelmingly the victims of acid attacks. According to a special report by Indian nongovernmental organization CEQUIN, 80 percent of victims are female, and of these 40 percent are girls younger than eighteen years of age (Bollineni 2010). Since 1994, the Progressive Women's Association has supported 8,886 female survivors of acid attacks (Ebrahim 2010). The phenomenon is by no means exclusive to Pakistan—Afghanistan, Bangladesh, Cambodia, and India have similar cases (Women Without Borders 2010).

Acid throwing is a part of the broader (sickeningly regular) phenomenon of honor killings, which are, quite literally, the killing of women and men to restore "honor," usually for the transgression of traditional values and social and gender norms. Like honor killings, acid attacks are about the restoration of masculine monopoly on social, political, and economic control and power. In Pakistan, patriarchy is perpetuated by religious and tribal ideology. Acid throwing demonstrates ideology at its most extreme. Women who are attacked with acid (or killed for "honor") are usually those who transgress gendered norms—women who divorce abusive husbands, reject traditional dress, exert independence from men, or show any manner of "immorality" as defined by men (Women Without Borders 2010). This form of violence against women in Pakistan takes place in the context of widespread domestic abuse—80 percent of wives in rural Pakistan fear physical violence from their husbands, while 50 percent of urban women have experienced domestic abuse (Toosi 2010). Yasmeen Rehman, a prominent women's advocate and parliamentarian, stated that domestic abuse in Pakistan is so engrained that it can be equated with habit (Toosi 2010). As a tool of masculine dominance, acid throwing is ideal. The physical disfigurement from acid burning is important. Survivors, wearing the scars of their attacks, are further violated through ostracism and shame within their community and vulnerable to further violent attacks (Women Without Borders 2010). Like honor killings, which end a woman's life, acid scars disable and remove women's ability to be independent and thus to transgress norms, subduing and subordinating them. Depending on the extent of their injuries, women may be unable to work. Furthermore, the disfigurement relegates women back into the private and invisible realm of their traditional gender role, reinforcing men's dominance of the public sphere and their monopoly on social, political, and economic agency. The permanent and public nature of the injuries from acid throwing allows for perpetrators to tangibly and visually validate their actions and reinforce their masculinity within their peer and social contexts. An acid survivor is a permanent reminder of the violent perpetrator's dominance.

In developed countries, too, the loss of masculinity through the loss of traditionally masculine functions is far more pronounced (Kersten 1996, 392). In this context, crimes, including violence against women (as a form of dominating the "weaker") are a way to compensate for the loss of other (traditional) ways to prove masculine identity. Recounted in Box 3.3, the story of

Box 3.3 THE PRICE OF AN EDUCATION

Rumana Monzur, a political science master's student and Fulbright scholar at the University of British Colombia (UBC), was brutally attacked in front of her five-year-old daughter by her husband on a trip home to Bangladesh in June 2011 (*Huffington Post* 2011). As a result of having her eyes gouged, part of her nose bitten off, and her neck gnawed, Rumana was left with permanent disfigurement (*Huffington Post* 2011). Doctors in India assessed her eyes and determined that they could not be repaired (Toope 2011). Rumana returned to Canada in July 2011 to seek further treatment from Canadian ophthalmology specialists, but after three surgeries the damage was deemed "catastrophic" (Lindsay 2011). Staff and students at UBC immediately rallied to help Rumana, establishing a fund to help with the expenses resulting from the attack (Toope 2011). The university also pledged to do whatever it could to ensure Rumana could finish her master's thesis, including offering space for her, her daughter, and her parents in the university's family housing units (*Huffington Post* 2011). Of the incident, Rumana said she thought her husband, Syeed Hasan Sumon, was jealous (*Huffington Post* 2011). The attack occurred during a dispute about Rumana's education. She wanted to return to UBC to continue her studies and undertake a PhD (*Huffington Post* 2011). The incident highlights the pervasive extent of domestic violence in Bangladesh and further illustrates the tension arising from women's advancement beyond the family household. Sumon reacted to his wife's rising social, economic, and educational advancement through violence and as a result Rumana will never see again. Importantly, she has eschewed the status of victim and maintained her commitment to both her studies and her daughter (Lindsay 2011). Sumon was arrested for the crime after several days of evading police but died in the bathroom of a medical university on December 5, 2011, while "undergoing treatment for several illnesses" (BBC 2011).

Rumana Monzur, a University of British Columbia graduate student and Bangladeshi citizen, shows how globalization and the educational opportunities it brings for women are double-edged swords. Some forms of violence against women typically associated with developing country contexts are increasingly part of the experience and the responsibility of global society, including universities in wealthy countries.

Research evidence from several regions supports the political economy perspective of this book, showing that a reduction in male incomes challenges norms of masculinity and exacerbates tensions between men and women. Surveys during project work in Asia and Africa reveal that the economic success of married women was sometimes accompanied by an increase in intrafamily violence and, in Costa Rica, with the dissolution of families (Seguino 2008, 48; Chant 2001; Schuler, Hashemi, and Badal 1998). In Latin America and the Caribbean, the severely inequitable distribution of wealth is one of the chief factors fueling a rise in the rates of domestic violence, which is also one of the highest rates in the world (Larrain 1999). Yet, because conventional economic analysis and human rights law do not consider power dynamics in the family household, "the relationship between high returns to business and poverty and violence [against women] at the household level remains invisible" (Sweetman 2008, 2).

Recreational Masculinities

In South Africa, where there is a history of state-sponsored violence and the contemporary context is mired by poverty, unemployment, crime, and deprivation, several forms of violence against women are prevalent. Rape, in particular, has been found to be extremely pervasive. In one epidemiological study, it has been argued that rape plays a crucial role in male peer group positioning and that it must be understood within the context of the limited number of other recreational opportunities available to poor, township and rural youth: "[c]ompetition over women has achieved overwhelming importance because it is one of the few available and affordable opportunities for entertainment and arenas where success [in masculinity] may be achieved and self-esteem gained" (Jewkes and Abrahams 2002, 1240). Given young men's poverty-ridden context, reciprocal relationships and the input of resources they require may not be realistic options. Rape and violence are thus more readily deployed to seek the same goals of masculine identity and status.

A recent study of fifteen South African men and their female partners recruited via two agencies that provide programs for victims and perpetrators of intimate violence also reveals the intersection between men's economic disempowerment and their violence against women (Boonzaier 2005). The study investigated how in a globalizing South Africa, where there are more economic opportunities for women and rising male unemployment, men attempt to maintain their hold on dominant forms of masculinity through violence against women. Interviews with men revealed that their ideas of "successful masculinity" were linked to their ability to become or remain economic providers for the family. Men facing chronic unemployment described feeling powerless and used this feeling as a justification for violence against women intimate partners (Boonzaier 2005, 100).

In a different context, that of globalizing Kuwait, men have also reacted against economic liberalization through violence. Studies examining the protest of Islamic fundamentalists against political, economic, and cultural liberalization have found that their resistance to economic restructuring is expressed through the prevalence of sexual and gender-based violence against women, which draws on traditional patriarchal discourses and objectifies women as symbols of liberalization (Tetreault 2003, 234). "[W]omen are implicated . . . not only because they are themselves objects of value and symbols of communal identity, but also because their emancipation introduces a new class of competitors for political and economic positions" (Tetreault 2003, 236). In the struggle between tradition and modern capitalism, women are subject to men's violence in their quest to maintain their dominant masculine identity and place.

Men lashed out violently against women in the democratic protests in Arab countries in 2010 and 2011, similarly to maintain their entitlements to political and economic positions, as women take up leadership roles in incipient democratic social movements and with the prospect of a new democratic regime that theoretically should redress gender inequalities in all rights and freedoms. On International Women's Day, March 8, 2011, the centenary of this day celebrating women workers, in Tahrir Square, Cairo, hundreds of women, many of whom had participated in the protests that toppled (President) Mubarak, chanted, "Now is the time—there is no freedom for men without freedom and equality for women." In a counterprotest, men objecting to the call for a new constitution allowing women to stand for the Egyptian presidency charged violently on the women while police and military stood by (Younnis 2011).

Soldiering Masculinities

Insufficient economic opportunities for men to provide for their families and as such live up to expectations of successful masculinity may encourage men to enlist as soldiers in militia or armies where women are usually unwelcome or a clear minority. Perpetrating violence against women or intimate partners is much more likely in this context. Chris Dolan (2002) argues that economically marginalized men in Northern Uganda welcomed the chance to restore their traditional male identity by following warmongers and becoming soldiers. However, as Chapter 7 discusses, soldiers in the Congo received only meager wages, if at all, and failed to achieve their expectation of successful masculinity (Eriksson Baaz and Stern 2009). Not only did they express their frustration at not being able to provide for their families and their fear that their wives would sleep with other men as a result, but they also used these feelings as justifications for individual and group rape. Box 3.4 explores the connection between masculine identities and guns as badges of masculinity that, whether intentionally or not, are used to perpetrate violence against women, including intimate partners.

Box 3.4 SMALL ARMS PERPETRATE VIOLENCE AGAINST WOMEN

Small arms and light weapons, firearms, or guns are possibly the most immediate tool in conflict. They are also an increasing tool in violence against women. The statistics are telling: 42 percent of worldwide homicides are committed with firearms; 40 percent of femicides in Mexico between 1985 and 2009 were committed with firearms (see Chapter 5); in Pakistan, the thriving gun-manufacturing market means that 65 percent of murdered women were killed using guns. In Venezuela, where there are anywhere from three to ten million illegal firearms, 99 percent of homicides annually are committed with firearms (Márquez 2011). In Amnesty International's (2011a) report on sexual violence in post-earthquake Haiti, guns were integral to men's perpetration of sexual violence. As Gerome (2011) points out, if rape during armed conflict is a threat to international peace and security, why not eliminate the small arms that facilitate it?

Guns are a source of masculine identity closely linked with power and subordination. They increase the likelihood of violence against women, and in the continuum of conflict, they legitimate it also. Men's predilection toward war and guns is not biologically innate, but socially constructed (Cockburn 2010, 143). But the continued attachment to guns deliberately maintains these gendered identities. Guns are a part of war and militarism, but they are used in all contexts to commit violence against women. Indeed, the *presence* of guns perpetuates conflict in the home and in public even after so-called war or armed conflict. The worldwide trend is that the low-income and least-educated segments of the population are increasing their possession of weapons—the same communities where family violence is often rife. Guns in the home can deliver fatal consequences when mixed with patriarchy and violence. In places such as Pakistan, where domestic violence is largely hidden, men use their guns to abuse women (Márquez 2011). In their study of torture committed by nonstate actors, Sarson and MacDonald (2009) found that 71 percent of survivors of ritual abuse/torture were terrorized with guns. A report by the Violence Policy Center (2010) in the United States similarly found that in addition to a means of committing murder, firearms were used in "hostile gun displays" as a common form of intimidation in domestic violence. In Montenegro, of 1,500 women seeking assistance from women's shelters, 90 percent were threatened with small arms by their partners (Gerome 2011). In domestic abuse cases, women are three to six times more likely to die if there is a gun in the house (Márquez 2011). In her mission to the United States, the UN special rapporteur on violence against women (2011, 28) noted the ubiquity of guns in domestic violence. One of her recommendations for remedies for women victims of violence was that guns should be confiscated by authorities at the first report of domestic violence.

David Capie (2011) analyzes the linkages between firearms and violence in Papua New Guinea (PNG). He cites the postconflict situation, ease in obtaining a firearm, high levels of crime, gang culture, and police corruption

(continued)

Box 3.4 (*continued*)

as contributing to high levels of sexual violence and gang rape in that country (Capie 2011, 45–46). PNG ranks 153 out of 187 countries on the Human Development Index (UNDP 2010), suggesting the intersection of extreme poverty and extreme violence. In such a context it is unsurprising that masculine identities are sought to overcome men's lack of economic power. Capie (2011, 50) shows how guns are a symbol of masculinity in PNG, not only for their real ability to subordinate but also because, as a highly sought after item, guns are viewed as superior to traditional weapons and the ultimate symbol of (economic and social) prestige and masculinity.

In 2009, the United States supported converting the working groups on an Arms Trade Treaty into preparatory committees for a 2012 draft text (IANSA Women's Network 2010). It was the first indication of support from the world's largest arms exporter and crucial player in the completion of a treaty (IANSA Women's Network 2010). IANSA—the international nongovernmental organization network against the proliferation of small arms—argues that any such treaty must include recognition of the gendered consequences of small arms. One of the pamphlets of a women's antimilitarism network studied by Cockburn (2010, 145) reads: "We need a redefinition of masculinity, strength, power and adventure; an end to war toys and the glorification of war and warriors." Like crime (see Box 3.1), small arms are the remnants of war and their association as symbols in the achievement of masculinity needs to be challenged if violence against women is to be eliminated. Criminal justice and small arms control risk irrelevance if they do not address the violent construction of masculinities.

Disaster Masculinities

The upheaval associated with the aftermath of disaster and the embrace of "strong men" in disaster-affected societies may be another risk factor for violent masculinities (discussed in greater depth in Chapter 9). In post-Katrina New Orleans, the "pervasive culture of masculinity" that developed among relief teams and volunteers in the context of hard physical reconstruction work and harsh living conditions was integral to the incidence of gendered violence and sexual assault of women volunteers (Luft 2008, 16). According to one volunteer in New Orleans, the physicality of the cleanup "created a machismo atmosphere of who could get the most amount of work done, and props to those who can" (Luft 2008, 16–17). Women working in New Orleans described it as an entirely male environment—not just in terms of the numbers of men and physical labor, but importantly, the structure of decision making and who was being listened to (Luft 2008, 17). Rachael Luft (2008, 17) labels this "disaster masculinity." In a postemergency environment with scant gender-sensitive organizational structure and little accountability, gender violence was highly plausible. Linking gender-based violence to the challenging of gender norms by female volunteers, she argues that it is not surprising "that a disaster zone characterized by a culture of heroic male adventure would display ambivalence about the boundary-transgressing women also positioned as disaster heroes" (Luft 2008, 26). In effect, masculinities may be threatened when women take up roles typically preserved for men and considered a marker of male identities as strong protectors.

Financial Risk-Taking Masculinities

The financial sector's culture of celebrating risk-taking behavior among men is one manifestation of the hegemonic business masculinity Connell refers to. The unregulated culture of finance also increases the risk of masculinities becoming violent. As Chapter 6 explores, the 2007 global financial crisis has been attributed in part to excessive risk taking and male "group think" in financial institutions. The crisis itself has been described as "a very male crisis" (European Commission 2010, 19) in part due to the concentration of men in the finance sector,[2] on corporate boards, and in institutions regulating finance and monetary flows and the notorious sexist culture on New York's Wall Street and the City, London's financial district (Prugl 2012). As the 2011 movie *Inside Job* depicts, afterhours visits to strip clubs and lap-dancing clubs, as well as hard drug taking, were daily practices among male financiers (see also Allen 2009). While there is no direct evidence of heightened violent behavior against women, as in the postdisaster context, it is made highly plausible in this context where masculine risk taking, power, and money collide.

Masculinity, Violence Against Women, and HIV/AIDS

We have seen how certain constructions of masculinity lead to various forms of violence against women so far in this chapter. But they also perpetuate that other major global epidemic, HIV/AIDS. Therefore, if we do not address and change the dominant forms of masculinity, we cannot hope to end the HIV/AIDS crisis, let alone violence against women on a global scale.

In South Africa, where over five million people are living with HIV, women make up 60 percent of people older than fifteen years living with HIV, and about 1.2 million children have been orphaned as a result of AIDS (UNAIDS 2009). Patriarchal norms and sexual violence undermine women's sexual and reproductive health. Likewise, intergenerational sex is an important factor contributing to the spread of HIV (Pettifor et al. 2004). Such relationships are frequent in South Africa owing to such factors as polygamy, subsistence needs, and materialism (Shisana et al. 2005). There is a substantial body of literature associating women's risk of HIV infection and violent and controlling masculinities (see Jewkes and Morrell 2010). Post-Apartheid South Africa has been the site of social, economic, and political upheaval. According to Lindegger and Quayle (2010, 47), this upheaval has significantly influenced gender identities. While eschewing gender uniformity, Lindegger and Quayle (2010, 43) nevertheless argue that "there is remarkable empirical consistency in constructions of hegemonic masculinity related to high-risk behavior for HIV transmission across geographical, cultural and linguistic divides in Africa and elsewhere." Risk taking, multiple sexual partners, unprotected sex, and sexual violence are markers of hegemonic masculinity, to which many South African men aspire (Brown, Sorrell, and Raffaelli 2005). The issue is racially fraught. Such constructions of South African masculinity have been lambasted by former president Thabo Mbeki, who criticized "racist" conceptualizations of African men as "rampant sexual beasts, unable to control our urges, unable to keep our legs crossed, unable to keep it in our pants" (*The Economist* 2004). Current gender violence in South Africa is possibly related to the idealization of traditional constructions of masculinity in response to the perceived threat of foreign human rights–based gender norms (Walker 2005). High levels of unemployment in South Africa challenge men's traditional breadwinner roles. A report by the South African National AIDS Council (SANAC) identified "limited support and leadership" as contributing to the lack of promotion of sexual and reproductive health, prevention of HIV/AIDS, and confrontation of the problem of violence against women (SANAC Women's Sector 2010 33). The president, Jacob Zuma, is himself a polygamist—a practice cited as contributing to HIV spread. Having served on the National AIDS Council, his ignorance stunned many when, during his trial in 2006 for the alleged rape of an HIV-positive woman, he stated that he took a shower after sex to lessen his chances of contracting HIV (Eetgerink 2006).

HIV intervention, especially prevention, necessitates "far more than information transmission and technological solutions (such as increased use of condoms) to modify male behavior" (Lindegger and Quayle 2010, 41). The construction of dangerous masculinities and behaviors must be challenged. There are several media campaigns and "edutainment" programs aimed at changing behaviors and raising awareness (Republic of South Africa [RSA] 2010, 14). Of these, two should be noted as importantly gender aware. Astonishingly, there are no data on the percentage of most at-risk populations (including women) reached with HIV prevention programs (RSA 2010, 18) and, hence, no way to accurately gauge which methods are effective.

"Brothers for Life" is a national media and advocacy campaign launched in 2009 that mainly targets men aged thirty and over. The campaign is a collaborative effort led by the South African government, foreign donors, intergovernmental organizations, and nongovernmental organizations (Brothers for Life 2011a). It features celebrities, sport stars, and reformed abusers and is specifically aimed at changing masculine behaviors that contribute to the spread of HIV/AIDS. Its slogan is "yenza kahle," which means "do the right thing" in Zulu. The manifesto reads:

> There is a new man in South Africa. A man who takes responsibility for his actions. A man who chooses a single partner over multiple chances with HIV. A man whose self worth is not determined by the number of women he can have. A man who makes no excuses for unprotected sex, even after drinking. A man who supports his partner and protects his children. A man who respects his woman and never lifts a hand to her. A man who knows that the choices we make today will determine whether we see tomorrow. I am that man. And you are my brother. (Brothers for Life 2011a)

Brothers for Life has a toll-free helpline for gender-based violence. The Springboks, South Africa's rugby team, have joined the latest "Brothers Against Violence" anti-gender-based violence campaign (Brothers for Life 2011b). In its "16 Points of Action to Stop Violence Against Women and Children," there is a strong emphasis on men reporting gender-based violence and men encouraging survivors to report their own abuse (Brothers for Life 2011c). Point number seven is "try to understand how your own attitudes and actions might perpetuate sexism and violence." There is also a strong emphasis on men disseminating the message of intolerance of gender-based violence and rallying the community, including abusers, to get behind the cause. Similar models of the program will be implemented in Tanzania, Zimbabwe, and Zambia because of South Africa's success. Brothers for Life has been endorsed as a model for best practices by Dr. Aaron Motsoaledi, minister of health in South Africa, because of its success in engaging over 350,000 men through mass media, advocacy, and interpersonal communication initiatives (John's Hopkins University Center for Communication Programs [JHUCCP] 2011).

Another program that addresses gender and HIV/AIDS was established with funding from cosmetics giant MAC. The MAC AIDS Fund Leadership Initiative (MAFLI) was launched in 2007 by the HIV Center and the UCLA Program in Global Health. The Human Sciences Research Council of South Africa (HSRC) became a partner in 2009. MAFLI is a fellowship training program aimed at cultivating "emerging leaders in South Africa who will make a major contribution to reducing the spread of HIV by addressing the link between HIV/AIDS prevention and gender inequality" (Ehrhardt et al.

2011). A goal of MAFLI was to form a South African–wide network on HIV prevention and gender (Ehrhardt et al. 2011). From 2007 to 2011, in four cohorts, the program trained forty-six fully funded fellows for one year and supervised the development of each fellow's HIV prevention plan for his or her community, continuing support for ten months (Ehrhardt et al. 2011). Most of the fellows were aged twenty-five to forty-five with a BA or MA, and 87 percent were women, of whom 80 percent were black, colored, or Indian (Ehrhardt et al. 2011). One fellow, Tshidi Maseko, an educational psychologist and co-founder and co-director of the Khanya Family Centre, included HIV and gender equity training with thirty-three staff at Khanya as a result of her participation in the training program, as well as introducing other HIV prevention services (Ehrhardt et al. 2011).

However, Lindegger and Quayle (2010, 49) warn of the potential for gender transformative discourses to fail to break through in meaningful ways beyond educational contexts. They think that men may appear responsive to educational initiatives that challenge dominant masculinities but may revert to unconstructive habits beyond the educative context (Lindegger and Quayle 2010, 49). Hence, a crucial challenge for the Brothers for Life program, and the MAFLI fellows, will be ensuring that the transformations observed in the programs also take place in the actual practice of men and masculinities (Lindegger and Quayle 2010, 49).

Gender helps us to understand why people behave as they do. Several characteristics of masculinity—such as risk taking, multiple sexual partners, lack of condom use, and violence—increase the risk of HIV infection. Prevention interventions based on gender equity will reduce not only new HIV infections but also violence against women and violation of women's human rights.

Involving Men in Efforts to End Violence Against Women

Violence against women is a men's issue, as the epigraph states. It is committed mainly by men and affects men's partners, wives, girlfriends, mothers, sisters, and daughters. Yet many men have become champions of nonviolence in the movement to end violence against women. Their activism demonstrates that the struggle to eliminate violence against women must be shared by both genders if we are to make inroads into one of the most hidden yet pervasive global problems of our time. We all have a role in ending violence, but men are crucial to this effort. Men's privileged gender position means that they control social discourse, laws, politics, law enforcement, and money and through these institutions can potentially end violence against women. It is men who must "deconstruct and reshape the dominant discourse on masculinity" (Kaufman 2001, 45). Ending violence against women is about "men changing" themselves, and encouraging others to do so, and "changing men"—breaking the silence and culture of impunity (Flood 2010, 9). Of course, this is hugely challenging, but the White Ribbon Campaign discussed in Box 3.5 is just one indication that the men's movement to end violence against women is gaining momentum.

Research by Casey and Smith (2010) suggests that three factors are critical in shaping men's involvement in efforts to end violence against women: personal, "sensitizing" experiences, which raise men's awareness of violence or gender inequalities; invitations for involvement; and making sense of these

---

Box 3.5 WHAT TYPE OF MAN ARE YOU?
THE WHITE RIBBON CAMPAIGN

The White Ribbon Campaign began in Canada in 1991 in the living room of Michael Kaufman. The group was formed in response to the "Montreal Massacre" of December 6, 1989, when an antifeminist man murdered fourteen female engineering students at the École Polytechnique. The men in the group were uncomfortable with the culture of silence that paralleled the abuse of women (Kaufman 2001, 45). As the symbol of the movement, the white ribbon would "neither be an act of contrition, nor a symbol of misplaced collective guilt; it did not indicate that the wearer was a great guy. Rather, wearing the ribbon was a personal pledge never to commit, condone or remain silent about violence against women" (Kaufman 2001, 45). UN Women has since become the formal partner of the campaign. It declared November 25 as "White Ribbon Day," beginning the sixteen days dedicated to activism to eliminate violence against women each year that ends on December 10, Human Rights Day. The campaign has spread around the world, most recently to Lebanon—the first White Ribbon Campaign in the Middle East (KAFA 2010). In New Zealand, the White Ribbon campaign has a number of major events: a White Ribbon Breakfast; a Giant Ribbon Pledge Project, which involves gathering signatures on sixty white fabric panels, which are sewn together to form a giant white ribbon that is displayed in prominent locations around New Zealand; and the White Ribbon Ride, led by the "Supa Maori Fellas," four Harley Davidson riding brothers who promote an alcohol-, drug-, and gang-patch-free motorcycle ride involving men from all over the country. Participants pledge "never to commit, condone or remain silent about violence towards women" (White Ribbon Ride 2011). White Ribbon Campaigns are also involved in year-round advocacy through media and outreach in schools, universities, and workplaces. Likewise, one of the White Ribbon's original aims was also to raise awareness about fatherhood and to redefine it as embracing, nurturing, and caregiving (Kaufman 2001, 49). Other groups, such as Sonke Gender Justice in South Africa, have mirrored such efforts at transforming fatherhood (Sonke Gender Justice Network 2011).

experiences in ways that are motivating. The annual motorcycle ride in New Zealand as part of the White Ribbon Campaign described in Box 3.5 registers with all three factors. However, Michael Flood (2010) cautions us not to over-estimate the success of programs to engage men in violence-against-women initiatives. The evidence is not yet in. However, the World Health Organization (2007), which evaluated fifty-seven interventions engaging men, reports that well-designed programs do show evidence of change in behavior and attitudes. In New Zealand, police attribute the record-high reporting of family violence (usually underreported) not necessarily to increased violence against women, but to the impact of antiviolence social marketing such as the "Say No to Violence" campaign and White Ribbon Ride (Davidson 2011).

Conclusion

A political economy perspective on gender relations compels us to secure men's economic and social rights, as well as women's. Masculinities are socially constructed and many; thus, they can be changed. We need to affirm nonviolent men and masculinities that are strong and caring but not necessarily imitating femininities. By resisting gender stereotypes, men's efforts to create alternate imaginings of nonviolent masculinities not only help to end violence against women but also enable men to take up healthier, emotionally in-touch and proud ways of being (Flood 2010, 10). The more that norms of care and responsibility are integrated into gender identities and not solely the imperative of statist "welfare" and dependency, the greater the challenge to neoliberal ideologies that maintain global economic and social inequality for women *and* men contributing not only to structural violence but also to violent societies (Snider 1998, 28).

Understanding masculinities is crucial to understanding and changing the political economy of violence against women. Men's campaigns to end violence against women are not about "blaming men"; they are based on the belief that men together with women can be a part of a different gender order (Kaufman 2001, 50). Shaming men not only will fail to effect change but also will reinforce men's internal contestation of gender relations that can lead to violence. We have seen how male violence against women can actually increase in globalizing contexts where women's social position is rising and their economic opportunities are expanding at the same time men are disenfranchised. Thus, for change to happen we need men to champion an end to violence against women, and we need women to champion these men and support alternate masculine identities.

| Crossing Borders to Make Ends Meet
Sex Trafficking, the Maid Trade, and Other
Gendered Forms of Labor Exploitation

The causes of human trafficking are rooted in a (global) economy in which
[women's] lives are commodities to be traded, used, and abused.

—BERNAT AND ZHILINA (2010, 3)[1]

Introduction

Economic globalization has increased the demand for women's cheap labor,
especially in the growing service sector. The employment of foreign-born
women extends across an increasingly broad range of economic sectors,
from prostitution and sex work, to domestic service and childcare, to highly
regulated occupations such as nursing. Migration has been one option for
women, as well as men, to receive an income and provide economic security
for themselves, their families, and often their countries, too. The expansion
of women's labor market participation in developed countries—which in the
decades since the 1980s has contributed more to global growth than India,
China, and the Internet combined (*The Economist* 2006)—and the reduction
of state welfare provisions have led to a growing demand for workers in
domestic, health, and social services, especially caregivers of children, the
elderly, and sick and invalid persons. As well, the globalization of business
and imported male migrant labor has fueled a very lucrative globalized sex
industry. The outcome of these globalizing processes is a significant feminizing of survival—not just of the women themselves, but of their households
and governments, in part due to the underdevelopment and indebtedness of
(formerly colonized) economies in the global South and protectionism and

financial austerity imposed by (formerly colonizer) economies in the global North. Crucially, violence has become part of the employment relationship in these thriving service industries due to the highly unequal power relations at work based on inequalities of gender, class, migrant status, and ethnicity. Migrant women workers are frequently exploited in poorly paid, and often unregulated, illegal employment as nurses, maids, nannies, and sex workers. They are inherently vulnerable to violence working in these conditions with low social status, living in degrading housing situations and lacking basic legal protections and opportunities for redress or alternative employment and income.

This chapter examines how the political economy of globalization encourages migration for employment but without attending to minimum social and labor standards that would protect against exploitation and violence. Poor women from racial and ethnic minorities with undocumented immigrant status are extremely vulnerable to violence in precarious and often illicit employment in services typically hidden from public view or the ambit of the law. Global structural conditions are thus responsible for exacerbating endemic violence against women. In order to prevent this violence, we must seek to regulate and/ or change these globalized forms of labor. Trafficking is deliberately discussed in this chapter as integral to global processes of labor exploitation and survival that are both highly feminized. Rather than fetishized (where a human relation is transformed into a commodity object), sex trafficking is conceived in this chapter as an extreme form of labor exploitation where power is exercised physically, economically, and psychologically to dominate, taking away the dignity and rights of the person, most of whom are women and girls.[2] Countertrafficking strategies and interventions that do not recognize this connection to labor and migration for economic livelihoods fail to address the structural causes and the consequences of violence against women. Rarely do they expand women's employment choices or bolster their ability to protect themselves against migration and employment-related violence.

This chapter consists of four parts. The first part examines the global and local environments that accentuate gendered inequalities, migration for precarious employment, and the attendant risks of violence. The second part considers women's survival strategies, especially the choice to migrate, given the need for their labor in developed countries and for their income in often impoverished families and countries. The third part investigates state responses to labor exploitation, highlighting the criminal justice approach adopted to stem trafficking in particular. I argue that governments in sending and receiving countries have failed to protect migrant women workers and to attend to the socioeconomic inequalities at the root of labor exploitation and trafficking. The fourth part analyzes a similar failure at the international level, noting how countertrafficking strategies tend to perpetuate violence against women with their focus almost solely on prosecution rather than prevention. The chapter concludes by considering alternative strategies for preventing violence suggested by a political economy perspective such as promoting decent work opportunities for migrant women workers.

Globalization, Gender Inequality, and Migration

Macrostructural Conditions

An understanding of the context of globalization is crucial for addressing transnational labor exploitation and trafficking in origin and destination countries, as well as at the global level. Global competition has expanded markets for cheaper female labor both in formal manufacturing economies and in informal economies associated with domestic and intimate services. Employment opportunities can no longer be satisfied by local markets where job losses are sustained in domestic industries due to more competitive and lower-cost industries, as well as protectionist policies in other countries. Corporations bargain hard with states to secure arrangements, such as special economic zones, which are discussed in Chapter 5, to limit labor standards and employees' rights (Cameron and Newman 2008, 26). State restructuring to facilitate global trade and investment and the failure of development policies have increased unemployment and poverty rates across countries. They have also reduced social services, requiring more women to become income earners for their families. The impact of this restructuring process is often referred to as the "feminization of poverty,"[3] and it is paralleled by the feminization of migration as more women look to urban areas and transnationally for the economic opportunities that are not afforded to them in their home region or country.

Developing countries actively encourage migration for remittances; foreign currency can, and does, form a vital part of GDP in these states, bolstering development and relieving domestic unemployment and the negative social consequences that flow from it (Cameron and Newman 2008, 21, 26; Chuang 2006, 144). Remittances from international migration in 2005 totaled $251 billion and have had a significant impact on diminishing poverty in developing countries (UNFPA 2006, 62). However, these remittances have been falling since the onset of the global financial crisis with households cutting back on services (see Box 4.1). The resulting impoverishment and indebtedness of economies in the global South have led to greater feminization of poverty and survival within and across households.

Box 4.1 IMPACT OF GLOBAL FINANCIAL
CRISIS ON WOMEN MIGRANT WORKERS

Migrants, especially the temporary ones, are generally among the first to lose their jobs in a global economic recession (Ghosh 2010, 89). "The combined effects of declines in both new immigration flows and migrant stocks, coupled with the spread of joblessness and a decline in the earnings of migrants and a growing feeling of economic uncertainty among them, led to a deceleration in the flows of remittances" (Ghosh 2011, 33). After the 2007 global financial crisis (GFC), migrant women and domestic workers were among the first to be laid off. This was in part due to prevailing gender and racist ideologies that consider their labor dispensable and in part because their part-time, flexible, and vulnerable work conditions made it easy for employers to fire them (Seguino 2009). In developing countries, women's incomes and family livelihoods disproportionately suffered after the crisis due to the drop in remittances from migrant women's care work, as well as women's employment concentration in export sectors such as manufacturing and high-value agriculture and the tightened conditions for microfinance lending to women farmers and entrepreneurs (Buvinic 2009, 4). Although we do not yet have any concrete evidence, it is likely that many more girls in low-income countries were pulled out of school as a result of the financial crisis, the loss of remittance income, and the loss of state support due to aid cutbacks from donor countries, and were likely led into sex work or trafficking as households coped with declining income.

Analysts expected that the global recession increased illegal migration because of fewer avenues for legal immigration in richer countries as unemployment rose and was attributed to immigrant workers (Ghosh 2010, 70). In this context, poverty is exacerbated and women and girls in poorer countries are especially vulnerable to exploitative employment and to trafficking. The International Organization on Migration predicts that with "the pressure for irregular migration thus building up, human traffickers could have a field day and see their trade flourish" (Ghosh 2010, 71). As more people go underground, there is a real possibility that exploitation and human rights abuses against migrants will increase, including violence (Ghosh 2010, 94, 103). Interestingly, despite the anti-immigration climate, some countries have deliberately sought to protect the supply of migrant domestic workers. For instance, in Europe, Italy confined its migrant quota to mainly domestic and personal care work (Ghosh 2010, 57). In Asia, although Malaysia revoked the job visas of 55,000 Bangladeshi immigrants and Thailand decided not to renew work permits for half a million migrant workers or issue new work permits, migrant domestic workers continued to flow into both countries during these restrictions. Indeed, Malaysia and Thailand even encouraged employers to lay off migrant workers to make room for domestic workers, which indicates just how crucial they are seen to be to the economy (Ghosh 2010, 60).

Box 4.1 (*continued*)

Overall, the crisis has had a disproportionate negative impact on women's and girls' incomes and livelihoods, which this book shows are linked to their increased risks of violence, due in part to men's responses to unemployment, economic displacement, and disempowerment. Economic and social security is crucial for both protecting and preventing violence against women; the GFC has thus set back efforts to eliminate violence and advance women's rights.

Migration has reinforced and deepened existing gender, race, and class inequalities. It is a gendered process inseparable from the devaluation of a broad range of jobs associated with "women's work" now carried out by a growing, mostly foreign female "serving class" especially in global cities (Sassen 2008, 1). Neoliberal economic policies have increased the number of women migrating for work, the type of work they inevitably do, and their situation of vulnerability to violence in often precarious employment positions. In 2005, women were nearly half of all economic migrants (95 out of 191 million) and they dominated in migration streams to developed countries. For example, women from Bolivia, Colombia, Ecuador, and Peru sent home a total of nearly $3.2 billion in remittances in 2010, more than the total remittances of male migrants (Chávez 2011; Arteaga 2010). As well as financially supporting their families, the pressures for women to migrate may include escaping from an unhappy marriage or a violent husband, or the social pressure to marry in patriarchal societies.[4] That is, women may be escaping violence in their home country only to experience further violence in a foreign country.

Violence may become part of the employment relationship due to the highly unequal power relations at work based on the combined oppressions of gender, class, nationality, and ethnicity. As nurses, maids, nannies, and sex workers, migrant women workers are often exploited and vulnerable to violence, working in poor conditions and lacking basic legal protections and opportunities for redress. Domestic workers do not enjoy the basic labor protections that most governments guarantee for other workers. They are typically excluded from standard labor laws such as minimum wage, regular payment of wages, a weekly day off, and paid leave. Employers evade domestic labor laws and governments rarely monitor their observance in the domestic sphere (Varia 2007, 1). Labor-sending countries often have an economic incentive to ignore their breach as they benefit from the high levels of remittances and may not wish to jeopardize their relations with relevant host countries.

Christine Chin's (1998) study of foreign female domestic servants in Malaysia describes how the government's export-led industrialization strategy is based on a system of social reproduction that imports poor women from Indonesia and the Philippines at minimal cost to work in the household/domestic sector, thus freeing up middle-class Malaysian women to work in the export sector (also Piper 2003, 724). The study recounts stories of violence and abuse of these women workers perpetrated by both male and female employers. It also reveals how female domestic workers are subject to public scrutiny and often derision in the popular media. The poor treatment of domestic workers has to do with their location in the private sphere, where, as nonfamily members, they provoke fears and where the normative assumption that a man is king in his own household reigns (Elias 2008).

Structural inequalities in global trade regimes allow freedom of movement for investors and professionals typically from developed countries but limit the movement and rights of low-skilled workers usually from developing countries. Human rights abuses and violence against migrant women are very common precisely because migrant domestic workers are not afforded the same basic labor protections guaranteed to other workers (Iredale and Piper 2003). Very few countries have ratified the international conventions that extend citizenship and labor rights to migrant workers. Just 23 percent of states have ratified the 1949 International Labour Organization (ILO) Convention on Migration for Employment, only 10 percent have ratified the 1975 ILO Convention Concerning Migration in Abusive Conditions and the Promotion of Equality of Opportunity and the Treatment of Migrant Workers, and a mere 17 percent have signed the 1990 International Convention on the Protection of the Rights of All Migrant Workers and Members of Their Families (ICMR; United Nations Population Fund 2006).[5] There are direct linkages between violence against migrant women workers and the failure of states to protect women's economic and social rights by monitoring labor standards and ensuring access to adequate housing, education, and alternative employment opportunities.[6]

Sex Trafficking—An Extreme Form of Labor Exploitation

Migrant women working in the sex sector and women and children trafficked for sexual exploitation or forced labor face extreme vulnerabilities. Although trafficking and migration for work are distinct phenomena, the parallels between them cannot be ignored given their similar structural causes and the fact that vulnerable migrant women and girls are prime targets for traffickers. Moreover, legal migration for domestic work can also have some of the characteristics of trafficking, for example, nonpayment of wages, contract substitution, and so forth (Asis 2008, 188). Human trafficking is "fishing in the stream of migration" (Coomaraswamy 2003). It is the dark underside of migration and inseparable from processes of globalization and trade liberalization (Truong 2001b). "Compared to other industries, the sex industry has attracted a disproportionate share of traffickers' interest," because it is illegal or partially decriminalized, there is certainty of demand, and it is extremely profitable, making it the perfect business for criminal networks (Cameron and Newman 2008, 31). Trafficking flows are generally from underdeveloped regions and states to more affluent regions and states (Cameron and Newman 2008, 22; see Seager 2008). Trafficking, therefore, needs to be discussed as an economic issue, relating to economic restructuring and economic and social rights, as well as an issue of violence against women, although it is not in the 1995 UN Fourth World Conference on Women's Beijing Platform for Action.[7] The trade in human beings is part of the globalization of trade in goods, investment, production, and services and also needs to be part of trade policy discussions at the World Trade Organization as well (Truong 2001b).

The flourishing of trafficking is linked with women's low socioeconomic status and their lack of economic rights in the context of neoliberal globalization (Lansink 2001). The majority of trafficked women have made a decision to migrate in search of better economic opportunities, not to be abducted or kidnapped or to work in indentured labor conditions. State policies that treat trafficked women as criminals or mere victims in need of rescue and rehabilitation fail to take account of their economic agency and their human rights in the prevention, protection, and prosecution of trafficking. States often seek to control women and police their bodies rather than empower them (Berman 2003; Sullivan 2003). Indeed, it is not migration for sex work that should be abolished, but rather the power relations between trafficked women and traffickers that involves physical, psychological, and economic violence against women, as well as violation of many other human rights. When slavery was abolished, for instance, it was the power relationship that was abolished, not working in the cotton fields or in domestic work (Lansink 2001, 8).

Globalization thus introduces new vulnerabilities to violence, as well as offering potential for empowerment through labor migration. But government policies that fail to attend to the basic social and economic entitlements of individuals and families make violence against women a more likely outcome than empowerment for women (SRVAW 2000). Restrictive immigration policies focused on national security and a narrow construal of economic interests lead to greater economic exploitation, physical abuse, and violence against migrant women workers. Research evidence shows that where countries have male-biased immigration laws, women migrants are more vulnerable to violence. This is because of several factors. First, where women are admitted into the country as a "dependent" on their husbands' visa, the power relations within the family shift, and there is an increase in the rates of domestic violence. Also, in these situations women are unable to leave their abusive husbands because they may then lose their visa. Second, where women are unable to secure legal migration, they may resort to trafficking or smuggling and working in the informal sector, where they are much more vulnerable to violence. Third, where visa and migration laws do not give migrant women full access to social services such as counseling or heath care, they are more vulnerable to violence. Finally, where women's visas are tied to their place of employment, they cannot leave without losing their immigration status, even if their employment situation is abusive (Varia 2007; Human Rights Watch 2008b).

Meso Forces—The Role of the State

Parallel to the transformation of the global political economy and its effects on the demand for migrants and on trafficking, governments are complicit in creating and perpetuating gendered inequalities that add to the "supply" of migrants, especially women. The case of China, discussed in Box 4.2, illustrates how government policies, in this case China's one-child family and pro-market policies, have had gendered consequences and how inattention to these consequences allows egregious violence against women, such as bride trafficking, to thrive.

Governments' failure to intervene in these discriminatory public employment conditions and private, social conditions renders them complicit in creating conditions for "supply" of labor (legal and illegal). In many countries, gender still determines which children are educated and to what level, and what work is most highly valued. Most often girls are denied a full education in view of their ultimate endpoint as a married woman in charge of the "household." The denial of girls' and women's rights to education and access to productive resources within the household is part of a broader and deeply embedded state and socially sanctioned ideology about women's gender roles. When this intersects with poverty, the result is the commodification of the marginalized—in this case the girl within the home—and increased vulnerability as families send or sell their children into migration streams.

Also within the private sphere and tacitly beyond the ambit of state intervention is domestic violence. Empirical evidence reveals that living in a dysfunctional family is one of the major causes for trafficking (Cameron and Newman 2008, 24; Kumar et al. 2001, 35). Gendered household relations

Box 4.2 CHINA'S TRAFFICKED BRIDES

In China, the combination of a Confucian patrilineal family system and the government's "one child" policy introduced in the 1970s has resulted in a consistently higher than usual sex ratio at birth: 116.9 male live births for every 100 females, and in rural areas as high as 130 males per 100 females (China National Bureau of Statistics 2004, 10; World Health Organization [WHO] et al. 2011, v). Son preference has given rise to China's "missing girls"—"missing" due to female infanticide and the widespread practice of sex-selective abortion (Banister 2004; Li 2007, 5). According to the 2000 census, the number of missing girls in China is estimated to be 40.9 million (Li 2007, 7). China's "missing girls" phenomenon (also prevalent, notably, in India) demonstrates how gendered power relations in the family interact with—and are perpetuated by—control over women by the state. Women, who are generally viewed as responsible for family planning in China, are under enormous pressure to produce sons, exposing them to violence and unsafe medical conditions (WHO et al. 2011, 5; China National Bureau of Statistics 2004, 22, 30). Prenatal sex selection has pervasive social and economic implications (UNFPA 2007a). Not the least implication is that the "entirely dominating system" sustains an environment of physical and structural violence against women (Li 2007, 6).

Among the effects of sex selection is the "marriage squeeze" that arises from the lack of marriageable women (Li 2007, 7). The proportion of excess males could eventually reach 20.7 percent in China (Li 2007, 7). The growing number of men who cannot find wives has given rise to trafficking of girls and women for forcible marriage from within China and from other countries such as Burma and Vietnam (Richburg 2009; WHO et al. 2011; Branigan 2011). Trafficking conditions, prevailing marital dynamics, gender norms, and frustrated Chinese masculinities increase the likelihood of violence against women. Trafficked women "are often unable to speak the local language, are deprived of their family environment and are under intense pressure to produce male children." (WHO et al. 2011, 5) Add to this the likelihood of sexual and domestic violence within these exploitative "marriages." Traditional Chinese attitudes that place women within the household render "invisible" the practices of bride kidnapping and trafficking, and the perpetuation of violence against women. Sex imbalances further entrench traditional views of the woman's home role, restricting women and girls' access to education and entry into the labor market—those resources that might enable them to protect themselves from violence (Guilmoto 2007, 12).

Addressing inheritance laws and domestic violence in China would have positive effects on the status of women, the number of females being born, and ultimately the exploitation of women in trafficking. China's hasty scramble to implement the "Care for Girls" program, while a necessary development, is likely "too little, too late" since the problem is the result of decades of skewed family planning (BBC News 2004).

and parental facilitation intersect with pervasive family violence that creates an irresistible combination of factors that lead to migration. First, domestic violence makes women more eager to leave the household for better conditions and independent economic opportunities; second, women are "battered" and vulnerable to trafficking physically and emotionally; third, as already stated, baseline gender inequality and patriarchal family dynamics reduce the likelihood of women's education and the better employment opportunities that are available with educational achievement (La Strada International 2008, 61–62; Bernat and Zhilina 2010, 3). Whether or not migration is deliberate or coercive, given the state-mediated gender inequalities in the family household and domestic violence, as well as the macrostructural conditions of globalization, we can see that "choice" is socially and economically constrained.

Women's Survival Strategies in a Global Economy

Migration has been one option for women to receive an income and provide economic security for their families and communities. Women are often chosen by their families to migrate based on the expectation that they will sacrifice themselves to a greater degree than men for the welfare of their families—that is, they will work harder, remit a higher proportion of their earnings, spend less on themselves, and endure worse living conditions (INSTRAW 2007; Kofman and Raghuram 2007).

Although organized crime is a fundamental characteristic of illegal migration and trafficking, it is not sufficient to explain the complexities of migration and the global labor market (Taylor and Jaimeson 1999). Women's survival strategies in the global economy simultaneously "push" and "pull" them into an increasingly diverse marketplace of goods and services where their vulnerability is a potential site for violence.

Push Factors

The supply of people available for export (legal and illegal) is the function of specific economic and social conditions in developing countries. We have seen how women flee from conditions of violence and oppression in the home, often perpetuated by the state (Bernat and Zhilina 2010, 3). However, the vast majority of women from Latin America and Asia are also fleeing the effects of structural adjustment policies being pursued in their countries of origin (Taylor and Jaimeson 1999, 262). We know that the majority of the world's poor are women and that women are disproportionately affected by such structural changes. However, the conditions of poverty are not entirely sufficient to explain migration, since migration requires resources. Theoretically, women should be *less* likely to migrate owing to their economic disadvantage and the fact that most opportunities for legal labor migration also tend to favor men's work, not informal "women's work" (Chuang 2006, 138). However, "survival migration" describes the "push" of poverty: families may sell their children and women may indenture themselves to pay the costs of migration. Poverty "challenges neo-liberal notions of individual choice" because it eliminates alternative means of survival but pushes women to choose migration as a way to escape oppressive economic and social conditions (Cameron and Newman 2008, 23). Thus, not all women are victims; often migration was their decision as an economic agent pursuing better access to productive resources and independence. Unfortunately, seeking alternate economic opportunities makes women especially vulnerable to the violence of traffickers (Asis 2008, 186). Poverty eliminates the ability to extract oneself from an exploitative situation, which is a crucial determinant of many trafficking situations where women may be initially compliant but are later unable to escape exploitative conditions (Cameron and Newman 2008, 22, 32).

The changeability of consent is what causes many people to confuse smuggling and trafficking. A woman "is a victim of trafficking if she is deceived about the conditions of work and then coerced or forced to work in exploitative conditions" (Cameron and Newman 2008, 33). Trafficking appears to play to the gendered expectations of women about what is acceptable work. Fake marriage is often promised to trafficked young girls. In Nepal, it was the second most prevalent means of trafficking young girls (Kumar et al. 2001, 21). Women are recruited for one gendered industry, such as domestic work, but are in fact forced into other gendered work, such as prostitution (Cameron and Newman 2008, 39). Because prostitution is unacceptable to many women, and often "professional prostitutes" can control their situation and clientele, traffickers target the most vulnerable women to become prostitutes in "cheap" conditions (Cameron and Newman 2008, 31).

Natural disasters and conflict-affected areas are also a significant feature of the supply of migrant women workers, as Chapters 8 and 9 examine. They create displaced people, especially women and children, who form "a vast reservoir of human beings living without rights, security, and, usually, any hope of a return home" (Taylor and Jaimeson 1999, 263). This is symptomatic of the general disorganization and lack of governance that disrupt normal immigration procedures and create conditions of unemployment and economic and physical insecurity (Cameron and Newman 2008, 47–48). In these conditions, criminal networks flourish and profit from a significant market opportunity to facilitate the delivery of exploitable labor. Traffickers also manipulate the suffering of female victims of violence in their own communities. In Guatemala, traffickers played on the shame of female victims of war rape, offering them working opportunities to escape the dishonor of returning to their families (Women, Health and Development Program and Pan American Health Organization 2004).

The push for migration involves the complex interaction of poverty, poor governance, and struggle for survival in a globalized "age of disposable people" where, as the Moldova case in Box 4.3 describes, women are more likely than men to be disposed of abroad. In this context, desperation leads to the choice to migrate, and demand ensures the steady flow of people within and across borders (Bales 1999).

Pull Factors

Women's survival strategies in the global economy generally fall into three economies of demand: cheap "sweat shop" manufacturing labor, domestic work, and sex work. The prospect of *any* job is a strong "pull" factor for survival migrants, and the certainty of supply perpetuates substandard labor conditions (Chuang 2006, 145; Taylor and Jaimeson 1999, 262). The demand arises from the dual work and family constitution of women's lives in the global North, aging populations, and declining fertility and birth rates, as well as the commodification of sex in popular culture and the transnationalism of the sex industry (Chuang 2006, 144–145).

As more women enter the workforce in the developed world, there is a deficit of care in the family household, making migrant domestic labor increasingly in demand. These household roles are underpaid and undervalued and therefore unattractive to many women in developed countries. A study by Anderson and Davidson (2003) found that employers of domestic workers in wealthy countries prefer to hire foreigners. The ethnic and racial difference of migrant domestic workers apparently "makes the hierarchy between employer and employee less socially awkward" for the more privileged employer (Chuang 2006, 146). A "global care chain" is established whereby wealthy, often European, women employ migrant women of color to replace their traditional caring roles, while these migrant domestic workers rely on other female family members to raise their own families back home in poorer communities and countries (Ehrenreich and Hochschild 2004). This recourse to the employment of migrant women roles is due not just to first world women relinquishing traditionally female household roles but also to men clinging to gendered notions of work/household responsibility rather than increasing their share of care and domestic work (Cameron and

Mimi Chakarova's 2011 film, *The Price of Sex* (www.priceofsex.org), exposes the shadowy world of sex trafficking across Europe and the Middle East told by the young women who were supposed to be silenced by shame, fear, and violence. The story begins in Moldova, where we are told that one Moldovan girl can be easily exchanged for one kilogram of cocaine or an AK47. Moldova has the undesirable repute of being both Europe's poorest country and Europe's biggest exporter of women. The discrepancy between rich and poor countries in Europe, the economic collapse of former communist countries, and the globalization of markets provide an opportunity for new forms of illicit trade. Moldova had the highest percentage of women workers under communism. Since the transition to capitalism, however, unemployment has skyrocketed to 15.4 percent, and women are a whopping 68 percent of those unemployed, according to the International Fund for Agricultural Development (Horn 2010). And as in many post-communist states, the role of women in Moldova has reverted to presocialist traditional roles that emphasize women as mothers or domestic caregivers. Yet Moldovan women are often breadwinners for their families, on lower salaries than men earn in Moldova or working "for higher pay and higher risks . . . abroad" (Horn 2010). Organized crime makes a business of exploiting people's lack of economic opportunity. Many of those who have migrated to other countries for work and opportunity have been deceived, made victims of traffickers and abusive employment practices abroad. Between 200,000 and 400,000 Moldovans have been trafficked for labor and sex work since the collapse of communism; unofficial estimates are even higher. The UN 2009 Trafficking in Persons Report estimates that 25,000 Moldovans were trafficked in 2008 alone (UNODC 2009). The state, with few resources and corrupt officials, offers little protection to its citizens. Meanwhile, the price is high for Moldovan women in trafficking destinations such as Dubai, where all races and classes of men demand sex (including the laborers building the city's glittering mirror glass skyscrapers). The race and nationality of women are ranked by male purchasers, with Eastern European white women commanding the highest price, followed by Middle Eastern women, African women, and Asian women.

Newman 2008, 41). Although domestic work is a frequent trafficking purpose, legal regulation of this work varies across countries. As with sex work, migrant women workers in the private, typically "invisible" sphere have a greater susceptibility to violence and exploitative conditions, which the Dominique Strauss-Kahn affair in Box 4.4 patently illustrates.

With respect to sex trafficking, the pull factors include the immense expansion of markets for sexual representations through pornography, mainstream television, and the Internet (True 2003; Taylor and Jaimeson 1999). Trafficking

Box 4.4 SEX, LIES, AND HAUTE FINANCE: THE "DSK AFFAIR"

There have been many scandals involving western politicians and their domestic help; more typically in the United States they have involved prospective women federal cabinet members failing to have their positions confirmed by Congress when they were found to have employed illegal immigrant women domestic workers to look after their household and children. In the DSK affair, the story is a sex scandal and involves a man having a very different relationship to domestic work and workers. But it reveals the same racial and nationality hierarchies as the cases involving powerful women. Here Dominique Strauss-Kahn (DSK), the head of the International Monetary Fund (IMF), savior of European bailouts, and former French socialist politician, was alleged to have raped a maid, Nafissatou Diallo, an immigrant in the United States from Guinea—a poor country in Africa, in receipt of an IMF loan and subject to IMF structural adjustment conditionality—in his New York presidential hotel suite. One of the gendered impacts of IMF policies Strauss-Kahn oversaw has been an increased migration of women seeking survival employment in foreign countries when harsh IMF austerity measures erode local economic opportunities. Migration can provide better opportunities and even empowerment for women, but it can also leave them vulnerable to abuse and violence, as is the case of DSK's exploits.

Since May 2011, evidence has emerged that the DSK affair was a setup, possibly by French political rivals of Strauss-Kahn supporting Sarkozy for president, and that DSK was warned about this when his phone went missing on the morning of the alleged rape (*Sydney Morning Herald* 2011). Whether true or not, the striking thing is that DSK likely committed sexual violence even after having been warned about such a plot. In the global media storm that followed the rape allegations, forcing DSK to resign from his IMF post and ending his political career, little attention was paid by journalists and political commentators to the woman who was the apparent victim of DSK's attack. The domestic migrant woman worker is almost invisible in the face of international politics and economics, just as the austerity policies, for which DSK has been held up as personally responsible as IMF chief, have reinforced the invisibility of women who have been negatively affected by his personal and public actions. In this real-life story, we see how women who migrate to work in the service industries of richer countries are especially vulnerable to sexual violence—and that labor and sexual exploitation often go together in the private sphere where service work often takes place, under the radar of law and available protection.

This is not a story with a happy ending, a "Pretty Woman" fantasy, or a "Cinderella" transformation.

must be viewed as a part of this globalized economy, which was established by often legitimate actors—entrepreneurs—but which international criminal groups have since infiltrated, mining sources of vulnerable labor in impoverished and often conflict-affected settings, as Chapter 8 recounts (Taylor and Jaimeson 1999, 274). The purpose of this chapter is to conceptualize labor, whether for sex, domestic work, or other social services, as part of the unequal power relationships between people given their relative social and economic circumstances within the global economy, where the threat of violence to maintain these relationships is always present.

State Failure to Prevent Violence Against Women Workers

State responses to labor migration are characterized by an almost universal failure to locate women's vulnerability to violence as a symptom of their gendered economic and social inequality. Migration is resisted by states through ever-restrictive immigration policies despite being absolutely necessary for their economies. Characterizing migrant laborers as "the other" makes it easier to deny them equal labor rights and the same working conditions as employees who are citizens (Cameron and Newman 2008, 46). The justifications for the control and limitation of migration are couched in terms of state "security" rather than concern about human beings. Women make up the majority of labor in the informal sector, reflecting their unequal economic position and the gendered division of household labor, which restricts their ability to enter the formal labor market. Segrave, Milivojevic, and Pickering (2009, 193) observe that "there is a form of sexual violence in women's economic, social and cultural exclusion metered out in the almost total absence of legitimate transnational migration options." The refusal of states to acknowledge the realities of migration, including the feminized circuits of survival, while benefiting from the transnational sex industry renders states complicit in the dangerous consequences of illegal migration, notably the violence of trafficking, as Box 4.5 illustrates in the case of Thailand (Asis 2008; Chuang 2006, 146). Yet ironically, trafficking has become the raison d'être of border control strategies (Segrave et al. 2009, 30).

Countering Trafficking but Discounting Violence

The resistance of all states, and not merely Thailand, to addressing the gendered social and economic inequalities that feed trafficking is in some respects unsurprising. Treating trafficking as a criminal justice issue has become the dominant international approach. It is far less resource intensive and politically challenging than developing long-term strategies to address

Box 4.5 THAILAND'S SEX TOURISM, TRAFFICKING,
AND THE THAI ECONOMY

Thailand's sex tourism and trafficking is a story of supply and demand intimately associated with the actions of the state and globalization processes. Leslie Jeffrey (2002) documents how the Thai sex industry grew out of demand by American servicemen in South-East Asia during the 1960s and 1970s. Although prostitution was a preexisting part of Thai society (and currently, the majority of customers are Thai men), "sex" did not become the well-organized industry that it is today until the influx of foreign (military) men encouraged by the 1967 "Rest and Recreation" agreement between the United States and Thailand (Diep 2004, 315). In the 1980s, Thailand introduced a policy agenda that allowed the sex industry to develop. Phongpaichit (1997) locates the emergence of trafficking in the Thai government's policy of encouraging women to emigrate and marry expatriate Thai men. At that time Thailand was undergoing restructuring toward an export-led economy. Restructuring created vast economic disparity between urban and rural areas as a result of the decline of the rural agricultural sector in which women were the majority of laborers (Singh and Hart 2007, 161). The loss of agricultural employment and the growth of the tourism industry catalyzed women's migration from rural to urban Thailand, where their most ready source of income was factory work, domestic service, or sex work (Jeffrey 2002, xiii). Encouraged by the International Monetary Fund and the World Bank, the Thai government actively developed its tourism and entertainment industries (Poulin 2003, 38), and the sex industry was an integral part of this expansion (Truong 1990). The government promoted sex tourism with advertising: "The one fruit of Thailand more delicious than durian [a local fruit], its young women" (Poulin 2003, 38). Poulin (2003, 40) describes this as the cultural "prostitutionalization" of Thai society, a reputation resented, yet economically beneficial to the Thai government. Although the government is less explicit about sex tourism now, owing in part to Thailand's reputation as a hub of sex trafficking, the tourism industry generates billions of dollars a year, and whether acknowledged by the government or not, sex tourism is a central part of this revenue (Singh and Hart 2007, 163; Bishop and Robinson 1998). The sex industry supports millions of people in all areas of the service sector (Singh and Hart 2007, 162), while remittances from sex workers to rural families have been estimated at $300 million annually (Lim 1998, 12). Sex work provides an income vastly greater than median wages, and its proliferation is arguably the result of an economically strategic choice for many women (Arnold and Bertone 2002, 32; Jeffrey 2002). In Thailand, as with other places, the nexus between poverty, gender inequality, and prostitution is hard to miss.

The receptive Thai environment for sex work has facilitated a burgeoning sex trafficking trade. Thailand is a source, transit, and destination country for human trafficking (Segrave et al. 2009, 23). Lim (1998) reported that the Thai underground economy amounted to over thirty-three billion dollars per

Box 4.5 (*continued*)

year, two-thirds attributed to the sex industry, amounting to 10–12 percent of GDP. Trafficking is estimated to be worth 500 million Bahts annually (approximately US$124 million) (Poulin 2003, 38). There is a significant domestic flow of migrants from rural northern Thailand to urban areas, but as fewer Thai women enter prostitution due to the improved standards of living (relative to other neighboring nations), trafficking of women and girls into Thailand from Burma, China, Vietnam, Cambodia, Laos, Russia, and Central Asia is increasing (Segrave et al. 2009, 24). The internal traffic of Thai females consists mostly of twelve- to sixteen-year-olds from the hill tribes of the North and Northeast (Arnold and Bertone 2002, 49; Dinan 2008). Without legal status, hill tribe ethnic minorities are considered "illegal aliens" and subject to arrest, deportation, extortion, and other forms of abuse and denied basic human rights such as voting, land ownership, movement, and educational qualifications. As such, their opportunities for employment are seriously limited, explaining their overrepresentation in the sex industry and vulnerability to trafficking. Foreign women "are generally at the bottom of the prostitution hierarchy," with Thai men choosing Thai prostitutes because foreign prostitutes are associated with "lower" and cheaper establishments (Poulin 2003, 39). This treatment further enhances their vulnerability to violence, combined with their social and cultural isolation and lesser earnings.

Thailand's legal framework includes the Prostitution Prevention and Suppression Act B.E. 2536 of 1996 and the Measures in Prevention and Suppression of Trafficking in Women and Children Act B.E. 2540 of 1997. The 1996 act partly decriminalizes prostitution and links it to poverty, social problems, and organized crime. Although it includes penalties for prostitutes themselves, it chiefly targets parents who sell their children for sex work, sex industry "entrepreneurs" that exploit prostitutes (including traffickers), and clients of underage prostitutes (Jeffrey 2002). However, these regimes sit uncomfortably with the Immigration Act, which does not distinguish between victims of trafficking and illegal migrants. Any migrant is charged with illegal entry and placed in the International Detention Center (IDC). A Memorandum of Understanding (MOU) was developed between the police and NGOs that provides for shelters instead of detention facilities prior to repatriation and includes treating foreign migrant children as Thai nationals (Derks 2000, 33). However, many police in Thailand refuse to recognize that the MOU overrides immigration law (Arnold and Bertone 2002, 47–48). Eventually, the Royal Thai Police in Bangkok issued a Royal directive stating that the MOU be enforced seriously (Arnold and Bertone 2002, 47–48).

Despite the putative legal response, the situation in Thailand is extremely complex due to the porous borders with poorer neighboring states and the potential for trafficking to dissolve into the enormous (voluntary) prostitution market, and because there are multiple government agencies involved. There are also competing agendas for inbound trafficking victims and Thai victims

(*continued*)

Box 4.5 *(continued)*

trafficked elsewhere (Segrave et al. 2009, 25). Thailand is unique because of the extensive international NGO network operating throughout the country to address trafficking, which has had a major impact on shaping the Thai responses (Segrave et al. 2009, 25). But these efforts are thoroughly dependent on the long-term commitment of the state to address the structural dimensions of trafficking. What is clear is that significant economic benefits come from the sex industry and trafficking. The illegality of prostitution and the state's tacit approval of the commercial sex industry are contradictory (Singh and Hart 2007, 162). Moreover, the lack of awareness, resources, and cooperation among police, as well as corruption, hinders effective law enforcement (Derks 2000, 34). A questionnaire is used to identify trafficked victims due to NGO pressure, for instance, but not all women are questioned using this "special" questionnaire. Essentially the screening process is random (Segrave et al. 2009, 50).

Sex trafficking is part of structural discrimination, nationally and internationally, as development is uneven and women are resources to be exploited in the growth of emerging economies such as Thailand (Poulin 2003, 39). Race-based discrimination combines with state prescribed laws of residence and citizenship, neglect, and outright discrimination on the part of the Thai police and government to exacerbate people's disadvantage (Cameron and Newman 2008, 43). Thailand conveys the complicity of states in trafficking through the creation of a highly lucrative sex industry "safe haven" (Diep 2004, 310).

the labor migration aspects of the problem. When the Palermo Protocol to Prevent, Suppress and Punish Trafficking in Persons, Especially Women and Children, an attachment to the Transnational Organized Crime Convention, was negotiated, UN member states agreed to criminalize trafficking and enforce other prosecutorial measures, but they failed to fully integrate human rights, especially women's rights, into the trafficking policy response (Segrave et al. 2009, 18). Countertrafficking strategies, championed above all by the United States, primarily seek to identify and prosecute the traffickers. Yet criminal prosecution has not proved effective in reducing trafficking (Chuang 2006, 138). It ignores the social and economic root causes of trafficking, which are usually more concerning to the "victims" themselves.

Countertrafficking strategies based on a gendered law-and-order approach necessitate a clear delineation between trafficking victims and illegal migrants. But the line between victim and illegal migrant is ambiguous: for instance, women who genuinely intend to migrate for sex work may pay middlemen to take them to another state but then end up in exploitative conditions beyond their control (Segrave et al. 2009, 52). Most women appear to bypass formal victim processes and are picked up by authorities and deported as illegal noncitizens. This attests to the failure of states to locate trafficking in broader patterns of migration. It demonstrates how the overall impetus for the system is maintaining the sanctity of national borders rather than protecting women's human rights (Segrave et al. 2009, 27–30). The binary of ideal victim and illegal noncitizen is necessary for this securitization.

In the criminal justice approach, trafficked women have two choices: either they choose "victimization" and become a witness or they choose not to cooperate and fall into the status of "illegal noncitizen." For many women this is not a choice but an ultimatum (Segrave et al. 2009, 80, 88). In their study of sex trafficking, Segrave et al. discovered that women all saw their encounters with police as "getting caught." The women interviewed "cited physical intimidation, verbal abuse, humiliation and mistreatment by police as common experiences" (Segrave et al. 2009, 59). While in police custody they would have no food, water, or toilet and would not know their rights (Segrave et al. 2009, 61). Yet cooperation was the only way they could access any kind of assistance, welfare, or victim migration status. The approach to criminal prosecution was also highly subjective. It starts with a system of identification that is almost entirely up to the discretion of officials, influenced by their prevailing gender and racial stereotypes and prejudices (Segrave et al. 2009, 53; Bernat et al. 2010, 4). Officials draw upon "women's *performance of victimization* . . . of [the] innocent and passive victim, subject to extremely exploitative conditions" (Segrave et al. 2009, 51 [emphasis added]). In an interview with Segrave et al. (2009, 141), a legal aid solicitor in Australia stated that "[w]omen who come across as naïve ones, they're treated more sympathetically. The ones that come across as streetwise and smart are absolutely ripped to shreds by the defense lawyers." During the prosecution process, women's complex stories of victimization were reduced to "manageable linear journeys in which 'the rescue' is always a desirable outcome for victims of trafficking regardless of what might be the end result of this process" (Segrave et al. 2009, 35).

The privileging of criminal justice satisfies the state because it is highly visual and seems as though the state is "doing something" while leaving immigration policy unchallenged. Similarly, countertrafficking is instrumentalist in that it produces measurable criminal justice outcomes but not necessarily protection of trafficked persons from further violence or the prevention of trafficking violence (Segrave et al. 2009, 123). There is no feeling of catharsis for victims of trafficking. This is because their experiences of violence are not simply physical but also social and economic. The findings of Segrave et al. (2009, 86) reveal that many women decided the possible benefits of cooperation, such as a long-term stay visa in Australia, which were not guaranteed, were not worth the cost. This is also the conclusion of the film *The Jammed*, which is based on actual transcripts of trafficking victims in Australia. In so-called successful prosecution cases, the victim's return home is brought about, allowing the receiving state to relinquish any further duty toward victims of trafficking. Virtually no emphasis is placed on empowering women in repatriation, enabling choice, or acknowledging their status as people who seek migration to improve their material access and independence, sometimes through sex work.

Countertrafficking initiatives are driven by the security prerogatives of the state and championed above all by the United States, as discussed in Box 4.6. They deny that "trafficking is fishing in the stream of migration," as stated by Radhika Coomaraswamy (2003), the first UN special rapporteur on violence against women. States frame trafficking as an issue of moral decline and transnational organized crime, evading their responsibility for labor exploitation (Segrave et al. 2009, 83). Consider the disparity in the approach of states to protecting migrant workers versus "trafficking victims": it took thirteen years for the International Convention on the Protection of the Rights of All Migrant Workers and Members of their Families (the Migrant Workers Convention) to enter into force, and just three years for the Palermo Protocol to be ratified at the United Nations (Chuang 2006). Yet egregious human rights violations are experienced by both groups, especially women, given that they are most likely to be trafficked and also the majority of the informal, "invisible" labor market. By making the victims of trafficking the target of law enforcement efforts, governments only exacerbate women's vulnerability to abuse and violence and deter them from turning to law enforcement officials for assistance (Gupta 2010). This is the major flaw in the US approach to monitoring Trafficking in Persons.

Toward Decent Work Alternatives

The failure of countertrafficking strategies demonstrates the lack of understanding of the gendered dimensions of the phenomenon: that structural conditions lead to the push to migrate, that trafficking takes advantage of gender-based exploitation, and that it is unlikely trafficked women can or want to return to their original conditions. Further, the criminal justice approach taken by the United States and most other countries pursues legal protection of victims but without providing alternative options for livelihood and survival. It addresses trafficking as if it were an "individual" problem rather than a form of violence against women embedded in gendered structures of poverty, underdevelopment, discrimination, and inequality in communities and

Box 4.6 US TRAFFICKING IN PERSONS MONITORING

The US Trafficking Victims Protection Act of 2000 sets out minimum standards for the implementation of measures to eliminate trafficking. The State Department reviews the efforts of individual countries classified as "source," "transit," or "destination" states. The system ranks countries according to a three-tier system, with the results published in an annual Trafficking in Persons (TIP) Report. Importantly, the United States issues sanctions against states classified as Tier 3—states that fail to meet US standards to address trafficking. There is a noteworthy correlation between Tier 3–classified states and those states with whom the United States has strained diplomatic relations: among them Cuba, North Korea, Venezuela, and Iran (Desyllas 2007, 67). Although formally the system provides for measures relating to the "3 Ps" of prevention, protection, and prosecution, the TIP system has entrenched a criminal justice approach and the realization of tangible prosecutorial outcomes. It mirrors a similar focus in the Palermo Protocol. The protocol couches the criminal justice provisions as hard obligations, while provisions to prevent trafficking are programmatic and aspirational (Chuang 2006, 148). The TIP Report and the Palermo Protocol framework together make up the gold standard of trafficking response. They are coercive—pressuring governments to adopt similar law-and-order responses to trafficking. So far the approach has elicited a broad response from governments, making the TIP system among the more influential of US human rights measures. But with its focus on criminal prosecution, the framework diverts attention away from socioeconomic and migratory causes of trafficking. The TIP/Palermo supremacy demonstrates the hegemonic position of the global North in constructing and defining trafficking and policy responses (Desyllas 2007, 58).

A criminal justice response assumes that effective law-and-order institutions are in place, which is not the case in many developing states. Many countries have signed or ratified the Palermo Protocol but lack the political will or capacity to create domestic laws, and programs to implement its basic aims (Cameron 2008, 90). The TIP/Palermo framework is largely unquestioned. Few analysts or scholars challenge the US TIP data or the focus on prosecution, despite the fact that "trafficking policy in the U.S. was formed and supported by religious leaders, neoconservatives, abolitionist feminists and NGOs." (Desyllas 2007, 65) Until 2005, the TIP Reports focused on sex trafficking rather than forced labor, and only in 2010 did the US government include an assessment of its own countertrafficking efforts. The 2010 TIP Report placed the United States in Tier 1—a government that has acknowledged the existence of human trafficking and whose measures "fully comply with the TVPA's minimum standards for the elimination of trafficking" (End Child Prostitution and Trafficking USA 2010). Segrave et al. (2008, 130) call the criminal justice system led by the United States "part of a performance for an international audience."

(continued)

Box 4.6 (*continued*)

The US response to trafficking can be located in a masculine context of violence and war, where the imperative to "combat" trafficking reflects the necessity of masculinity to rescue innocent and childlike female "victims" from "the barbaric crime of trafficking" (Desyllas 2007, 65, 71). A political economy understanding of the structural causes of trafficking cannot be easily reconciled with the crusading approach of the United States. By placing the burden of proof on the "victims" in order to access temporary visas and other welfare, the system caters to law enforcement rather than protection or prevention outcomes. Establishing international countertrafficking measures designed mainly to prosecute individual criminals, the system alleviates states' responsibility to examine the deeper causes of trafficking, including the feminization of survival and migration, and overlooks states' own complicity in creating an environment where trafficking can thrive.

globally. States and the international community have a responsibility to change these structural conditions such that better economic and social options are created for vulnerable women and girls, giving them actual choices—which they don't have in either their original or trafficked situation. Rather than restricting women and girls' right to migrate and seek work, "the real challenge lies in creating the guarantees for them to do so safely and with dignity" (Varia 2007). Migration can increase women's self-esteem, personal autonomy, and social and economic status. It may enable them to generate the income to become property owners in their local communities and to begin small businesses. It will almost certainly improve their bargaining position within patrilineal or gendered households and allow them to enjoy increased social recognition from the community as a whole—all of which are factors predicted and proven to lessen women's vulnerability to violence (Ramírez, Domínguez, and Morais 2005).

One approach is to formalize informal sector employment, extending the same working conditions, rights, benefits, and protections to noncitizens as are available to citizens. The landmark ILO Convention 189 (International Labour Organization 2011) and 201st Recommendation adopted in 2010 does just that for domestic workers worldwide,[8] many of whom are migrants or members of other disadvantaged communities and who are particularly vulnerable to discrimination in respect of conditions of employment and work, and to other abuses of human rights (International Labour Organization 2011). The convention recognizes and values the contribution of domestic work to local and global economies. It promotes regulation as the best way to protect women and prevent violence and abuse by making domestic working conditions "visible" and on a par with regular employment. Individuals and civil society organizations now need to keep the pressure on states to implement the convention in national laws and policies following the ILO guidance in Recommendation 201 and to change the social norms that make it acceptable for us to exploit the vulnerable labor of other human beings.

With respect to preventing trafficking as an inherently violent practice targeting women and girls, rather than focusing on prosecution, state and global policies need to address the fundamental structural conditions of trafficking (Cameron and Newman 2008, 21). For instance, states need to develop non-discriminatory local employment opportunities specifically aimed at young women as potential employees, as well as provide access to key social and economic rights. As Gupta (2010) stated in Geneva in 2010, trafficking survivors "want more than a bed in a shelter or a condom in a brothel. They want access to safe housing, education and training, jobs, land and livelihoods." Legal protection without viable economic options and individual rehabilitation without community development and empowerment are unlikely to stop the lure of trafficking (Gupta 2010). The European Parliament, in its 2010 Resolution on Preventing Trafficking in Humans, holds states accountable for ending trafficking. It calls for an annual joint report by Eurojust, Europol, and Frontex (the European Union border security agency) on the key causes and factors in countries of origin and destination facilitating human trafficking. The report would be presented to the European Parliament, national parliaments, and the European Commission and Council and involve a public hearing, including NGO and civil society participation. It mandates data collection on criminal modus operandi and trafficking routes and an evaluation mechanism for EU country implementation of trafficking policies. Compared with the US Trafficking in Persons system of monitoring, the broader and less punitive mandate of this proposed European Parliament reporting system could begin to address the social and economic drivers of trafficking, rather than merely its criminal facilitators.

Conclusion

Violence against women is intimately connected to women's labor and working conditions in an increasingly globalized and competitive market economy. This chapter has argued that state security and criminalization approaches do not attend to the socioeconomic disadvantage and inequalities at the root of labor abuse and trafficking. States have collectively failed to recognize that trafficking is inseparable from global migration processes and to understand trafficking's embeddedness in uneven development and gendered inequalities. They have also not met their obligations to achieve progressive realization of social, economic, and cultural rights under international human rights agreements. In so doing, states are powerless to prevent ongoing and endemic violence against women. International antitrafficking initiatives are counterproductive as well. The lack of protection and alternative livelihoods afforded to women victims makes it difficult to prosecute traffickers and has hardly affected the flourishing of the illegal trade. Above all, the narrow focus on trafficking, especially for sex work, has allowed states to consistently ignore the broader issue of the abuse, exploitation, and unfair and unequal treatment of migrant workers, especially in the domestic service sectors, where women and girls predominate.

| New Spaces of Gender Violence
Economic Transition and Trade Liberalization

Introduction

Transitions to capitalism and liberalization of trade have facilitated the integration of economies without protecting local production, people's livelihoods, gender equality, and human rights. The destabilization of social and economic life by macroeconomic policies, including structural adjustment policies, is associated with growing inequalities and increasing levels of violence against women in several regions, including Europe and the former Soviet Union, Latin America, Africa, and Asia (UNICEF 1989).

The growth of trade has facilitated the globalization of export-oriented, labor-intensive industries. The creation of "free trade" or special economic zones, exempt from many government regulations, exacerbates gendered inequalities and creates unregulated environments in which violence against women thrives. These industries have largely employed women's labor, often young, migrant women from rural areas hired on temporary contracts at lower wages than men with minimal benefits. Violence against women workers, including abuse of reproductive rights, sexual harassment, rape and sexual violence, and, most egregiously, "femicide," the gender-based murder of women, has been prevalent in many of these free trade zones in developing countries, where extractive industries involved in exporting natural resources for advanced production elsewhere and new manufacturing industries for global consumer markets have been established (SRVAW 2005b, 2006b, 2011). Violence against women can be seen as a response by men to larger, changing socioeconomic conditions, as discussed in Chapter 3 (Scheper-Hughes and Bourgois 2004, 5). Rapid change in entitlements to employment and assets, and acquisition of newfound resources and power can produce gendered imbalances that greatly increase violence against women. This has been the case in the transitions to capitalism in Eastern Europe and China after 1989 (Chan et al. 2008).

The first part of this chapter explores cases of both manufacturing and extractive export industries from Mexico, Guatemala, the Pacific Islands, and Africa and their impact on violence against women. The second part considers the role of international financial institutions that have extended development loans for export industries that have exacerbated sexual and gender-based violence. The chapter concludes by reflecting on initiatives that could forge *nonviolent economies* that improve gender-equal livelihoods and opportunities as a way to diminish violence against women.

Violent Transitions: Gender, Markets, and Trade Liberalization

The market transitions in Central and Eastern Europe and the former Soviet Union since 1989 have led to widespread increases in poverty, unemployment, hardship, income inequality, stress, and violence against women. These factors have also indirectly raised women's vulnerability to violence by encouraging more risk-taking behavior, more alcohol and drug abuse, the breakdown of social support networks, and the economic dependence of women on their partners (UNICEF 1999; True 2003). Box 5.1 discusses the case of Russia: the high levels of domestic violence, as well as other forms of violence, in the post-communist transition and the societal acceptance of this violence as women's economic and social status has declined in the post-Soviet era.

Some have viewed Eastern Europe, including Russia and Central Asia, as "test regions" for judging the impact of neoliberal macroeconomic policies (Elson 2002). Rather than revealing positive impacts of market reform, almost all the countries in these regions have exhibited regressions in women's economic and social status (see SRVAW 2006c). The biggest regression globally in the economic status of women has been in Eastern Europe, according to Social Watch's 2008 Gender Equity Index. In addition to increases in rape and domestic violence, this region has seen hundreds of thousands of young women trafficked for prostitution and other indentured labor each year due to the consequences of economic liberalization, as seen in Chapter 4. Yet most analyses of the impact of globalization and liberalization have focused on the public sphere exploitation of women workers by multinational corporations or the impact of state austerity policies on women, rather than the increased violence against intimate partners as a result of economic transition and integration—and the rapidly changing,

Like other former communist states that have transitioned from command to market economies, Russia's transition from the Soviet era to capitalism has not been gender neutral (Paci 2002; True 2003). A report by the World Bank states: "GDP has fallen, absolute poverty has increased five-fold and employment and wages have plummeted. Mortality rates have increased sharply while fertility rates have dropped" (Paci 2002, ix). Transition in Russia has had "contradictory effects" on women (SRVAW 2006c, 5). Transition has pushed women from previously high levels of full-time, secure employment into precarious employment in marginal, low-paying and low-status sectors of the economy (Weiler 2004, 69–70). The effects of liberalization in Russia have led to an increase in unemployment, crime, and privatization, as well as cuts to social welfare, all of which have severely affected women and increased their economic dependence on men (Weiler 2004, 64–65). Economic dependence is especially problematic in the context of Russia's high rates of violence against women. Domestic violence is believed to be the most widespread form of violence against women in Russia, although trafficking, rape, sexual harassment, military violence, prison violence, and racially motivated violence are also present (SRVAW 2006c, 8). The collapse of the Soviet Union spelled the end of state monopoly on liquor production, leading to widespread alcohol abuse and contributing to Russia's endemic domestic violence problem (Weiler 2004, 65). Russian politicians have often toyed with limiting excise taxes on alcohol to increase their popularity in democratic elections without considering the impact on domestic violence against women. This is not surprising since transition has resulted in a general loss of status for women, furthered by growing sexualization and commodification of Russian women to the extent that sexual violence—from harassment to trafficking—has become a major problem (Weiler 2004, 70). The Special Rapporteur on Violence Against Women in her mission noticed the additional burden for women from the multifaceted hardships in the North Caucasus region, where economics, politics, culture, and conflict intersect to undermine women's rights (SRVAW 2006c, 5). Assessing the post-communist increase in violence against women in Russia is tricky. No government statistics are gathered on women assaulted or killed by their partner (Human Rights Watch 1998), and the data that are gathered are usually inconsistent (SRVAW 2006c, 8). Nonetheless, available statistics show that 80 percent of all violent crimes are cases of domestic violence. Approximately 14,000 women are killed by their family members annually, usually by their husbands (International Helsinki Federation for Human Rights 2000, 381). Official data, and likely most predictions, largely underestimate the actual levels of violence because of the lack of reporting of domestic violence incidents (Paci 2002, 75). Human Rights Watch estimated in 1998 that only 5–10

(continued)

Box 5.1 (*continued*)

percent of victims report to police (Human Rights Watch 1998). Although battery and sexual assault are criminalized, social stigma pressures victims to keep silent and "solve it" within the family (SRVAW 2006c, 9). Due to severe housing shortages and privatization, many women cannot leave the family home (SRVAW 2006c, 10). Moreover, there is a serious shortage of domestic violence shelters in Russia: only 5 shelters throughout the federation and 120 crisis centers (SRVAW 2006c, 13). For their part, police are reluctant to report domestic violence crimes that will not receive a conviction.

Under communism, the ultimate goal was to reach a society where all classes, ethnicities, and sexes were equal. Now, under Article 19 of the 1993 Constitution, women and men have equal rights before the law. However, the prevalence of violence against women, particularly arising from the unequal power relations within the household, makes Russia the site of an increasing gap between constitutional equality and real inequality in family relationships (Pascall and Manning 2000, 251). One of the most significant explanations for the surge in violence against women in posttransition Russia is the revitalization of patriarchal values. Preexisting forms of sexism have become more salient in the post-communist transition (Weiler 2004, 58; also True 2003). Previously gender-neutral Soviet policy "appears to have been replaced by the outlook that a woman's primary task is to care for the family and children" (SRVAW 2006c, 5). Even Russian activists refer to domestic violence as "violence in the family"—appealing to neotraditional gender ideologies that argue for women's protection in the home (Johnson 2007, 293). Indeed, in many meetings held by the special rapporteur, authorities referred to an ancient Russian proverb: "a beating man is a loving man!" (SRVAW 2006c, 9).

unregulated, and increasingly unequal environment that supports economic exploitation of women in the private sphere.

Despite being widely touted as a catalyst for development and prosperity, there is increasing evidence that trade liberalization, together with a whole host of other neoliberal economic reforms on which it is dependent, is heightening the prevalence of various forms of violence against women and girls. Export processing zones (EPZs) have helped countries diversify their traditional commodity export base. For example, Mauritius (which is now targeting financial services) used the zone strategy to shift from sugar to manufactured exports, Sri Lanka from rubber and tea to garments, and Costa Rica from coffee and bananas to garments and microprocessors (International Labour Office 2003, 2). But as the next section discusses, the volatility of commodity export markets, and the civil conflict over resources they often exacerbate, has been traded for a manufacturing export industry driven by multinationals off the backs of poor, migrant women.

Manufacturing Export Processing Zones and Abuse of Women Workers

In the 1970s and 1980s, manufacturing industries have set up in the special economic zones of developing countries to lower labor and other costs of production. Women, typically young migrants from rural areas, became the majority of the workforce in these EPZ industries, where normal labor conditions and benefits did not apply (Buchanan 1995; Fernández-Kelly 1983, 1993; Peterson 2003). Export industries such as textiles, footwear, and food processing, where 80 percent or more of the workers are women, have also been the ones most subject to cost cutting and restructuring because they are continually subject to import competition and seek to maintain competitiveness in global trade. As such, women workers employed in these industries are often more vulnerable than men to changes in the trading environment (True 2009a, 3).[1] The ease of capital mobility contributes to their insecurity and often leads these women to work for lower wages and conditions than they should be afforded.

Violence against women is a commonplace abuse of power in EPZ workplaces (Raworth 2004, 25). Take the case of Kenya, where EPZs were developed as a strategy to address widespread unemployment—a direct condition of structural adjustment programs imposed by the World Bank and International Monetary Fund (IMF) (Karega 2002, 4–5). Over 40 EPZs produce around 10 percent of the nation's exports and employ over 40,000 workers (PlusNews 2008), and in EPZ textile industries, women make up the majority of workers (Karega 2002, 4). Here competition between men and women for casual jobs has given rise to a frequent exchange of sex for employment by women heedless of the HIV risk because they are desperate to secure any form of employment (PlusNews 2008). This occurrence is noted as commonplace in other EPZs also (Raworth 2004, 25). In Kenya, EPZ companies use nonregistered organizations to recruit casuals on their behalf. The insecure and ad hoc nature of the work means that many workers are not union members. Employers are reportedly aware of sexual harassment but claim to be powerless to intervene unless women come forward and complain, which they usually do not (PlusNews 2008). A study commissioned by the International Labor Rights Fund (ILRF) revealed that 95 percent of all women in Kenya who had suffered workplace sexual abuse were afraid to report the problem for fear of losing their jobs, because those women who did report were either fired or demoted (Karega 2002). Over 90 percent of all respondents in the ILRF study had experienced or observed sexual abuse within the EPZs (Karega 2002). The majority of the women interviewed were young (between twenty and thirty years old) and poor, and almost half were single mothers with school-age children dependent on their income (Karega 2002). A study of Sri Lankan EPZ workers by Hancock, Middleton, and Moore (2010, 12) also found widespread verbal abuse, sexual harassment, forced sex, and intimidation but a similar lack of reporting: of the 1,571 women respondents who had experienced harassment or violence, none had reported it officially.

Sexual harassment can occur when supervisors retain the check-in card of female workers, forcing them to go to the supervisor to retrieve it, at which point the supervisor can request that the women remain behind after work (Karega 2002, 24–25). The Clean Clothes Campaign reports the high prevalence of "body searches" of women factory workers, including at the Levi Strauss facility in Sandanski (Bulgaria) (Ascoly and Finney 2005, 43). In Lesotho, daily body searches required women to take off their clothes, and menstruating women had to remove their pads to show that they were not stealing anything (Ascoly and Finney 2005, 43). Where sexual harassment and other violence against women is perpetrated by employers, women's unequal position of power and need for income virtually guarantee their silence. The culture of impunity is further evidenced by the fact that 70 percent of the men interviewed for the ILRF study viewed sexual harassment of women workers as normal and natural behavior (Karega 2002). In Sri Lanka, unequal gender relations and gender norms in Sri Lankan society prevent reporting, because any sexual harassment is attributed to a woman's lack of modesty—women are concerned not only about their job but also about their reputation and future marriageability (Hancock et al. 2010, 12).

Women from China and Vietnam who went to the EPZ in American Samoa confronted Daewoosa factory management after they discovered they were earning below minimum wage and living in rat- and roach-infested rooms with inadequate meals of cabbage soup and rice. The women stopped working due to nonpayment of wages, but on November 28, 2000, they were harassed and beaten by armed security guards. On another occasion, when workers refused to work until they were paid, the company withheld food for two days (Ascoly and Finney 2005, 27). In April 2002, the Samoa High Court ordered the company to pay workers $3.5 million in compensation and provide them with assistance to either return home or go to the United States. The factory owner was convicted of human trafficking the following year (Ascoly and Finney 2005, 27). The Women's International League for Peace and Freedom (WILPF) reported that strikers at the Phils Jeon Garment factory in the Philippine EPZ "Cavite zone" were taken by surprise by ten masked men who, according to the strikers, bound and blindfolded them, loaded them into a waiting truck, and dropped them outside the gate of the Cavite EPZ. Many believe the attacks were sanctioned by the Philippine Economic Zone Authority (PEZA) and its police force, who routinely failed to investigate how the masked men entered the EPZ (WILPF 2007).

Women also face the risk of violence when they leave work late at night after long shifts in EPZs (Raworth 2004, 25; Patel 2010). The International Labour Office (2003) notes this risk and advises that special measures should be taken to ensure adequate transport and security. In Lesotho, women have been raped leaving garment factories late at night, but management refused to provide safe transport (Ascoly and Finney 2005, 43). Likewise, garment workers in Bangladesh reported that working long hours and arriving home late, at two o'clock in the morning, can provoke suspicion and threats by husbands and male relatives, "especially when their employers—hiding evidence of excessive overtime—had punched their official hour cards to show that they left the factory at six in the evening" (Raworth 2004, 28).

Ciudad Juarez—The Femicide Capital

The cases of femicide in Ciudad Juarez—the EPZ on the US-Mexico border where *maquiladora* (the Spanish term for the multinational manufacturing factories employing more than 50 percent women workers) are located—are the most egregious form of violence against women associated with EPZs. They manifest the severe, destabilizing effects of neoliberal globalization. It is estimated that many of the more than 400 young women who have been murdered or have disappeared in Ciudad Juarez since 1993 were employed in these factories.[2] Thousands of young rural women with formal education but no family responsibilities came to Mexico's tax-free border cities when the 1992 NAFTA agreement liberalized trade with the United States and the Mexican government created these zones to attract foreign investment. The maquiladora system replaced the *bracero* program, in which Mexican workers, particularly men, were brought to the United States as contract workers and then repatriated at the end of the season. The effect of this had been to move a significant percentage of the Mexican male population to the northern states of Mexico, near the border (Fernández-Kelly 1983).

The young women *maquiladora* workers were treated as dispensable and constructed as "cheap labor" relative to the men, leading to high male unemployment in the border cities and towns (Livingstone 2004, 60). This construction inherently devalued the young women workers. Studies show that their influx resulted in lower wages for all, which, combined with male unemployment, led to a generalized resentment toward young women workers. Both the multinational firms and the state authorities concerned failed to protect these women from targeted, violent abuse (Camacho 2005, 259; also Weissman 2004–2005; Staudt 2009). Camacho (2005, 267) argues that just as women were emerging as new, consequential political and economic actors, their citizen and human rights to personal security were dispensed with.

The femicides in Ciudad Juarez were the subject of the UN Human Rights Commission's first inquiry under the optional protocol of the UN Convention on the Elimination of All Forms of Discrimination Against Women (CEDAW) undertaken by the CEDAW Committee (CEDAW 2005; SRVAW 2006b). The report of the committee revealed the inherent vulnerability to violence of women in the border city: "they were young, come from other parts of Mexico, living in poverty, working in *maquilas* where protection for their personal security was poor, subject to deception and force" (CEDAW 2005, para. 63–64). The committee observed that the women did not enjoy their basic social and economic rights, including the right to decent work, education, health care, housing, sanitation infrastructure, and lighting (para. 289). The panel recommended that Mexico ensure compliance with the human rights provisions of CEDAW (para. 290) (Chinkin 2008, 37). However, as Box 5.2, about the Cotton Field decision by the Inter-American Court of Human Rights, shows, the struggle to recognize the femicides that have occurred in Ciudad Juarez and to end state impunity toward this violence against women is ongoing.

Ciudad Juarez is not entirely unique as an export processing zone infamous for femicide and violence against women. Similar patterns of violence have been observed in other states, including neighboring Central American states such as Guatemala and El Salvador (SRVAW 2004, 2005b; Cabrera 2010). Many women work in informal sectors and *maquilas* in urban areas that escape regulation and where human rights violations such as physical, sexual, and psychological abuse and penalization of pregnant workers are common (SRVAW 2005b, 7, 11). MADRE, an international women's human rights organization, reports that over the last decade 5,000 women and girls have been murdered in Guatemala, and UN Rapporteur on Violence Against Women Yakin Ertürk reported that the majority of victims were poor women between thirteen and thirty years of age, who were abducted, gang raped, tortured, mutilated, and killed (SRVAW 2005b, 9). The most frequent victims were housewives (24 percent), domestic workers (13.6 percent), and students (11 percent) (SRVAW 2005b, 10). Ertürk also found that the body parts frequently injured were the head and thorax, a modus operandi reminiscent of torture methods used in the counterinsurgency (SRVAW 2005b, 10). Only 2 percent of the femicides registered in Guatemala between 2005 and 2007 have been solved (Cabrera 2010, 41). On April 9, 2008, the Guatemalan

The establishment of multinational *maquila* factories in Ciudad Juarez has
led to significant economic growth in the city. However, with high levels of
male unemployment and migration of young women from rural areas to
work for low pay in the factories, this growth has not improved the social
and economic livelihoods of all residents. Extreme forms of violence against
women have occurred in an environment of increasing violence and inequality. Local and state impunity for this violence has brought widespread
international censure.

On November 6 and 7, 2001 the bodies of eight women and girls, who
had been sexually tortured, were discovered in an old cotton field in the city
(a site of a previous era of global capitalism). The discovery shocked local
and international communities, who had known about the disappearances
and homicides of women in Ciudad Juarez since 1993. The Mexican state
imprisoned and tortured two men for the homicide and rape of the women.
One died in prison shortly thereafter (the other was later acquitted for lack
of evidence). A year later, in 2002, the mothers of three of the women (two
of them minors, or "girls"), Laura Berenice Ramos Monarrez, Esmeralda
Herrera Monreal, and Claudia Iveth Gonzalez, petitioned the Inter-American
Commission on Human Rights (IACHR) requesting an investigation of the
crimes given the Mexican state's impunity and ineffective response. Each
case had to be filed separately rather than as one case for eight victims, and
the Mexican government pressured the Inter-American Court of Human
Rights (IACHR) to reject the cases. The mothers, and those who supported
and represented them in the cases, experienced intimidation, harassment,
and violence (De Cicco 2009).

After having published two key reports on violence against women in Ciudad Juarez and on access to justice for women living with violence, the Inter-
American Court agreed to hear the three cases as one, "the Cotton Field" case
in 2007. The court argued that the cases had to be heard together because
they "occurred in the context of impunity for violent acts that disproportionately affected women as a group, which had allowed these acts of violence to
continue, creating a pattern of conduct."

On December 10, 2009, the IACHR issued the judgement of the "Cotton
Field" case (*Case of Gonzalez et al. ["Cotton Field"] v. Mexico*) condemning
the Mexican state for violating the human rights of three young women
who were disappeared, tortured, and murdered in Ciudad Juarez, Mexico,
as well as for violation of the human rights of their mothers and next of kin
(Red Mesa de Mujeres and CLADEM 2010). The decision established fifteen
remedies that the state had to implement to close the case, including reparations, remembrance of victims, and measures to prevent discrimination and
violence against women with regard to the rights violated.

(*continued*)

Box 5.2 (*continued*)

However, the court decision is a form of reparation in itself for women's human rights. The court concluded that a context of violence against women exists in Ciudad Juarez, and in so doing, it established a precedent and methodology for determining what constitutes violence against women perpetrated by the state. The crimes were defined as "femicide" by the legal briefs, the expert witness reports, national reports from the Chamber of Deputies of the National Congress, and evidence from civil organizations and amicus curiae documents. Article 21 of the Mexican General Law on Access of Women to a Life Free of Violence states that femicide is "the extreme form of gender violence against women, resulting from the violation of their human rights in the public and private sphere, comprising a series of misogynous conducts that can lead to the impunity of the State and society, and may culminate in the homicide or other forms of violent death of women." The court used the term "gender-based murders of women," also known as femicide, but did not find it necessary to decide on whether the murders of women in Ciudad Juarez constituted gender-based murders other than those of the murders of the three women in this case. The court "stated that since 1993 homicides involving women have increased in the city and that a culture of discrimination against women has been influential in this." It found that "the State's intentions, methods and response to these crimes were evidence that the victims were discriminated against on the basis of their sex." Specific evidence of this was found in:

- The authorities' inefficient responses and indifferent attitudes to the investigation of these crimes;
- The fact that in case of female homicides that involved elements of sexual violence, levels of impunity were highest of all;
- The extraordinarily high levels of violence, including sexual violence involved in homicides against women; and
- The ongoing perpetration of violence against women in Ciudad Juarez (Red Mesa de Mujeres and CLADEM 2010, 23–32).

Violence has been escalating in Ciudad Juarez, and campaigns have sought to discredit human rights organizations and propound "the myth of femicide." The year 2009 registered the highest number of murders of women in the city. Red Mesa de Mujeres and CLADEM are engaged in ongoing monitoring of the Mexican state's compliance with the Cotton Field decision and remedies, many of which remain unfulfilled two years later.

Congress passed a law against femicide and other forms of violence against women, which includes tougher prison sentences and recognizes economic violence in the denial of access to work and access to property (Cabrera 2010, 41). However, the enduring environment of impunity and the steadily increasing incidence of femicide in Guatemala reveal the normalization of institutionalized gender inequality and violence (Manz 2008, 154).

Gendered Violence and Extractive Export Industries

Trade liberalization has heightened various forms of violence against women workers in extractive export industries, as well as manufacturing industries. International financial institutions' (IFIs) funding of extractive industries accentuates rather than reduces the risk and prevalence of violence against women in the communities where these industries are supported. The World Bank has acknowledged that less developed countries' reliance on primary commodity exports is one of the leading causes of violent, armed conflict (World Bank 2003). Extractive industries employ women in unregulated and unsafe working conditions and contribute to the rise of sexual violence, prostitution, and conflict. Regardless, in 2010 the World Bank spent $50 million on its Growth with Governance in the Mineral Sector project, in contrast to $3.2 million spent on all its gender-based violence prevention projects in 2010 combined (D'Almeida 2011b). According to Monti Aguirre, a Latin American campaigner at US-based NGO International Rivers, "resource extraction development projects supported by IFIs nearly always leave women out of the benefits side of the equation" (quoted in D'Almeida 2011b).

In their report *Broken Promises*, Gender Action and Friends of the Earth International (2011) analyzed the gender differential impacts of the Chad-Cameroon Oil Pipeline in Chad and the impacts of the West Africa Gas Pipeline (WAGP) in Nigeria, Ghana, and Togo. The World Bank and European Investment Bank (EIB) partially financed both pipelines, providing financial security to the consortiums of oil and gas multinationals. The study found that women have suffered disproportionately from the projects. Women were noticeably absent from all stages of the projects, including community consultations about the projects. In preparation for the WAGP, "[Friends of the Earth] Nigeria could not find a single woman who was selected for community consultation in project planning or execution; the views of women were not represented at the community level or to pipeline's company representatives" (Gender Action and Friends of the Earth International 2011, 16). The short-term boom in unskilled labor opportunities went to men (Gender Action and Friends of the Earth International 2011, 7). As a result of this gender bias in employment, prostitution increased, as did domestic violence and women's sexual subordination to men (Gender Action and Friends of the Earth International 2011, 8). In the case of the Chad-Cameroon pipeline, the 10 percent value of the land compensation for loss of crops was allocated to male heads of households, often without being disclosed to women, despite the fact that women make up over 70 percent of the agricultural workforce in those countries (Gender Action and Friends of the Earth International

2011, 13, 10, 8). In Nigeria and Ghana, women cannot own land, and in Togo, women have only limited access to formal land rights, usually through their spouses. Consequently, compensation also went exclusively to men (Gender Action and Friends of the Earth International 2011, 17–22). Yet we know that when productive resources, including financial capital and income-generating land, are disproportionately distributed to men, gender inequalities increase and women face greater risk of violence and, at the same time, have less capacity to protect themselves from this violence.

The environmental impacts of projects involving the destruction of forests and fisheries, loss of wildlife, and decrease in soil fertility directly affecting food production, water quality, air quality, medicine, and fuels were devastating for local communities (Gender Action and Friends of the Earth International 2011). Not only were promises broken, but also women's livelihoods were worsened due to the loss of lands for subsistence farming and depletion of fish stocks central to female fishing communities (Gender Action and Friends of the Earth International 2011, iv). The WAGP project depreciated women's already marginalized purchasing power and influence in their communities (Gender Action and Friends of the Earth International 2011, 15).

An earlier Gender Action study of IFIs' oil investments noted the gendered impacts of a pipeline project in Azerbaijan and Georgia and an oil and gas project on Sakhalin Island, Russia (Bacheva, Kochladze, and Dennis 2006). Both projects were funded by the World Bank and European Bank for Reconstruction and Development. The pipelines were promoted by project sponsors and the IFIs as "a model of development and poverty alleviation," yet neither had policies to safeguard women's rights (Bacheva et al. 2006, 3, 18). The study outlined similar negative consequences of the projects for women: damage to subsistence sources (loss of material and productive resources), lack of employment opportunities for women, increased migration of male workers (and an associated increase in prostitution), and increases in sexually transmitted infections and stillbirths (Bacheva et al. 2006). The few women employed by the projects that Gender Action interviewed stated that they worked in the workers' camps as cooks or cleaners, with employment contracts from one to three months, and worked for long hours with little pay and no holidays (Bacheva et al. 2006, 18). Local women's groups reported an increase in sexual harassment complaints but stated that women endured the sexual harassment in order to keep their jobs (Bacheva et al. 2006, 18). Gender Action noted that the corollary of increased prostitution was an increase in trafficking and health problems (Bacheva et al. 2006, 18, 19, 29). The study reveals that extractive development projects "almost as a rule increase both the burden for local women and gender inequality"

(Bacheva et al. 2006, 3). The case of World Bank funding of infrastructure and incentives for the mining industry in the Democratic Republic of the Congo in Box 5.3 illustrates these negative impacts on women and how they exacerbate gendered violence.

Box 5.3 INTERNATIONAL FINANCIAL INSTITUTIONS, EXTRACTIVE INDUSTRY, AND SEXUAL VIOLENCE: THE DEMOCRATIC REPUBLIC OF CONGO

In the Democratic Republic of Congo (DRC), gender-based violence is widespread and systematic (Meger 2010). In many cases it is linked with extractive industries, particularly artisanal and small-scale mining, where women and children often make up the majority of laborers (Arend and Ajinkya 2011, 1). Women and their families rely on the income from mining, yet they are paid less and are vulnerable to physical abuse and sexual exploitation at the hands of employers and militia who run the operations. In 2002, the World Bank helped the DRC to revise its Mining Code in order to attract foreign private investment but ignored gender-based violence endemic among mining communities (Arend and Ajinkya 2011, 1). The World Bank also funds various infrastructure projects to strengthen mining as a poverty alleviation strategy, but its strategies are tellingly silent on the linkages to gender-based violence. For instance, the World Bank's $50 million Growth in Governance in the Mineral Sector project identifies gender-based violence as among the human rights violations caused by the mineral trade but does not have any policies or initiatives to address it (Arend and Ajinkya 2011, 2). The World Bank's $120 million Private Sector Development and Competitiveness project, designed to lift postconflict Congo out of extreme underdevelopment, identifies mining, transport, telecom, and energy as the sectors that could help the Congo to achieve economic growth (Arend and Ajinkya 2011, 4). The project encourages those industries that are proven to have a disproportionately detrimental effect on women and that seriously increase violence against women. The lack of gender-sensitive monitoring and sex-disaggregated data are major impediments to assessing the impact of the project on women's access to productive resources, which are often deterrents to violence (Arend and Ajinkya 2011, 4).

Migrant Male Workers and Sexual Violence in the Pacific

Trade liberalization and foreign investment in extraction industries typically involve importing foreign male workers. If the local economic context is impoverished, their presence may encourage the development of prostitution and sex trafficking, as well as gender-based violence. For example, the liberalization of the fisheries and forestry industries in the Pacific that import foreign male workers from Asia has encouraged the development of prostitution and sex trafficking on shore and has been linked to gender-based violence, child prostitution, and HIV/AIDS (Pacific Islands Forum Secretariat 2008). Trade liberalization also encourages fiscal policy discipline, new forms of taxation to recover lost tariff revenue, and the reprioritization of public spending toward provision of pro-growth infrastructure and pro-poor services. This restructuring of government budgets in semisubsistence countries has significant gender impacts, as already low-income households face economic austerity. In this situation, women are more vulnerable to domestic violence and may also turn to employment in sweatshop manufacturing, the sex industry, and other precarious places of employment where violence is more likely.

The liberalization of the fisheries industry has led to the development of an unregulated sex industry in many Pacific ports in Fiji, Papua New Guinea[3] and Kiribati due to the nature of male enclaves working in foreign fishing fleets (Sullivan and Ram-Bidesi 2008, 20, 44). In Kiribati, a word has even been coined for the women who are involved in the sex trade with Asian (particularly Korean) seafarers—*te korekorea*—reflecting the incipient nature of the sex trade in South Tarawa (Sullivan and Ram-Bidesi 2008, 31; UNESCAP 2009, 58). While the sex trade can be a source of income for women and their families in Pacific communities, it also has serious and harmful implications for many women (Sullivan and Ram-Bidesi 2008, 22). Women are more susceptible to sexually transmitted diseases and are vulnerable to substance-induced violence at the hands of male seafarers (Sullivan and Ram-Bidesi 2008, 31). Evidence from Kiribati also suggests that girls as young as fifteen are involved in the trade, lured to the source of income in Pacific communities that have few employment opportunities (Vunisea 2005). A case study of Padang province in Papua New Guinea has also linked the development of tuna canneries by multinational firms to an increase in the sex trade and violence against women and girls (Pacific Network on Globalization [PANG] 2008).

In the Solomon Islands, local government officials have accused foreign logging companies of exploiting not only their natural forestry resources but also teenage girls. Loggers from Asian countries working for multinational companies are said to employ these girls to work as domestic live-in servants, subjecting them to sexual abuse and leaving them pregnant when they return home (Radio Australia 2008). Large-scale commercial logging started in the Pacific over forty years ago, but in the early 1980s there was an influx of logging industry multinationals into the Pacific, based mostly in Southeast Asia (Kabutaulaka 1997; PANG 2008, 21). For example, during the period from

1981 to 1983, the number of logging licenses given to foreign companies increased fourfold in the Solomon Islands alone (Fraser 1997, 41). Logging has become one of the central exports of the Solomon Islands, making up about 50 percent of GDP (Kabutaulaka 1997). In Papua New Guinea, logging makes up a significant portion of the GDP, although figures are changeable due to illegal logging. The trade is surrounded with problems, as the overseeing bodies in the Pacific do not have the resources to ensure compliance with tax, environmental, or labor standards. In addition, there have been many concerns involving corruption and conflicts of interest in government.

One of the least reported and acknowledged side effects of the rapid growth of the logging trade is its effects on the society around it. The nature of the work, involving a transient male labor force with good cash incomes, entices young women into domestic work and to sell sexual services to these men. For these women, their work makes them vulnerable to violence and abuse, especially given the lack of legal and social institutions prohibiting them. The evidence that forced prostitution takes place—including child prostitution—has been gathered by a range of Pacific NGOs. In the Solomon Islands, the Christian Care Centre of the Church of Melanesia undertook most of the field work for the United Nations reports on the issue (Herbert 2007; UNESCAP 2009). Their findings make for disturbing reading. Prostitution in the Solomon Islands is largely unorganized and is often coordinated through the woman or girl's family. It frequently takes the form of temporary marriages with very young girls. The Papua New Guinea country study in the UN Economic and Social Commission for Asia and the Pacific Report provides examples of Malaysian and Korean logging workers buying (part-time) wives and girlfriends from parents with large payments such as gifts of houses and cars (UNESCAP 2009, 58). There is also routine prostitution that takes place at locations around logging sites, in hotels and bars, and even in schools and at beaches (UNESCAP 2006, 37). The women and girls who marry or work in these circumstances rarely see the benefit of their work, as it often goes to extended families.[4] More egregiously, they are often unable to remarry and reintegrate into village life (UNESCAP 2006, 43).

Gender Action and Friends of the Earth International argue that the World Bank has ample evidence of the negative social and environmental impacts of extractive industries, as well as an internal report on the links between extractive industry and armed conflict (Gender Action and Friends of the Earth International 2011, 4). Yet, extractive industry is the model of development, growth, and poverty alleviation that is being championed by IFIs. "The same IFIs that claim to reduce poverty and support women's empowerment in fact fund gender-blind extractive industry projects" that increase poverty and undermine women's economic and social rights in developing countries (Gender Action and Friends of the Earth International 2011, 1). The rhetoric that consistently falls short of concrete action and the evidence-based knowledge that this approach to development is harmful to women render IFIs not only grossly negligent but also complicit in structural and physical violence against women.

Toward Nonviolent Economies

Government intervention is needed to address the harms generated by manufacturing and extractive industries across global regions, and specifically to eliminate the sexual abuse and exploitation of women and girls that have come with the increase in the multinational-led export trade. Prosecuting perpetrators of violence, protecting women from violence, and preventing violence against women under conditions of globalization in transnational border regions where justice and social support systems are weak at best and multiple actors are involved is particularly challenging. However, there are some policy and legal tools available for addressing violence against women in these contexts. The Cotton Field decision and monitoring discussed in this chapter illustrate how even in the most severe cases of femicide activists are working to bring about a change in pervasive local and state impunity toward violence against women.

Governments have the option of shifting away from low-cost models of foreign investment and trade, for instance, supporting manufacturing garment, footwear, or food processing industries based on higher-quality, differentiated, and value-added production with better conditions for employees.[5] Moving into higher-value and higher-quality export production would be beneficial for women, who would continue to enjoy formal employment but with better pay and conditions. This movement into higher-quality production would also involve an investment in human capital and skills training, improving women's knowledge base and future employability, all of which serve as deterrents to violence.

At a minimum, however, equity and employment provisions need to be part of national legal frameworks and trade agreements so that foreign companies in these manufacturing or extractive industries must provide decent working conditions for all workers—female and male—and are held accountable for discrimination, abuse, and violence. Box 5.4 discusses one initiative to promote greater corporate social responsibility for current gender inequalities in the global political economy. The Women's Empowerment Principles promoted by the UN Global Compact and UN Women seek to harness corporate power to change society, as well as business practices and

Box 5.4 THE UN GLOBAL COMPACT-UNIFEM WOMEN'S EMPOWERMENT PRINCIPLES

The Women's Empowerment Principles, or WEPs, are a global corporate code of conduct on women's human rights developed through an international multistakeholder consultation process in March 2009 and launched in March 2010. They focus on corporate responsibility to address the rights of *all* women *across the board* and not just at the boardroom table. There are seven women's empowerment principles, each with key elements and indicators to monitor their impact: (1) leadership for gender equality; (2) equal opportunity, inclusion, and nondiscrimination; (3) health, safety, and freedom from violence; (4) education and training; (5) enterprise development, supply chain, and marketing practices; (6) community leadership and engagement; and (7) transparency, measurement, and reporting. CEOs commit to promoting women's empowerment through these principles. The WEPs emphasize that equality lies in promoting women's leadership (equal outcomes), having work/life balance policies in employment, and ensuring women are included as equals (equal treatment) at work. For instance, a key element drawn from principle 2 suggests that companies "proactively recruit and appoint women to managerial and executive positions and to the corporate board of directors" in order to promote workplace practices and policies free from gender discrimination.

Principle 7 suggests that companies "make public their policies and implementation plan for promoting gender equality; establish benchmarks that quantify inclusion of women at all levels; measure and report on progress, both internally and externally, using data disaggregated by sex" (UN Global Compact/ UNIFEM 2010, 3). The United Nations keeps track of how businesses are doing on the initiatives. A working document that contains examples of "best practice" initiatives shows how key multinational businesses in energy, finance, services/ tourism, and manufacturing sectors have implemented processes aligning with the principles (UN Global Compact 2010). These practices are voluntary and are not audited by the United Nations or independently, but they raise awareness of the many ways in which businesses can promote gender equality.

The WEPs encourage corporations to deploy their financial power to change society, for instance, by fundraising for ending domestic violence internationally or assisting women-owned enterprises (UN Global Compact/ UNIFEM 2010, 5). They complement rather than replace government regulatory approaches that seek to mitigate corporate power and its impacts on gender inequalities and violence.

policies, to provide greater economic opportunities for women and to end violence against women at home and at work. Corporations through the power of markets have a major impact on economic development, as well as on the economic and social rights of women and men and their vulnerability to violence (UN/UNIFEM 2010, ii).

| Boom, Bust, and
Beating

International Financial Institutions,
Crises, and Violence against Women

Introduction

This chapter examines how the liberalization of the financial system, particularly international development loans, and the collapse of credit in the United States and Europe, which brought about the global financial crisis in 2007, have accentuated the high prevalence of violence against women around the world. International financial institutions such as the World Bank and International Monetary Fund finance development loans in export trade–oriented industries, often conditional on the adoption of economic reforms, including cuts in state budgets for public services. These loans, intended for economic development, fail to address the gendered nature of underdevelopment, perpetuating women's poverty and inequality and further exacerbating sexual and gender-based violence.

The macro-financial mechanisms accentuating violence against women in developed countries are not dissimilar from those affecting gender-based violence in developing countries. All the evidence to date suggests that the global financial crisis (GFC) has had a disproportionate impact on women. Large increases in domestic violence have been reported in the wake of the financial crisis in many countries as the crisis spills over into housing mortgage foreclosures, job losses, stress, and poverty. These economic and social impacts are all research-based determinants of violence that increase the likelihood of being a victim or a perpetrator of violence within families and societies. Government responses to the financial crisis have largely compounded these impacts on women. Following fiscal stimulus packages to stabilize economies, states have begun to limit or cut public expenditures, including state sector jobs (which employ significantly more women than men) in health and education areas, for instance. These austerity policies have set back women's economic and social status relative to men, putting more women than before in precarious situations with respect to housing, employment, and livelihoods where they are more vulnerable to violence and less able to protect themselves.

This chapter consists of two main parts. The first part examines the practices of international financial institutions and their development lending as part of the problem rather than the solution to ending violence against women. The second part analyzes the neoliberal financial logic of boom and bust and how these economic cycles affect gendered relations in societies facing economic crisis and escalate the risk factors for heightened violence against women.

International Financial Institutions, Development Loans, and Violence

> Now, every time a local movement or women's collective calls me and says "help us," behind the crisis, behind the destruction, there's always World Bank lending.
>
> —VANDANA SHIVA (in D'Almeida 2011b)

International financial institutions (IFIs) grant loans to developing countries to alleviate poverty, improve livelihoods, and promote economic development. Given all the rhetoric about gender equality being "smart economics" and at the same time the existing knowledge about feminization of poverty, the dominance of women in informal agriculture, and the effects of conflict on women and children in developing countries, we would expect that, at a minimum, development projects financed by the World Bank and other IFIs would be gender sensitive. However, research by Washington-based financial institutions watchdog Gender Action reveals stark gender blindness by IFIs with negative implications for efforts to eliminate violence against women. And so explains the epigraph by feminist environmentalist Vandana Shiva that wherever there is a crisis for women in the developing world, there is a failure of World Bank lending to, among other things, comprehend women's economic contribution. Gender Action's research reveals that the World Bank's investments in "gender and social inclusion" have actually decreased in recent years, from 6 percent of the bank's budget in fiscal year 2006 to 2 percent in 2010 (D'Almeida 2011a). IFIs spend a miniscule amount on projects addressing gender-based violence, implicitly seeing violence as a social and political issue rather than an economic issue. They often finance projects, especially in extractive industries, that exacerbate gender-based violence and discrimination, as discussed in Chapter 5. In the rare cases where gender-based violence is acknowledged, it is framed as an economic cost rather than a human rights violation or something to be addressed as a first-order priority before economic empowerment or development can occur. The projects that acknowledge the costs of violence, for instance, do not include strategies to actually address this violence. Where a project states it will address gendered violence, there is often no mechanism to quantify the effects or measure the success of the project (Arend 2011, 5). Gender Action makes three key recommendations to IFIs to strategically rethink their approach to gender issues. These recommendations, listed in Box 6.1, could form the basis for human rights organizations to monitor IFIs and hold them accountable for their performance on stated commitments to development, gender equality, and eradication of violence.

International Financial Institutions' Gender-Based Violence Projects

In 2010, the World Bank had an annual budget of $58.8 billion (Gender Action 2011; D'Almeida 2011a). However, it currently funds only three investments that focus on gender-based violence. These investments total $12.5 million, or 0.02 percent of the World Bank's 2010 budget (Arend 2011, 5). Following the earthquake in Haiti, women were the targets of rampant sexual violence, as discussed in Chapter 8 (Amnesty International 2011). Gender Action criticized the World Bank's failure to fund any initiatives dealing with this violence and itself secured $500,000 from the World Bank for investment (Zuckerman, Young, and Vitale 2010). This amount was 0.2 percent of all World Bank investments in postearthquake Haiti (Arend 2011, 5). In the Congo, the World Bank has invested $1.98 million (0.01 percent of its

Sub-Saharan Africa budget) to address sexual violence in a country now known as the rape capital of the world given the endemic nature of sexual violence there, including the use of rape as a strategic tool of war, described extensively in Chapter 7 (Arend 2011, 5). In Cote d'Ivoire, the World Bank pledged $730,000—just 0.006 percent of its Sub-Saharan Africa budget— for a project aimed at decreasing violence against women. The case of the World Bank's multidam project in Lesotho described in Box 6.2 shows how the omission of crucial gendered knowledge from development projects perpetuates existing inequalities and engenders new forms of violence against women.

Gender differentials are not measured in the World Bank's $80 million Total War Against AIDS project in Kenya or its $19 million HIV and Health project in the Republic of Congo, despite women's greater vulnerability than men to contracting HIV and to experiencing male violence as HIV carriers (Gender Action 2011, 1). The lack of sex-disaggregated data in most of the World Bank projects illustrates the gender-blind nature of project funding and design, but it also makes it impossible to evaluate the quality of projects and therein hold the World Bank to account (Arend 2011, 5). The World Bank claims to be a global leader in reproductive health in its 2010 Reproductive Health Action Plan (D'Almeida 2011a). Yet this focus, like the marginal attention to gender-based violence, reveals that reproductive health is not viewed by the World Bank as a human right but instead as an input to maximize women's economic output: "As long as women are healthy, they are better able to be economically productive" (Elizabeth Arend, quoted in D'Almeida 2011a).

Similar trends are suggested by Gender Action's investigations into other IFI funding of projects designed to counter gender-based violence. The regional IFIs' funding allocations attest to the rhetorical nature of their gender policy, which recognize in theory the impacts of gender inequality and violence on development. The African Development Bank (AfDB) has currently made one investment for $7.1 million (0.5 percent of its 2005 annual budget) in the Support to Mano-River HIV/AIDS Control project in Cote D'Ivoire (Arend 2011, 2). While it mentions linkages between violence against women and HIV/AIDS, the project fails to integrate interventions to address gender violence into health care, instead focusing on "educational messages" to reduce violence while failing to engage men and boys in this awareness raising (Arend 2011, 2). Similarly, the Inter-American Development Bank (IDB) has only made one investment in tackling violence against women and sexual reproductive health, in the Dominican Republic in 2007. Yet with a budget of $164,000, it constitutes a mere 2.6 percent of the IDB's $6.2

Box 6.2 LESOTHO, THE WORLD BANK'S MULTIDAM PROJECT, AND VIOLENCE AGAINST WOMEN

Yvonne Braun (2010) engaged in ethnographic research in rural Lesotho communities affected by the Lesotho Highlands Water Project (LHWP)—a large scale, internationally financed multidam project—to assess its gendered impacts. The eight-million-dollar project between the Lesotho and South African governments was partially funded by the World Bank, the African Development Bank (AfDB), the European Union, and several other European funding agencies. Braun (2010, 86) found that the project, touted as a national development strategy for poverty reduction, created detrimental gender and labor stratification within some of the poorest communities in Lesotho that vastly outweighed any potential benefits, such as new roads. She continually encountered the prevalence of prostitution around the development areas. Consequently, she altered her research agenda to investigate the indirect channels that women used to access development funds.

Because most jobs went to foreign men, and temporary jobs to local men, women's employment options were domestic work and prostitution. By excluding opportunities for women in the dam project, women were pushed into unregulated, low-wage work with substantial risk of violence, sexually transmitted infections, HIV, and so on. Rising concerns about HIV meant that many men solicited younger girls for sex on the assumption that they were more likely to have had fewer partners or to be virgins than adult sex workers (Braun 2010, 90–91). Braun describes how access to credit and compensation for appropriated land that was previously shared, and on which women were the primary laborers, went exclusively to men. Not only did the multidam project not fulfill its poverty-reduction mandate, but also it reinforced women's secondary status and hegemonic masculinity (Braun 2010, 81). This occurred at a time when Basotho migrant workers were made redundant from South African mines and an influx of white foreign males virtually monopolized the project's secure jobs. Women experienced gender-based violence perpetrated by these male laborers involved in the projects.

Braun's work describes the crisis of masculinity as a result of this unemployment and the marginalization of women as agents of development. The study demonstrates how gender-blind development projects devalue women's labor in agricultural food production and in the household, excluding them from the benefits of so-called development. Reinforcing male ownership and patriarchal authority in the household with their dam project, the IFIs heightened the risk and the prevalence of violence against women in Lesotho.

million Gender Mainstreaming Budget (and 0.001 percent of the IDB's total budget for 2007). By contrast, the IDB's HIV-related projects in Suriname and Honduras completely neglect gender-based violence as a cause of HIV infection and do not acknowledge the increased vulnerability to violence experienced by HIV-positive women (Gender Action 2011).

Gender Action (2011) reports disturbing levels of violence against women in Eastern Europe and Central Asia, yet the European Development Bank (EDB) has no projects on women's human rights or gender-based violence. In Azerbaijan, 99 percent of women respondents reported their subjection to some form of physical abuse (Arend 2011, 3). In Turkey, Moldova, and Armenia, many women thought physical abuse could be justified for such things as refusing sex (Arend 2011, 3). Undoubtedly, such attitudes toward violence contribute to the widespread sex trafficking crimes in these countries, and for which Moldova in particular is infamously known, as Chapter 4 details.

For its part, the Asian Development Bank (ADB) has made only one gender-specific investment in the last decade. This investment, for $10 million in Nepal, aims to improve women's knowledge of—and access to—legal institutions that address gender-based violence rather than any socioeconomic causes of that violence. Moreover, the project includes no measures to assess its impact on reducing violence against Nepalese women (Arend 2011, 4). The majority of ADB HIV projects likewise fail to comprehend and respond to the mutually reinforcing relationship between gendered violence and risk of HIV infection. Among twenty-two projects over ten years, only three acknowledge this HIV risk. In Papua New Guinea, for instance, where sexual violence is widespread, the ADB's (2007) Lae Port Development project, which aims to develop the Lae port, an important feature of the island's export-based economy, makes no mention of gender-based violence and its impact on women or development (Arend 2011, 4).[1] Yet the project intends to improve the livelihood of those directly or indirectly affected by the port and to reduce the incidence of HIV/AIDS through financing gender-responsive programs (Asian Development Bank 2007).

Moreover, it should be noted that no current IFI investments in gender-based violence, sexual and reproductive health, or HIV/AIDS acknowledge or address gender-based violence against men and boys (Arend 2011, 4). Thus, the gender perspective of IFIs is theoretically, as well as practically, flawed in that it neglects to examine and target gender relations, focusing merely on women's social and economic activities. Chapter 3 of this book, which attends to the construction of masculinities and advocates men as champions of ending violence against women, explicitly challenges such reductionist, and frankly, sexist, approaches.

Financial Crises and Violence Against Women

Women are often the hardest hit by economic transition, financial crises, and rising unemployment. "Economic and political insecurity provoke private and public backlash against women's rights that may be expressed through violence and articulated in the form of defending cultures and traditions" (Montreal Principles on Women's Economic, Social and Cultural Rights 2004, 3). Widespread discrimination against women and girls in education, employment, and business and the lack of a state social safety net can mean they are not protected from violence when economies rapidly expand and contract, boom and bust. Economic liberalization and export-oriented development in East Asia in the 1980s had detrimental impacts on women and girls due to patriarchal family-firm structures and the lesser value attributed to women's paid and unpaid labor. There is considerable evidence that fast-paced economic growth in East Asian countries such as Korea, Taiwan, China, and Hong Kong was accelerated by increasing women's employment, while at the same time gender wage gaps in the labor market were widened (Seguino 2000, 2008; Berik 2004; Kongar 2008). Accelerated gendered economic inequalities are risk factors for increased violence against women and girls, although because of limited data it is not possible to empirically support this theory in this case.

When the Asian financial crisis hit in 1997–98, the impact on women and girls was disproportionate. Girls were removed from school to help at home and save on school fees or were forced to seek work in the sex sector to support household incomes as a result of cutbacks in public services, jobs, and wages (Truong 2001a; Young 2003; Hoskyns and Rai 2008). In some East Asian countries, women's paid labor intensified, while in others, notably South Korea, their labor participation shrank. The resulting increased financial burdens strained intrahousehold relationships and boosted suicides, family violence, and abandonment (Floro and Dymski 2000). In Argentina, economic crises had similarly deleterious and gendered effects compounded by decades of state-perpetrated violence under the previous military dictatorship, as Box 6.3 recounts.

Given the experiences in many countries and regions in the 1990s as a result of liberalized financial credit and loans, the social and economic impacts of consequent financial crises were well known when the global financial crisis ensued in 2007.

Barbara Sutton (2010) analyzed the effects of the previous military dictatorship regime in Argentina and its more recent financial collapse in 2001 on women's bodies—both physical violence against women and structural violence against women associated with the feminization of poverty and economic inequality. She considers the economic crisis as the context for increased violence rather than a singular cause of this violence. The crisis created a violent environment primed for aggression in families, communities, workplaces, and larger society involving the violent suppression of social protection and labor conflict, as well as rising crimes against property and personal safety (Sutton 2010, 143). Sutton (2010, 160) argues that "the body is the place where micro interpersonal relations and wider social structures intersect" and that women's experiences of violence are "affected by ideologies that represent women as disposable objects, of economic inequalities that limit women's opportunities to escape violence, of state authorities that refuse to take such violence seriously, and of institutionalized discourses that teach women they cannot make fundamental decisions over their own lives and bodies." After the collapse of the Argentine peso–US dollar exchange rate parity, the currency depreciated 400 percent and unemployment climbed to 25 percent, and many people struggle to survive in such severe economic conditions. The structural violence of the economic crisis compounded with the interpersonal violence exerted by men against women. "Domestic violence was one way in which some men seemed to channel the frustrations caused by unemployment, by their inability to be proper breadwinners, by their wives' work outside the home, and by the test this situation presented to hegemonic masculinity" (Sutton 2010, 145; Causa and Ojam 2008).

Argentina's economic crisis fueled opportunities for increased violence against women, as well as different forms of such violence. For instance, it "pushed many women into occupations that inherently expose them to multiple forms of violence such as prostitution." A survey by AMMAR (Asociacion de Mujeres Meretrices de la Argentina) found that prostitution in Buenos Aires increased 42.85 percent after the 2001 crisis. The secretary of AMMAR interviewed by Sutton noted that "many sex workers are heads of households. Before, they were domestic workers or at least had some job, but now they don't know what to do. They must bring some money home" (Sutton 2010, 147). Homeless men and women, who had jobs before the economic collapse, turned to informal self-employment collecting cardboard in the streets for recycling factories in exchange for cash. Women cartoneros were commonly subject to sexual harassment, "a concomitant effect of both crisis-induced poverty and of gendered assumptions about her supposedly 'out of place' female body" (Sutton 2010, 49). Poor women no longer had the means for transport to seek support from women's police stations. Unfortunately, preexisting gendered discrimination and attitudes have meant that throughout the economic crisis, violent street crimes receive more attention than the domestic violence disproportionately affecting women (Sutton 2010, 148).

The 2007 Global Financial Crisis Impact on Domestic Violence

The political economy approach to violence against women is especially relevant in the context of the global financial crisis. The crisis has had a disproportionately negative impact on women and girls' education, employment, and livelihoods, which, as Chapter 2 of this book shows, are linked to increased risks of violence due in part to men's responses to economic displacement and disempowerment, as discussed in Chapter 3. "It is those who have least to lose—women who are unemployed or on low incomes, pregnant women, families, single mothers and pensioners, victims of sexual, domestic or other violence—who [will] lose most" (Fawcett Society 2011, 1).

In almost all regions of the world, the impact of the financial crisis with the overnight disappearance of credit and drastic fall in demand has been more detrimental for women's unemployment than for men's, especially in those places where women work in informal and insecure sectors (International Labour Organization 2011). As we discussed in Chapter 4, migrant women and domestic workers were among the first to be laid off due to prevailing gender ideologies that consider their labor dispensable, as well as their part-time, flexible, and vulnerable work conditions (Seguino 2009; Harikrishnan 2010). In developing countries, women's incomes and family livelihoods disproportionately suffered due to women's employment concentration in export sectors such as manufacturing and high-value agriculture, the drop in remittances from migrant women's care work, and the tightened conditions for microfinance lending to women farmers and entrepreneurs (Buvinic/World Bank 2009). The World Bank predicted that up to 53 million more people would be driven to poverty in developing countries in 2009 as a result of the GFC, bringing the total number of those living on less than two dollars a day to over 1.5 billion. Girls in poor and low-income countries that had preexisting low female schooling are highly vulnerable to being pulled out of school and may be led into sex work or trafficking as households cope with declining household income (Buvinic/Work Bank 2009; Kaufman and Crawford 2011). These impacts will lead to serious setbacks in the realization of gender equality and efforts to protect, prevent, and, ultimately, eliminate violence against women.

Women are more directly exposed to the impact of the GFC as employees than they were in previous economic recessions in the 1980s and 1990s (Rake 2009, 2). In 2011, for instance, the number of women out of work in the United Kingdom was at a twenty-three-year high (Hill 2011). More women are now formally employed, but they also enter the economy on unequal footing, increasing their vulnerability to economic downturns relative to men (Rake 2009, 2). For women, the recession creates a "triple jeopardy": they are pushed out of the workforce, reducing their incomes; the rising cost of living reduces the purchasing power of income; and welfare and public sector cuts undermine women's access to services, including their access to justice and protection from violence (Fawcett Society 2011). In the United Kingdom, as in many other countries, women are more likely than men to live in poverty, be single parents, have insecure employment, rely on state help, and experience violence. The impact of the recession on women cannot be measured purely by unemployment statistics, because many women work in unpaid household roles or work on temporary paid contracts, and in both cases they are less likely to register as "unemployed" if their partner is still employed (Rake 2009, 4).

Government responses to the financial crisis have also disproportionately affected women compared with men. The fiscal stimulus packages rolled out by governments immediately after the collapse of credit and designed to stem domestic economic collapse and global trade protectionism were rapidly replaced by initiatives to reduce government budgets by cutting public services around the world. For example, in Britain, 65 percent of all public sector workers are female, meaning that 38 percent of all employed women work in public sector jobs in public administration, education, and health (Rake 2009, 5; Bennhold 2011). Two-thirds of the 130,000 jobs lost in local authorities since the first quarter of 2010 were held by women (Hill 2011). Women also make up the majority of employees in the retail and hospitality sectors that were badly hit by postrecession contraction of consumer spending (Rake 2009, 5). Because women make up over half of workers on temporary contracts and 42 percent of women in the workforce work part time, they have limited employment rights and less access to redundancy pay than men (Rake 2009, 6). What does all this mean for the risk and prevalence of violence against women?

In Britain, 90 percent of lone-parent households are led by single mothers, and 43 percent of children living in poverty come from single-parent families (Rake 2009, 4). These proportions are likely to increase as the burden of the recession on women takes its toll in job losses and cuts to services. Women may also be more likely to lose their job during maternity leave after the GFC, although it is officially illegal and discriminatory. Research released by the UK Equalities Office shows that 24 percent of men think that in difficult economic times it "makes more sense for people [sic] on maternity leave to be made redundant first" (Gentleman 2009). Hence, the recession is "likely to force many new mothers into uncomfortable compromises about the amount of time spent with their newborns," as women who are financially insecure take shorter periods of leave so that they don't lose their jobs (Rake 2009, 5).

In the context of economic hardship brought about by recession, violence against women is being accentuated rather than eliminated, contrary to the purpose of campaigns worldwide. In the immediate aftermath of the 2007 meltdown, it was predicted that domestic violence would increase. Social scientists know from the experience of the 1930s Great Depression "that divorce rates can fall while family conflict and domestic violence rates rise" as a result of economic shock and austerity (Warner 2010). Evidence already suggests that the financial stress associated with mortgage arrears and unemployment has contributed to a rise in intimate partner violence (O'Hara 2010). A general pattern of increases in domestic violence as a result of the financial crisis has been observed in the United Kingdom, Ireland, and the United States: In the United Kingdom domestic violence rose 35 percent in 2010 (Carr 2011). An Irish NGO, Women's Aid, has documented the surge in domestic violence in badly affected Ireland since the 2007 global financial crisis (Women's Aid 2009; Harney 2011). In Ireland, there was a 21 percent rise in 2008 of the number of women who accessed domestic violence services compared to 2007 (Harney 2011, 27). This number rose even further in 2009, up 43 percent from 2007 figures (O'Hara 2010). Women's Grid (2011) reported that attacks on women in the home have soared by more than 2,000 a week since the start of the recession. In the United States, the situation is similarly grim. A survey released by Mary Kay (2011), a US cosmetics corporation, found that 80 percent of shelters nationwide reported an increase in domestic violence cases for the third year in a row; 73 percent of these cases were attributed to "financial issues," including job loss. In 2009 in New York during the midst of the crisis, courts dealt with a swell in cases, which is an "indirect but still jarring measure of economic stresses" (Glaberson 2009). Cases involving charges such as assault by family members were up 18 percent across New York State (Glaberson 2009).

Examining data from the US Census and from the National Survey of Families and Households (NSFH), researchers from the National Institute of Justice (2004) found that there was a higher risk of intimate partner violence in times of "economic distress." They identified women, especially African American women, as most at risk of being victims of violence. Recession has the potential to create poverty anew, as well as exacerbate preexisting poverty, and women are most likely to bear the brunt of violent consequences. The National Institute of Justice report (2004) found that women living in disadvantaged neighborhoods were more than twice as likely to be the victims of intimate partner violence compared with women in more advantaged neighborhoods. In 2009, the *Washington Post* reported two families that had been murdered in the Washington area by patriarchs who then committed suicide (Katz and Hacskaylo 2009). The incidents were linked to severe financial stress, debts, and depression caused by the recession. Most alarming was that neither family had a known history of domestic abuse (Katz and Hacskaylo 2009). While economic recession can exacerbate preexisting poverty, it can also push new families into situations of violence.

In Ireland, Women's Aid (2009) found that men were using the recession to excuse their abusive behavior. Viewed in the context of gendered household relations and the toll that financial strain can take on masculinities (read: men's sense of identity and material entitlement), the increased financial pressure of recessionary hardship can "escalate stress . . . [and] can be used as an excuse to legitimize controlling behaviors" (Sharon Cosgrove, chief executive of Sonas Housing, quoted in Stack 2011). In the US National Institute of Justice study (2004, 2), women whose male partners experienced two or more periods of unemployment over the five-year study were almost three times as likely to be victims of intimate partner violence as were women whose partners were in stable jobs. Research in Ireland (Harney 2011) and the United States (Renzetti 2009) indicates that the decline in the economy is challenging the long-standing breadwinner model as a measure of masculine "success" and perpetuating other (physical) forms of dominance. Similarly, men's unemployment increases their proximity to their partners, allowing them the opportunity for closer scrutiny and control (Sharma 2009). Many women who were preexisting victims of domestic violence reported that the economic downturn had led to more frequent and dangerous abuse (Women's Aid 2009). According to Safe Ireland's service development manager, the recession has changed the type of abuse women are presenting with (O'Hara 2010). In the United States, 56 percent of shelters have also noticed the abuse is more violent now than before the economic downturn (Mary Kay Inc. 2011).

Lack of income and material support is a major reason why women in developed countries do not leave violent husbands (Kelleher Associates and O'Connor 1995). During a recession, economically dependent women are even less able to escape domestic violence due to a lack of economic alternatives and the likely resulting effect of poverty on their children (Renzetti 2009, 1). The UK charity Refuge noted that some women suffer more abuse because the economic climate makes them less likely to leave violent partners (Wardrop 2008). Safe Ireland and Women's Aid (2009) note that "economic" or "financial" abuse is a commonly cited feature of recessionary escalation of domestic abuse (O'Hara 2010). Male partners control financial resources and trap women in a situation of economic dependence. Tactics include denying female partners access to the family finances, arranging all social welfare in the male abuser's name, arranging all debt in the female partner's name, denying the female partner money for food for herself and her children and to pay household bills, forging the female partner's signature on checks, and forcing the female partner to put the husband's name only on the deeds of the house (Women's Aid 2009). According to Harney (2011, 34), during separation men will often keep the house and use the family home "as a bait" to attract the children back. Domestic violence similarly has negative impacts on women's employment (Women's Aid 2011). In the United States, 65 percent of women in shelters reported they were unable to find employment due to the economy (Mary Kay Inc. 2011). Effectively, women's "choices" oscillate between abuse and poverty (Women's Aid 2011).

Family violence services in affected countries, especially the United Kingdom, Ireland, and the United States, are struggling to cope with the demand for their help while simultaneously dealing with funding cuts from austerity-driven governments.[2] One Irish charity recorded a 163 percent rise in the numbers it supported in 2010 (Stack 2011). As it is, Ireland reportedly lags far behind on the UK and Council of Europe standards for the number of refuges per head of population (one family unit per 10,000 people). Due to a prerecession lack of family violence support services and cuts to both their public and private funding, many Irish refuges have had to turn women away, leaving many women little choice but to remain in abusive relationships (Harney 2011, 35, 30). The Health Services Executive, which provides 80 percent of domestic violence services, had a budget cut of 7 percent in 2010 (O'Hara 2011).

The United States has also faced austerity cuts in domestic violence support services. In 2010, domestic violence programs laid off or did not replace 2,007 staff positions due to a lack of funding (National Network to End Domestic Violence [NNEDV] 2011). In July 2009, Governor of California Arnold Schwarzenegger cut sixteen million dollars from the state's domestic violence program, more than 40 percent of shelters' annual funding. Other essential domestic violence services—legal services, counseling, twenty-four-hour services, emergency centers—have also been eliminated in that state (McKinley 2009). Other US states and local authorities have suffered similar setbacks, such as Topeka, Kansas, featured in Box 6.4, but none on the scale of California's "zeroing out" of funding (McKinley 2009).

At a time when victims of domestic violence are most in need, funding cuts make it impossible to continue to maintain the same level and quality of

In 2011, the Topeka City Council in Kansas decriminalized domestic violence. The move was a response to the district attorney of Shawnee County
announcing that he no longer had the financial resources to pursue misdemeanor domestic violence cases (which make up half of all of misdemeanor
prosecutions) due to budget cuts (Sulzberger 2011). The city council chose
to decriminalize domestic violence rather than pay for domestic violence
prosecutions themselves, placing the onus back on the district attorney since
domestic violence is still a state crime (Sulzberger 2011). The district attorney
has stated that he will review cases sent to him by Topeka police and pursue
them on a case-by-case basis (Covert 2011). So far, eighteen people have
been arrested but released without charges of domestic violence because no
agency is accepting new cases (Sulzberger 2011). The game of political hot
potato is especially disconcerting at a time when domestic violence services
are struggling to deal with the swollen demand for support. The move sends
a dangerous message: "one, that it's not a priority, and two, that it's not very
serious" (Covert 2011).

service. Shelters in the United States do not anticipate a reduction in demand,
either: 89 percent expect their overall situation during the next year will be
worse or the same due to the economy (Mary Kay Inc. 2011). There is some
evidence that domestic violence groups' advocacy is reaping rewards. The
National Network to End Domestic Violence in the United States applauded
Congress for passing an appropriations bill that includes significant funding for domestic violence services (NNEDV 2011). The bill includes twenty-
five million dollars for the Violence Against Women Act of 1994 (VAWA,
reauthorized in 2005), the Transitional Housing Program funding temporary housing programs, and an array of social services for domestic and
sexual violence victims after they leave emergency shelter. However, this
funding and guidance to state and local housing authorities, as well as support for employment programs for battered women, is a long time coming—
more than fifteen years after the original Violence Against Women Act was
passed. In 2008, Vice President Biden introduced a bill to enlist and train
100,000 lawyers to represent domestic violence victims. President Obama's
2011 federal budget included $130 million to help victims find shelter, coun-
seling, and legal assistance (Prupis 2010). Although these resources signal
strong US government commitment to ending violence against women,
they also reveal the consistent privileging of legal prosecution and justice
support over economic and social rights support for victims. It is likely, for

instance, that more funds will be spent on legal assistance than on shelter and counseling.

The disproportionate burden of the recession on women—whether the result of government policy or by virtue of state inaction—sends a very damaging message to business, "that equality measures are there for the good times only and that the Government is prepared to trade on women's employment rights at this difficult time" (Rake 2009, 8). Moreover, when governments target cuts at domestic violence prevention, this entrenches the message of impunity; the state becomes a perpetrator of violence against women as it is unable and unwilling to address the problem despite rhetorical commitments in law and policy.

Let Finance Be the Servant: Women in Economic and Political Governance

The world over, economic decision-making institutions have drawn their leadership from one narrow demographic: white men. Brigitte Young (2010) coins the phrase "global financial governance without women." Her research reveals the striking absence of women from the G20, central banking, and other global policymaking institutions after the global financial crisis of 2007–08. Economically, as well as politically, men have plotted the course to the recession and men have plotted the course out. The 2009 Fawcett Society report states that "recent select committee hearings have shown male domination not only at the top of the banks but among the ranks of financial journalists, in senior positions in regulatory bodies and even among the MPs who are scrutinizing the decisions" (Rake 2009, 3). A recession is an opportunity to fix what is broken and an opportunity to change governance. Among international organizations, it has become "almost self-evident that improving the gender balance in the decision-making process," as well as women's participation in the labor market, will have major economic benefits (European Commission 2010, 18; World Bank 2006; Hausmann, Tyson, and Zahidi 2010). The Fawcett Society report argues that the recent collapse in UK financial institutions has given new impetus to the need for greater diversity among economic decision makers to promote balanced risk taking and economic stability. Like a growing number of countries that have passed "quota laws" for corporate boards, including Norway, followed by Italy, Spain, France, the Netherlands, Belgium, and Iceland, it makes the case for legislation that would impose quotas for female board members on FTSE-listed companies (Rake 2009, 2).[3] Following the introduction of quotas, Norway's female representation in the boardroom has soared from 6 percent to 44 percent in six

Box 6.5 ICELAND

When Iceland became the first casualty of the global financial crisis, many blamed the collapse of the small state's banking sector on a young, overconfident, male, business-school elite, as well as reckless financial deregulation and spending (at one stage eleven times its gross domestic product) at the behest of male politicians (O'Connor 2008). When former Icelandic prime minister Geir Haarde was forced to resign amid widespread public outrage, Icelanders chose Johanna Sigurdardottir, a former flight attendant, and a union representative, to be prime minister. She is not the country's first female prime minister, but she is the world's first openly gay country leader. In 2011, *Foreign Policy* magazine named Sigurdardottir as one the top 100 "Global Thinkers," the tagline reading: "for showing how good women are at fixing what men break." The piece contends that Sigurdardottir has presided over a feminist revolution (*Foreign Policy* 2011). Certainly Iceland has moved toward greater gender parity in political representation—nearly half the country's legislature is now female, as are four of its ten cabinet members (*Foreign Policy* 2011). Sigurdardottir has supported high-profile campaigns against rape and domestic violence—Iceland has among the highest rates of domestic violence among the Nordic countries (Nikolov 2010)—exacerbated by the recession (Parbring 2010). A law legalizing same-sex marriage passed unanimously, allowing Sigurdardottir to wed her long-time partner in 2010 (*Foreign Policy* 2011).

Economically, Iceland has still had to implement austerity measures but has made much lighter cuts to social welfare programs than other European countries (*Foreign Policy* 2011). The recession was much shorter than many at the International Monetary Fund predicted (Inman 2010). Significantly, and in contrast to the PIGS countries (Portugal, Ireland, Greece, and Spain), Iceland chose to allow its private banks to fail—the taxpayer refusing to bail out the mistakes of an elite few (Jolly 2010). Although there was a substantial fall in currency value, the krona, Iceland showed faster signs of recovery, indicating growth in the third quarter of 2010 mainly due to exports helped by the weaker krona (Inman 2010). When the banks were nationalized in 2008 following the crisis, women were appointed to top positions: Elín Sigfúsdóttir and Birna Einarsdóttir became chief executives of New Landsbanki and New Glitnir, respectively (O'Connor 2008). Their appointments were an attempt to signal a new culture within the banking system (O'Connor 2008).

Igniting the debate about choice versus coercion, Iceland has followed the lead of other Nordic states by criminalizing the purchase of sex and banning strip clubs, for feminist rather than religious reasons (Bindel 2010). "Once you break past the glass ceiling and have more than one third of female politicians," Kolbrún Halldórsdóttir (the parliamentarian who proposed the ban), comments, "something changes. Feminist energy seems to permeate everything" (Bindel 2010). Although recessions have society-wide implications, ensuring that women have a say in how the economy is organized helps to ensure that public policies do not exacerbate their burden.

years, while the figures in the United Kingdom and other countries such as the United States, Australia, and New Zealand have regressed or stagnated (Rake 2009, 3; see Armstrong and Walby 2012).

Box 6.5 presents a fascinating case of one of the worst financial recession-affected countries—Iceland—that had one of the most promising recoveries, which has deliberately limited the effects of the recession on the most vulnerable groups in society; this contrasts with the mounting criticism of the public sector cuts and their impact on poor women among other groups in the United Kingdom. Other states and women's movements should take heed: cutting the public sector to save private sector financiers will only increase gender inequalities; not only would this not be "smart economics" (to cite the World Bank slogan), but also it would exacerbate violence against women and other societal ills that take generations to turn back.

Conclusion

This chapter has shown how global finance affects the prevalence of violence against women today. Here we have examined the negative impacts of finance on women's economic and social situations, and their heightened vulnerability to violence as a result of gender-blind development projects and the economic shock caused by an unregulated, some say testosterone-driven, financial system. But finance need not only have negative effects, exacerbating violence against women. If finance is made the servant of public governance rather than the master, it could make a significant difference to eliminating violence against women by resourcing women's capacities and initiatives and enabling their economic independence, which provides an alternative to living with violence, as well as protection from violence. That is to say, violence against women is not merely an economic cost on the balance sheet of international financial institutions; indeed, if stopping violence against women is elevated to be core business in IFIs and in governments, then it is highly probable that economic development will be not only be advanced but also sustained through women's enhanced capacities, including their participation in key financial governance roles.

| Old and New Tactics of War

Sexual Violence in Armed Conflict

Wars and conflicts, wherever they are fought, invariably usher in
sickeningly high levels of violence against women and girls.

—AMNESTY INTERNATIONAL

If you look at the front-line discussion of wars—the troops, the politics,
the borders, the weapons, the armies—that is a men's story. How you
actually exist and continue on living in war—that's a woman's story.

—PBS WOMEN, War and Conflict Series

Introduction

*now being brought to
light: has always happened,
but U.N. is just now
beginning to notice*

Sexual and gender-based violence is a defining characteristic of contemporary
conflict.[1] It is well documented that the gravest violence against women increases as a direct result of armed conflict. How do we explain this violence?
What are its causes and consequences from a political economy perspective?
If we understand violence against women to be linked to the broader struggle
to control power and productive resources in recent armed conflicts, then
what are the remedies for ending this scourge of sexual violence against
women? This chapter addresses these key questions. It consists of four main
parts. First, I describe the problem of sexual violence in armed conflict, international definitions, and responses to it. Second, I put forward a political
economy analysis of sexual violence that many argue is increasingly prevalent
in recent conflicts. This analysis is strongly critical of the narrow, international framing of systemic sexual violence during war as an exceptional form
of gender-based violence. I argue that UN security interventions to protect
against mass sexual violence in war fail to adequately conceptualize it as part

of the continuum of gender-based violence that transgresses familiar soldier-civilian, male-female, state-nonstate perpetrator, and war-peace boundaries and thrives under conditions of globalized conflict, significantly hampering any violence protection efforts. Third, I illustrate with examples from recent conflicts some of the economic and political mechanisms that suggest that sexual violence against women in conflict-affected societies is linked to global processes, including competition over resources, struggle for economic and political power, and the reproduction of militarized masculinities through war and profit. Fourth, I consider the practical implications of this political economy analysis of the drivers and impacts of sexual violence in conflict for international operations that seek not only to protect against or prosecute the perpetrators of this violence but also to prevent it in the long run.

Defining Conflict-Related Violence Against Women

Prior to 1993 and the UN Vienna Conference on Human Rights, violations of human rights, particularly violence against women, including sexual violence, occurring in the so-called private sphere were not explicitly recognized. Rape and other violence against women, whether perpetrated by family members or others, were considered gender specific and falling outside of state jurisdiction in many countries. By definition, such violence was not deemed universal and was unable to be included in human rights frameworks. This all changed with the mobilization of the women's human rights movements and the achievement of the recognition of "women's rights (and violations thereof) as human rights" at the Vienna conference.

Current international definitions of sexual violence are broad, encompassing sexual slavery, enforced prostitution, forced pregnancy, enforced sterilization, or any other forms of sexual violence of comparable gravity that may include indecent assault, trafficking, inappropriate medical examinations, and strip searches.[2] Sexual violence is not seen as synonymous only with rape, although rape is often the form of violence most reported and discussed by international actors, especially the global media. The large-scale rape of women and girls, for example, has been a military strategy in countless historical and contemporary conflicts, most recently in eastern Congo and in the Darfur region of western Sudan (Kelly 2000; Moser and Clark 2001; WHO Regional Office for Europe and Instituto Superiore di Sanita 2001). In Darfur, there are reports of thousands of women who were raped and tortured and who lost their husbands and livelihoods as a result of the conflict (Human Rights Watch 2008a; Hampton 2005; Askin 2006). During the Rwandan genocide, an estimated quarter- to half-million women and girls were reportedly raped (Amnesty International 2004). In Sierra Leone, up to 64,000 women were sexually assaulted by combatants during the war (Physicians for Human Rights 2002; Mackenzie 2009). Rape and other sexual violence also took place on a mass scale during conflicts over the past twenty years in Bosnia-Herzegovina, East Timor, and Liberia.

Of course, scholars recognize that rape occurred in past, historical conflicts and sometimes systematically (Bock 1983). The interaction between ethnic identity and conflict is addressed, but gender identity and conflict have, until recently, remained under the radar of most scholars, national governments, and international organizations, even though they cut across all groups. However, rape has been framed and recognized as a "weapon" rather than part of the "spoils" of war only in the last decade, since the establishment of the International Criminal Court and Criminal Tribunals (Chappell 2008; Women's Initiatives for Gender Justice and Nobel Women's Initiative 2010). Depending on the circumstances of the offense, sexual violence now constitutes a war crime, a crime against humanity (under the Geneva War Crimes Convention), an act of torture (under the UN Torture Convention), or a constituent act with respect to genocide (under the UN Genocide Convention; see Jones 2010).

After the Vienna Conference on Human Rights in 1993, the global advocacy for women's human rights pushed to the foreground the specific contexts in which the most egregious violations of women's rights take place. At the 1995 UN Conference on Women in Beijing, among the twelve critical areas of concern were not only violence against women but also the impact of armed conflict on women.

Since 2000, the United Nations Security Council (UNSC) has passed five resolutions seeking to address the situation of women and girls in conflict and postconflict. These are listed chronologically in Box 7.1. The "mother" resolution, Resolution 1325, on women, peace, and security broadly addressed the impact of armed conflict on women and girls, calling for the mainstreaming of a gender perspective in all UN peace operations and women's participation in peace negotiations and peace-building efforts. In 2004, the Economic and Social Council of the United Nations noted the importance of implementing Resolution 1325 and requested that the secretary-general ensure that all UN entities develop and implement gender action plans.[3] As a result, member states are expected to strengthen their national commitments and capacity to implement Resolution 1325 by adopting national and regional action plans that coordinate efforts to promote 1325 at all levels and across policy areas. These plans need to designate specific measures, clear targets, and benchmarks for full implementation by the year 2015. The

NO.	YEAR	SUMMARY
1325	2000	Women, peace, and security— participation of women in peace negotiations and peace building, and gender mainstreaming in peace operations
1820	2008	Recognizes sexual violence as an explicit tactic of war
1888	2009	Action-oriented follow-up—special representative to the secretary-general (SRSG) on sexual violence, women protection advisers, annual reports on implementation of Resolutions 1820 and 1888
1889	2009	Demand for collection of quantitative data and reporting of sexual violence
1960	2010	Ten-year anniversary reaffirming Resolution 1325 targeting rape, abuse, and violence against women in armed conflict

Norwegian government's action plan for the implementation of Resolution 1325, for example, makes protecting women from gender-based violence a major concern of humanitarian assistance and peace and reconciliation efforts, and a total of more than 400 million NOK has been budgeted for the follow-up to Resolution 1325 since 2007. In addition, administrative measures have been put in place to request that all developing country partners report on implementation of Resolution 1325.

The four UNSC resolutions since 2008 (Resolutions 1820, 1888, 1889, and 1960) have all focused on ending sexual violence perpetrated against women in conflict and on the integration of issues of sexual violence within all UN peace negotiations and related operations. These resolutions have been instigated in particular by the United States (under Secretary of State Condoleezza Rice and subsequently Secretary of State Hillary Clinton). Implementing Resolution 1820 on ending sexual violence in conflict commits the Security Council to considering appropriate steps to end such atrocities and to punish their perpetrators. The UN secretary-general is required to report to the Security Council evidence of the use of sexual violence against civilians in situations of conflict and post-conflict, actions taken to implement this resolution, and, further, timely strategies for ceasing this practice and measuring progress on its prevention. There is a lack of political will in many governments to end the culture of impunity toward violence against women, which suggests more must be done to document the violations of women's human rights in conflict and postconflict settings and to collect data on its causes and consequences for peace and reconstruction processes (Bernard et al. 2008).

In Resolution 1888, ending sexual violence in conflict is also elevated above other forms of violence against women and all other issues and objectives relating to women and gender equality in peace and security, including the importance of women's participation in conflict resolution and peace building. Paragraph 3 in both Resolutions 1820 and 1888 demand that all parties to armed conflict "train troops on the categorical prohibition of all forms of sexual violence against civilians" and "debunk[ing] myths that fuel sexual violence," challenging the assumption that rape is a spoil of war or a normal practice of masculinity. With these resolutions, the United Nations has shifted from a primarily humanitarian response for women survivors of war to expressing its readiness in international security terms to protect against, prosecute, and ultimately prevent mass sexual violence during conflict (Bachelet 2011). Resolution 1888 called for a new position of "Special Representative to the UN Secretary-General on Sexual Violence in Conflict" (paragraph 4) and a team of rapidly deployable experts to bolster national rule-of-law responses (paragraph 8). In January 2010, Margot Wallstrom, former deputy commissioner of the European Communities, was named to the position with the mandate of mainstreaming sexual violence prevention into international security policy and programming.

Despite these substantial international efforts by the United Nations and women's advocates worldwide, the scourge of sexual violence in recent conflicts has hardly lessened. In 2007, speaking on behalf of the United Nations, Secretary-General Ban Ki Moon acknowledged that:

> [I]n no other area is our collective failure to ensure effective protection for civilians more apparent . . . than in terms of the masses of women and girls whose lives are destroyed each year by sexual violence perpetrated in conflict.

And this UN failure is ongoing. In late July and August 2010, an estimated 500 women and girls were raped by armed men in remote villages in Walikale territory in North Kivu and Shabunda territory in South Kivu, eastern Congo (South Kivu province), while UN peacekeeping troops were stationed just twenty-five miles away from the pillaged villages. There was no protection, let alone a preventative UN response. One former force commander had stated, "it is more dangerous to be a woman than to be a soldier right now in Eastern DRC" (Cammaert 2008). Conflict in this region is by definition a war against women given the strikingly commonplace nature of rape and sexual slavery.[4] Wallstrom, who visited the region in October 2010, after a high-level panel was convened by the UN high commissioner for human rights in August 2010, heard directly from sixty-one selected victims of sexual violence in the Democratic Republic of the Congo, including seven victims from the August rapes, about their needs and perceptions of remedies and reparations available to them (OHCHR 2011).

For all their good intentions, the UNSC resolutions on women, peace, and security and gender mainstreaming efforts in UN peacekeeping operations have yet to bring about a change in the international reality that men both make wars and get to negotiate the terms of peace. A feminist perspective on war and security illuminates some of the reasons for this failure by pointing out the underlying gendered structures of war and peace in the international state system. Commonplace images of male aggressor/female nurturer and male warrior/female peacemaker greatly constrain efforts to bring about sustainable peace and security. Feminists observe how prevailing gender norms of masculinity and femininity perpetuate war making. Social constructions of hypermasculinity in military training motivate soldiers (men and women) to fight and to protect "women and children" through killing, and to suppress (feminine) emotions associated with bodily pain and caring, while the experience of war and conflict also shapes norms of masculinity, explaining why soldiers so often continue to act out violently against women on the home front or after the conflict is over.

Feminists define peace and security, not in idealized ways often associated with *women*, but in broad, multidimensional terms that include the elimination of all social hierarchies that lead to political and economic injustice (Tickner 1992; Enloe 1989, 1994; Cockburn 2010, 2012). Such a perspective focuses on the *insecurity* of individuals, particularly of marginalized and disempowered populations. It views military security as often antithetical to individual security, particularly for vulnerable groups. Too much stress on defense helps to legitimate a militarized social order that overvalorizes the use of violence, whether state sanctioned or not.

From a feminist perspective, putting the UNSC resolutions on women, peace, and security into practice requires changing our conception of international security to incorporate the provision of not just military and political security but also community security for women, men, girls, and boys. Now is a propitious moment to bring about such change. The scale and the brutality of recent sexual violence in conflict have focused political attention on long-term solutions. This book's argument is that eliminating violence against women in conflict depends ultimately on efforts to transform the social and economic gender inequalities that constrain women's participation and underlie their vulnerability in conflict settings. But this has not been the predominant approach of the United Nations.

that take too long to implement and actually have an effect

Securitizing Sexual Violence

UN Action Against Sexual Violence in Conflict[5] argues that conflict-related sexual violence is exceptional and "not simply another form of gender-based violence" (Holmes 2010). The United Nations asks, "*When* is sexual violence a security issue?" and applies a six-pillar test as shown in Box 7.2.

We might ask, "When is sexual violence ever *not* a security issue for victims, and especially for women?" As Box 7.3 retells, I observed this contrary questioning among women's human rights activists at an Office for the High Commissioner on Human Rights expert meeting on violence against women in Geneva in November 2010.

The United Nations prioritizes sexual violence as a threat to security and an impediment to peace when the perpetrators of this violence are from a belligerent party and light weapons are proliferated, or when there is a breakdown of law and order, militarization of fuel and water collection sites, and targeting of ethnic and other minorities or populations in contested territories. Concerned solely with situations where rape and other sexual violence "against women and children" are used or commissioned as a systematic tactic of war by military authorities, the United Nations wants, above all, to determine who is legally accountable for the violence and to prosecute them for the crimes (including with the adoption of sanctions; SCR 1820, paragraph

---

Box 7.2 SECURITIZING SEXUAL VIOLENCE

Six-pillar test

1. Crime of concern to the international community as a whole
2. Command responsibility is entailed
3. Civilians targeted
4. Climate of impunity—sexual violence "normalized" after conflict
5. Cross-broader implications such as displacement or trafficking
6. Ceasefire violation

Box 7.3 PARTICIPANT OBSERVATION

In her role as the UN special representative on sexual violence in conflict, Margot Wallstrom's mandate is to ask the question, "When is sexual violence a security issue?" There is stunned silence in the Geneva Office of the High Commissioner for Human Rights (OHCHR) "expert" workshop on violence against women. But when is sexual violence *not* a security issue for women? Activists sitting around the room are incredulous. They are politely told that we are talking about whether or not sexual violence is a security issue for states, not for women. Are states not composed of people, half of whom are women? Why is there this difference? Where is the feminist intervention here? Is it such a success to have gotten sexual violence on the international security agenda? Will this stop the violence against women? Will it make a difference to women's lives? These are the questions feminists ask when they scrutinize UN Security Council decisions. Why is it that a UN resolution and agenda on sexual violence—touted as an example of high-level international action on gender injustice—could be so indicative of the way women's security needs continue to be marginalized by the state security agenda and egregious violence against women silently perpetuated?

5; SCR 1888, paragraph 10). To do this, they need to establish a causal connection between the sexual violence and the purposes of the conflict. As a result, the United Nations is deaf and blind to the continuum of violence by all parties with or without rational cause, where perpetrators cannot necessarily be named but the violence is life threatening for the victims.

Unequal relationships of power between men and women are deemed to be insufficient explanatory variables for wartime sexual violence since they cannot tell us what form of violence is used, where it is used, and why it is commanded. Yet this conceptualization of conflict-related sexual violence and its causes is flawed. Rape and other sexual violence does not only occur in war because it is commanded or the best or most efficient way to achieve a particular military end, nor does tactical sexual violence occur in isolation from other forms of violence against civilians and soldiers. A political economy approach challenges the UN "securitization" framework for (1) its poor understanding of the root causes of violence, (2) its failure to effectively protect against or prevent sexual violence, and (3) its consequent silencing of a whole range of forms of egregious violence against civilians not directly related to the strategic purposes of a war. In the words of Cora Weiss, president of The Hague Appeal for Peace and UN representative for the International Peace Bureau, "we cannot pluck rape out of war and let the war go on. We must not make war safe for women" (Weiss 2011).

Political Economy and the War Story

A political economy approach seeks to uncover the political and economic power inequalities that fuel conflict-related sexual violence and to use that understanding to inform efforts to end this violence and, indeed, all violence against women. It does not view rape or other sexual violence as an inherent part of masculinity or war involving any race, ethnicity, religion, sexuality, or nationality. Rather, it conceives of gender identities and hierarchies as constructed in particular cultural, political, and economic contexts and therefore as amenable to change. Nor does a political economy perspective view war as a necessary or permanent feature of human societies. As this book has consistently argued, all forms of violence against women have a *material* basis that may, over time, become embedded in cultural practices. That is, they are rooted in and heightened by unequal social relations often in impoverished or destabilizing economic and political contexts characterized by stress, displacement, and struggles to obtain and distribute resources for survival or basic needs.

Those who seek power and authority try to gain control over productive and reproductive resources, including over the allocation of women's paid and unpaid labor, often in return for "protection" from violence. The causes of armed conflict are themselves often linked with attempts to control economic resources such as oil, metal, diamonds, drugs, or contested territorial and ethno-political boundaries of groups (El Jack 2003, 8). Violence against women may be one way to achieve this control whether planned or not. *a means to an end* Broadly speaking then, rape and other gender-based violence are related to the economic and political bases of the conflict in at least three ways—even if a causal "security" connection cannot always be empirically documented. First, this violence may enable the extraction of productive resources, whether assets, land, or labor, by dishonoring girls or women and their families and thus maiming a community given that in many conflict-affected countries women traditionally carry out much of the agricultural labor and/or meet basic subsistence needs. For example, in the Ugandan civil war, women were reportedly raped in order to extract resources from them— women are the major agricultural laborers, so soldiers attempted to stop women from being able to work, effectively cutting the food supply of the "enemy." In some cases the soldiers accomplished this goal further by amputating limbs (Human Rights Watch 1997, 23; Turshen 2000, 813). *1 Example - use sexual violence to get whatever they want in way they want - no matter who is killed*

Second, gender-based or sexual violence in conflict may stem from the impoverished situation in which many male soldiers working for government armies or armed militia find themselves. It is important to state that no context, impoverished or not, justifies acts of violence. However, working without regular pay or proximity to their own wives/partners but with a sense of entitlement as "male breadwinners" due to traditional gender divisions of labor, soldiers may rape with impunity or tacit approval of commanding officers, rationalizing it as a form of compensation: "taking what's mine or what's due to me." Even when a political settlement has been achieved, organized crime may perpetuate political violence and violence against women. For example, in their analysis of the discourses soldiers in the Congo use to explain the sexualized violence they commit, Maria Eriksson Baaz and Maria Stern (2009) show how the soldiers' explanations are "crafted out of statist norms around heterosexuality and masculinity produced within their society's military institutions and armed forces" (2009, 514). Moreover, they reveal how militarized masculinities in the Congo are actively constructed against femininity and using degrading images of women. In interviews, soldiers expressed their frustration at not being able to be a "real man," that is, providing for their wives and children and receiving in return the fulfillment of sexual and other needs. They discussed how this frustration "manifested in a negative and sexualized image of women" (Baaz and Stern 2009, 507).

In conflict situations also, men may feel powerless and unable to fulfill their duty to protect their families (Dolan 2002).[6] Insufficient economic opportunities for men to provide for their families (and as such live up to expectations of successful masculinity) may encourage conflict in the first place. This can arouse their resentment and erupt in violence against women family members, especially if women are the economic providers (UNFPA 2008, 7). Indeed, women often become heads of households during times of conflict as men may be fighting, be killed, or elect to leave the affected area to look for work elsewhere. In these cases, the loss of a certain political and economic status as masculine breadwinner is linked to acts of violence that can be interpreted as men seeking to reclaim their dominant status or entitlement in a wartime political economy.

Third, during times of economic or political breakdown and crisis, existing gender inequalities and discrimination are often exacerbated and more easily exploited by those in power—predominantly men—through sexual and other gender-based violence. These inequalities, especially women's lack of access to the same economic and social resources as men in every country in the world, mean that women are less able than men to protect themselves from violence or abuse and from being in situations such as poor housing or employment where they are highly vulnerable to such violence.

Rather than illuminate these political-economic dimensions of sexual violence against women, international security approaches, this chapter contends, obscure them. If we take the UN view that sexual violence is only a security issue requiring a protective response when it passes the "six-pillar test," then we will fail to see the incidence of such mass-scale violence, let alone predict or stop it. The UN failure to protect against sexual violence in conflict is conceptually, as well as practically, based. Both the theory of *why* and *when* sexual violence occurs in conflict and the implementation to prevent it are flawed. International security interventions that operationalize a narrow, legalistic definition of wartime sexual violence fail to adequately conceptualize this violence as part of a continuum of gender-based violence that transgresses familiar soldier-civilian, male-female, state-nonstate perpetrator, and war-peace boundaries and thrives under conditions of globalized conflict. Flawed conceptualizations significantly hamper any violence protection efforts and ensure that they are dead in the water, even before UN peacekeepers have received their predeployment training, codes of conduct, and checklists to prevent sexual violence. Let me illustrate this challenge to international security conceptions of sexual violence with the example of the conflict in the Democratic Republic of the Congo (DRC), coined "the epicenter of rape as a weapon of war" by some UN officials.

The Democratic Republic of the Congo—an Epicenter for Sexual and Gender-Based Violence?

The Congo has been plagued by conflict for over fifteen years, involving neighboring states Rwanda and Uganda and various armed rebel groups including the Lord's Resistance Army (LRA) and the Democratic Forces for the Liberation of Rwanda (FDLR), particularly in the East and South where lucrative mineral resources such as diamonds, cooper, and zinc lie. Although government troops have been at war, the different phases of the conflict have been similarly characterized by civilian deaths, injuries, and torture. It is in this context that the mass prevalence of rape and sexual violence is seen. Yet UN officials, aid workers, scholars, and the Congolese themselves cannot explain why. The case is begging for a political economy analysis (and solution). Despite the UNSC demand for quantitative data on sexual violence in conflict, comprehensive data are extremely limited for some obvious reasons. In many conflict-affected countries there is poor government infrastructure, and populations are often isolated and inaccessible due to the conflict. Victims of violence have strong cultural disincentives to report sexual violence and little government, legal, or material support to do so. In the most recent study of the incidence of rape in the Congo based on extrapolations from a household survey done in 2007 of 3,436 Congolese women

GBV is still present in contemporary war bc govn'ts dont do anything to stupit or provide support to women

aged fifteen to forty-nine nationwide, public health researchers Amber Peterman, Tia Palermo, and Karyn Bredenkamp (2011) found that approximately 12 percent were raped at least once in their lifetime and 3 percent were raped in the one-year period before the survey. The study indicates that the problem is much bigger and more pervasive than previously thought. Women have reported alarming levels of sexual abuse in the capital and in provinces far from the Congo's war-torn East, a sign that the problem extends beyond the nation's primary conflict zone—to western, northern, and eastern Congo (Peterman, Palermo, and Bredenkamp 2011). At the same time, compared with women in Kinshasa, women in North Kivu, where much of the armed conflict has taken place, were significantly more likely to report all types of sexual violence. Reports of sexual violence were largely independent of individual-level background factors, suggesting a strong correlation with structural factors, including the overall economic decline in the postcolonial period and the lack of government presence.

Conflict-Related Sexual Violence Begins at Home

Crucially, the study revealed that twice as many women, or approximately 22 percent, had been forced by their partners to have sex or perform sexual acts against their will. This finding implies pervasive sexual abuse in the private home (Peterman et al. 2011; Gettleman 2011).[7] "Not only is sexual violence more generalized," but also, as Peterman et al. (2011) state, "findings suggest that future policies and programs should focus on abuse within families." However, the UN Security Council mandate to eliminate sexual violence in armed conflict in the UN mission in the DRC (MONUC), while appropriate given the gravity of sexual violence in that country, risks rendering domestic violence and abuse invisible, which the major survey's research suggests is at the root of all conflict-related violence. Insofar as violence against women at home is a normal occurrence, such violence can easily become a legitimate practice among soldiers and an integral part of a strategy to terrorize civilians and extract resources. But if this connection is not recognized in the very conceptualization of conflict-related violence and a boundary is established demarcating sexual violence with a causal connection to the conflict from domestic violence occurring in the home or privately, then interventions to stop the violence that focus only on belligerent armed groups or target territories will be ineffective in *any* timeframe.

The quantitative evidence of generalized domestic violence against women in the Congo is supported by good qualitative evidence in other country cases that intimate partner violence against women greatly increases during and after conflict (Mooney 2005; World Bank 2007). The UN special rapporteur on violence against women's mission reports with respect to conflict-affected countries show clear linkages between violence against women, conflict, and militarism (SRVAW 2001, 2004, 2005a, 2005b, 2006a, 2008).

Women may become aware of impending conflict in ways that may not be visible to others. For example, in the Solomon Islands, women became aware of the threat of impending conflict when prisoners were released and it became more dangerous to gather forest products because of the risk of attack. In other contexts, women have decreased rates of market engagement when social tensions have risen in advance of conflict. Women everywhere are also often aware of increased circulation and accumulation of small arms in homes or communities (see Capie 2011). In some cases, elevated levels of domestic violence are associated with impending conflict. Women need to be engaged by decision makers in early warning processes (UNIFEM 2010).

Rational Acts of Rational Men?

As one UN official commented, "we can't develop our peacekeeping programs without understanding the perpetrators and victims better."[8] Data collection is a precondition for the implementation of Resolution 1820, which requires the Security Council to monitor sexual violence through regular and systematic reporting by peacekeeping missions. UN reports, scholarly studies, and press commentary document sexual violence perpetrated by all parties against all victims. However, the primary focus has been on violence against women perpetrated by armed illicit or military groups. While no one disputes that armed men engage in rape against civilian populations, the story of who is raping whom turns out to be significantly more complicated than the popular narrative suggests. Studies of rapists are rare (for an exception see Eriksson Baaz and Stern [2009]), although the United Nations suggests that data on perpetrators is preferable and more easily collected than that on victims.[9]

As we saw with the Peterman et al. (2011) study, rapes by civilians account for a large percentage of rape cases in the DRC. A study by the Harvard Humanitarian Initiative (HHI; 2010) funded by Oxfam found a huge increase in the number of civilian-perpetrated rapes between 2004 and 2008.[10] While the majority of rapists were either soldiers or militiamen, the report also shows a shocking seventeen-fold increase in rapes carried out by civilians. This spike in civilian rape coincides with military activities in the Congo. Approximately 40 percent of the rapes of the more than 4,000 victims surveyed in the HHI study were committed by civilians. Sixty percent were gang raped by armed men, but more than half of these assaults (56 percent) took place in the supposed safety of the family home at night (while 16 percent took place in fields and almost 15 percent in the forest), often in the presence of the victim's husband and children—revealing the strongly emphasized connection between domestic and conflict-related violence. Sexual slavery was also reported, affecting 12 percent of the women in the sample, with some women being held captive for years. In their sample, Peterman et al. (2011) found that 22.5 percent of rapes in the sample were perpetrated by husbands and other intimate partners, not by soldiers sweeping through a village. It also found an extraordinarily high rate of rape in Equateur province, far from the violence of North and South Kivu and Ituri. This finding suggests that civilian-perpetrated rape is not directly caused by conflict and the presence of multiple armed groups but is part of a more generalized trend in the context of a conflict-ridden society with higher levels of poverty and corruption than non-conflict-affected countries, not to mention the levels of socioeconomic stress and instability (World Bank 2011).

Seemingly contrary to UN narratives, not all rapists in the Congo are men, and not all victims are women. Kirsten Johnson et al., in a 2010 study involving interviews in over 1,000 households in the conflict-affected eastern Congo, found that women self-reported committing 41 percent of acts of sexual violence against other women and 10 percent of acts against men (Johnson et al. 2010).[11] Since there are very few women fighting in Congolese armed groups or even in the national army, this supports the Oxfam/HHI conclusion emphasizing community-based, civilian-perpetrated rape. At the same time, sexual and other violence against men and boys has taken place most egregiously when men/boys are forced to perpetrate violence even against family members. In those cases we can hardly speak of victims or perpetrators and indeed, that common identity boundary in studies of violence is often unhelpful in a context such as the DRC, where sexual violence is so widespread.

Even if we assume that rape and other sexual violence is perpetrated by armed forces or militia, it is questionable to what extent this violence is tactical and conflict related rather than generalized and community based, given the evidence on civilian sexual violence and violence perpetrated in private homes. Eriksson Baaz and Stern (2010, 16) argue that "while sexual and other violence is often used to humiliate and intimidate, this humiliation and intimidation is much less strategic and much more complex than a combat strategy to further military/political gains."

Whose Stories of Violence Do We Tell?

While researchers reveal a different picture of sexual violence than that framed in the UN definition of conflict-related sexual violence, this framing is nonetheless compelling in terms of the resources that are directed to respond to sexual violence that meets the six-pillar test. Not surprisingly, politically savvy victims seek to fit their experience of violence into the UN frame. Victims have a powerful incentive to self-report sexual violence, renarrating their stories using UN criteria. Official data collection of rape and other sexual violence perpetrated by belligerent armed parties is geared toward legal proceedings and counts only those victims/perpetrators that can be prosecuted. Consequently, there are huge problems with politicized and biased data collection. There is a tendency to identify obvious, publicized cases of sexual violence—not silent cases that take place in private. Yet feminists argue that this public/private boundary masking violations of human rights is precisely why violence against women still takes place below the radar of the rule of law in many countries. Moreover, governments may decide to collect certain data on sexual violence to avoid facing up to the involvement of their own military organizations.

For example, in the DRC, the data collection overstates public, sexual violence committed against politically aware victims; sexual violence perpetrated by national security forces is systematically underreported compared with that perpetrated by nongovernment armed groups. Gang rapes are similarly overreported compared with isolated cases where women victims experience violence alone and not in a group of women (Roth 2010). In Columbia, official recognition and collection of sexual violence data on armed groups began only in 2009, despite fifty years of ongoing conflict. But data are not collected on paramilitary groups. The Columbian government says that sexual violence does not exist among these groups (Roth et al. 2011). Further, sexual violence data are collected and coded as domestic violence in the case of homicides and displaced women (battered women who have left) only, and data do not rely on the testimony of victims who have major disincentives to report sexual violence given the dishonor and blame-the-victim stigma associated with rape especially.

Many methodological issues plague the collection of sexual violence data in conflict-affected countries. A reflexive, feminist-informed methodology that is sensitive to victims' voices and experiences needs to inform the research process of conceptualizing, collecting, analyzing, contextualizing, and qualifying data on sexual violence for particular audiences in often politicized settings (see Ackerly and True 2008, 2010).[12] It is not just good statisticians that are required but good qualitative researchers with research ethics that require them to attend to biases, including gender biases, throughout the research and who can link qualitative and quantitative data on sexual violence in conflict to allow for rigorous interpretations (Roth et al. 2011).

A political economy lens finds the framing of conflict-related sexual violence as an exceptional form of gender-based violence to be exclusionary, effectively silencing most victims of violence who cannot fit their stories into the UN frame, and misguided. It is clear that the conceptualization of sexual violence, as well as research process—how we collect data and what data we collect—determines what we see and know about sexual violence, its causes, and its consequences. Our data collection also has significant implications not only for investigating cases of sexual violence but also for the interventions intended to prevent and protect against that violence. In the January 2008 peace settlement in the Congo, not a single woman was present at the negotiating table despite Resolution 1325 and despite the widespread rape and other violence against women in that conflict (Lewis 2008). Women were not consulted or engaged. We have yet to see a major, demonstrable impact of Resolution 1325 on the terms of peace negotiations, and little collective action has resulted yet from Resolutions 1820, 1888, and 1960. There are major problems with the conception of sexual violence in these resolutions and, consequently, with their practical implementation.

After the Violence: Prosecution Versus Prevention

If states, the United Nations, and other international actors have failed to develop sufficient early warning mechanisms to detect and protect against outbreaks of sexual violence in conflict areas, then they have also failed to adequately respond after the violence. As I have argued in this chapter, this collective failure is due in part to the poor conceptualization of sexual violence reflected in the UNSC resolutions (also Shepherd 2008). By and large, the UNSC resolutions do not address the underlying gender roles that celebrate masculine aggression and impunity toward men's violence against women, and the gendered socioeconomic inequalities that affect women's vulnerability to sexual violence in conflict. The resolutions are also based on a narrow, traditional conception of state security that, in the context of UN peace-building administrations, privileges physical security and electoral machinery over social and economic security. The practical application of this concept of security has negatively affected women's ability to access their human rights to basic needs such as housing, food, health, income or employment, and education.

The UN Action Against Sexual Violence in Conflict has largely pursued a legal justice approach to ending sexual violence and attending to victims. Much of the substance of the UNSC Resolutions 1820 and 1889 is concerned with peacekeeping/policing, criminal accountability, and legal prosecution responses to sexual violence. Only paragraph 13 in Resolution 1889 encourages states with the support of the international community "to increase access to health care, psychosocial support, legal assistance and *socioeconomic reintegration* services for victims of sexual violence, in particular in rural areas" (my emphasis).

Yet increased international attention to sexual violence in the DRC has led to a substantial increase of funding without any good evaluation of the real needs on the ground and the complexity of the issues. The Office of the Senior Adviser and Coordinator for Sexual Violence in the Comprehensive Strategy on Combating Sexual Violence in the DRC released notes in 2009 that "efforts are unevenly distributed. . . . The programmatic focus is essentially on two sectors: medical and judicial support to sexual violence survivors, while the remaining sectors show very few interventions" (IRIN News 2009).

Significant international resources have been made available to prosecute perpetrators of sexual violence by bolstering legal institutions and judicial capacity and establishing legal aid and remedies for primarily women victims, as Box 7.4 describes in the case of Goma, DRC. These resources massively outweigh those available for socioeconomic support for victims, such as providing resources and education for sexual violence service providers and for longer-term projects to assist victims with economic livelihoods, including income-generating projects and help with finding employment or education for themselves and their families. Yet when the UN panel visited the Congo in October 2010 to meet with victims of sexual violence from across several regions and groups, they found the physical, psychological, and material needs of victims largely unmet (OHCHR 2011). The victims themselves conveyed to the panel what they wanted most: health and education, especially for their children, and "socio-economic reintegration programs, with attention to ensure that they are sustainable and tailored to the economic context" (OHCHR 2011, paragraph 5). Many victims interviewed by the panel, reflecting the broader population of sexual violence victims,

> [a]re unable to seek justice through the courts because they cannot identify their perpetrators or in some cases their perpetrators have not been arrested, leaving these victims with no possibility of access to reparation through judicial proceedings, as the justice system does not provide reparations in absence of the perpetrator. (OHCHR 2011, paragraph 8)

There are clear tradeoffs between legal versus socioeconomic remedies for sexual violence in terms of the channeling of financial and human resources and the whole purpose of official sexual violence data collection. The little socioeconomic support available to women and men civilians may be prioritized for victims of sexual violence or specifically rape. For example,

Box 7.4 PREVENTING AND PROTECTING AGAINST
VIOLENCE: GOMA, DRC

The sectors receiving proportionally the least funding and attention are prevention and reintegration. "Just treating the results of sexual violence is a catastrophe. No one is really treating the root or the entirety of the situation. If you just care for the raped women, you will be caring for them up until infinity," said Butros Kalere of Women for Women.

"Sexual violence is not just a physical problem, but we often don't have enough funding and thus, we are limited to real work only for the immediate victims," the organization's community health coordinator, Jean Robert Liko-fata Esanga, told IRIN, adding that its programs that focus on prevention, rehabilitation, and reintegration continually suffer underfunding.

Effective prevention programming, according to Tasha Gill, child protection officer with the UN Children's Fund (UNICEF) in the DRC, "employs advocacy and awareness to mobilize the communities through community leaders, identifying the issues and working towards longer-term changes within local social norms, while alternately working towards protecting those who are most vulnerable."

Even organizations that specialize in protection are feeling the pinch. "We usually try to reduce vulnerability and protect 1,000 women in the communities on the outskirts of Goma by providing them with skills training, literacy and financing a portion of their activities," explained an employee of one such NGO. "Now that our donor wants us to work more in an 'emergency' setting and we are confined to working in the IDP camps, it is very difficult as the population is always in flux. It's hard to keep track of them and be consistent with the training."

The United Nations' ideal plan for reintegration includes a "survivor-centered skill approach." While some NGOs have funding to provide women with the opportunity to learn skills during their hospital stays, their use of those skills upon their return can be restricted by location and availability of material. For example, women are restricted in practicing their sewing skills by lack of access to a sewing machine, while literacy skills are restricted by the lack of schools. "Medical, protection, and legal/justice services and psycho-social care are part of treating sexual violence, but these services also need to include enabling women to be able to provide for their families . . . for them to feel like they can move on and take care of their children," Wendy Marsh, an independent expert on sexual violence, told IRIN (2009).

while rape victims in eastern Congo have a good chance of getting needed medical services, a woman suffering from breast cancer or a woman in another part of the country giving birth are unlikely to have access to treatment. The focus on rape and the subsequent burst of humanitarian focus on the crisis creates perverse incentives for women to falsely present themselves as rape victims in order to access health care (Eriksson Baaz and Stern 2009). There is ongoing debate about individual versus collective reparations for victims of sexual violence in conflict. Some argue that resources allocated to collective projects to improve maternal health care, for instance, should be prioritized over compensation for individual women victims. The National Strategy to Combat Gender-Based Violence in the Congo envisions a reparations fund for victims whose perpetrators are unidentified or insolvent but not for targeted improvements to public infrastructure to benefit women especially (OHCHR 2011).

Currently, many victims are excluded from redress and in precarious social and economic situations, making it highly likely that they will experience further violence. The Congo has one of the most progressive laws on rape in Africa, but few rapists are prosecuted (Harvard Humanitarian Initiative 2010). The penal code was revised in 2006 to "prevent and severely reprimand infractions relating to sexual violence and to ensure systematic support for the victims of these crimes." Under this code, sexual conduct with someone younger than the age of eighteen is now automatically defined as rape, despite the legal age of marriage being fifteen years. However, the law is largely ignored and the economic barriers to bringing a sexual violence case to court are insurmountable for most victims. Fees are required to submit police complaints, and the police themselves do not have the resources to pursue investigations. Perpetrators are often in the family, and bringing a case may mean the loss of economic livelihood for the family, just as reporting a case of sexual violence at work may mean losing one's job (IRIN News 2011). The rule of law is at any rate only one avenue for ending the culture of impunity for sexual and gender-based violence. It does not address, for instance, the cycle of violence and poverty, which is the major theme of this book.

A political economy approach suggests the need to bring about a real, substantive improvement in women's material lives to prevent further vulnerability to violence. Implementing this approach would mean reinventing international efforts to prevent sexual and gender-based violence. Current initiatives such as predeployment training for peacekeepers to prevent sexual violence and the UN Women's roster of international gender experts who can be rapidly deployed to work on legal issues (criminal, constitutional, electoral/party) treat women as the passive victims requiring special protection from the international community rather than agents of political and economic change (Bachelet 2011).

A new policy consensus on women's rights and security must be informed by a political economy approach that identifies the social and economic inequalities between women and men and culturally embedded notions of masculinity as the root causes of gender-based and sexual violence in conflict and postconflict. Such an approach calls for a systematic human or community security response that must be backed by specifically targeted mandates, resources, training, and incentives to be effective. Already, twelve UN agencies have collaborated in the UN Action Against Sexual Violence in Conflict, but this mandate should be expanded further to embrace the promotion, as well as the protection, of women's human rights, especially their economic and social rights, in UN peace operations.

Better collaboration across UN agencies in developing a multidimensional security, human rights, and development strategy in conflict and post-conflict settings would make a demonstrable difference to the practical implementation of violence prevention. For instance, with respect to internally displaced persons in conflict-affected areas, closer attention to information sharing, coordination, and collaboration between UN Human Rights Council and Department of Peacekeeping Operations (UNDPKO) would improve social, political, and economic outcomes for women and children. The UN Refugee Agency's (UNHCR) community development approach to gender mainstreaming potentially complements UNDPKO's approach to physical security and gender-based violence in understanding the fundamental protection challenges and contributions of internally displaced women and children in conflict (Women's Refugee Commission 2007).

Conclusion

As we have seen in this chapter and previous chapters, the prevalence of violence against women is linked to—and accentuated by—globalized processes of gendered conflict, resource competition, and survival. How else can we account for the scourge of sexual violence in conflict areas in countries as diverse as the DRC, East Timor, Guatemala, and Colombia? The political economy approach advanced in this chapter and this book resists subsuming gender issues within larger international security concerns (Hansen 2000; Blanchard 2003), as we have seen with the elevation of sexual violence in armed conflict above all other forms of gender-based violence in the UN Security Council.

Lacking any thoroughgoing analysis of the complex social, political, and economic inequalities that shape women's and men's vulnerability to becoming victims or perpetrators of violence, the United Nations' near-exclusive focus on sexual violence against women in the recent Security Council resolutions and the UN Secretary-General's Action Plan on gender-responsive peace building reinforces gender stereotypes of women as victims and objects of male protection—and men as the power holders. By contrast, a transformative political economy approach addresses the root causes of sexual violence in conflict including, not least, the gendered economic inequalities in natural resources and political inequalities in state decision-making power, feminized peacekeeping economies consisting of the global trade in sex and domestic workers, masculine breadwinner and soldiering identities, and the unequal family-household relations that support them. These gendered political economies all make up major parts of the war story.

Rather than international security and legal actions responding to selected instances of sexual violence, practical, community-based responses that take into account social and economic needs, as well as access to justice and rights in states with typically weak legal and administrative institutions, are called for. Prioritizing state security and electoral machinery over gender-aware human security is destabilizing in the long run. If women are unable to achieve sustainable social and economic livelihoods, their vulnerability to violence, especially to sexual slavery and trafficking, as well as the violence of poverty, continues in so-called peacetime. Yet states and the United Nations, in responding to sexual violence in conflict, have focused on legal prosecution and reforming juridical structures and hardly at all on alterations in economic and social structures. The next chapter examines the ongoing violence against women in postpolitical settlement in former conflict-affected areas. I ask what can be done to stop this violence and how can a political economy approach, with its attention to the underlying structures of socioeconomic inequality that fuel violence against women, reconceptualize peace building?

| # Rebuilding With or Without Women?

Gendered Violence in Postconflict Peace and Reconstruction

Women face appalling violence—especially sexual violence—in the anarchy generated by conflict and its aftermath. . . . Yet post-conflict gender-based violence often remains below the radar screen, since a cessation of conflict is often mistaken for the full return of peace.

—BAN KI MOON (United Nations Secretary-General 2009)[1]

Men are more likely to die during conflicts whereas women die more often of indirect causes, after the conflict is over.

—ORMHAUG, MEIER, AND HERNES (2009)

Introduction

Women and children make up more than 80 percent of those displaced in refugee camps and resettlement zones after political settlement of conflict (World Bank 2011). They are frequently subject to rape, sexual slavery and abuse, early and forced marriage, forced pregnancy, trafficking for prostitution, and other indentured labor. In many contexts there is a spike of sexual and gender-based violence once fighting stops and the conflict between armed groups is stabilized. The war against women goes on: "A ceasefire that stops the guns but doesn't stop the rape means that sexual and gender-based violence can continue occurring."[2] But how far and in what ways does the poor economic and political status of women exacerbate this violence against women after conflict and hinder peace-building and reconstruction efforts? Following our discussion of the impact of armed conflict on gendered violence in Chapter 7, this chapter examines the interplay between the economic and political marginalization or empowerment of women and their experience of violence in postconflict settings.

As we saw in the previous chapter, the mandates of the UN Security Council resolutions are hugely significant for the international recognition they have given to gross violations of women's human rights in conflict and after conflict. Violence against women, and to some extent gender-based violence against men and boys as well, are now considered serious threats to international peace and security. But much more must be done by the United Nations and its member states to actually implement these resolutions and support the role of women in peace-building decision making and economic reconstruction in places as diverse as East Timor, Aceh, Indonesia, Mindanao province in the Philippines, Iraq, Afghanistan, Colombia, Guatemala, the Congo, and Darfur. This chapter applies the political economy approach advanced in this book to show that the social and economic livelihoods of women and men must be equally prioritized if peace is to be sustainable and violence ended in all its forms.

Violence Against Women After Conflict—The Evidence

As the epigraph from Ormhaug et al. (2009) notes, existing data on violent deaths in a range of conflict-affected areas confirm that men are more often victims of violence *during* wartime but that there is a high number of female deaths *after* conflict officially ends. The 2011 World Bank Development report concurs that while the direct impact of armed conflict falls directly on young males, who are the majority of fighting forces, women and children suffer disproportionately from war's indirect effects. Analyzing adult mortality as a result of armed conflict, political scientists Li and Wen (2005) find that over time women's mortality attributable to war is as high as men's due to war's lingering social and economic effects.[3] Moreover, a global review of fifty countries found sizeable increases in gender-based violence following a major war (Bastick, Grimm, and Kunz 2007). Let us further examine the available evidence on the apparent spike in violence against women after conflict before considering why and how it has come about.

Even after a political settlement has been achieved, organized crime, other groups, and individuals may perpetuate political violence and violence against women. Evidence of increased postconflict violence against women includes greater prevalence of domestic violence, sexual violence and abuse associated with transactional sex in refugee and internally displaced person (IDP) camps, forced pregnancy and marriage, and trafficking for prostitution. In Liberia, 74 percent of women surveyed reported sexual abuse prior to displacement and 54 percent during displacement (UNFPA 2006).[4] In Cartagena, Colombia, 8 percent of females experienced sexual violence prior to displacement and 11 percent during displacement (UNFPA 2006).[5] In Burma, where a military regime governs and there is ongoing conflict, an estimated 40,000 Burmese women are trafficked into Thailand each year to work in factories, brothels, and domestic settings (Human Rights Documentation Unit and Burmese Women's Union 2000).

Domestic violence may escalate above already high levels due to the heightened militarization of society and the celebration of armed masculinity that continues despite the formal laying down of guns and amnesty. Accounts of increased domestic violence have been reported in several different postconflict countries including East Timor (Hall 2009; Hall and True 2009), Liberia (Couldrey and Morris 2007), and Afghanistan (Abirafeh 2007). Soldiers who are no longer able to wield small arms in public may use them as an expression of their power in the private realm in acts of violence against intimate partners or other family members (see Cockburn 2012). The public reintegration of soldiers into peacetime civilian life often does not help with their adjustment to private family relationships destabilized by war. For example, during the war in southern Sudan, daughters became economic bargaining chips, increasing forced and early marriage, as well as rape within marriage and domestic violence. Childbearing was also considered a patriotic obligation for women in the struggle for self-determination. These gendered experiences and pervasive violence against women resulted in many men having a sense of entitlement to sexual services both inside and outside marriage after the war (UNDP 2010).

After conflict, women refugees, internally displaced persons, and their families are vulnerable to gender-based and sexual violence in camps and resettlement zones. This vulnerability to violence is compounded for women and children who suffer the stigmatization of being raped during the war (UNFPA 2007b).[6] At the end of 2009, forty-two million people in the world had been forced to leave or flee homes due to conflict, including fifteen million refugees outside their country of nationality and twenty-seven million internally displaced persons as a result of civil armed conflicts. Frequently, when men are killed in conflict, they leave women behind to become heads of households responsible for their family's survival. In addition to heightened physical insecurity, women can be forced into risky income generation activities, such as sex work, to feed their families, which exacerbates the likelihood that they will experience violence or abuse. In camps and postconflict settlements, women and girls often exchange sexual services for food and protection from men with more resources. Abysmally, such exchanges and associated sexual violence have been found to occur at the hands of international peacekeepers and staff responsible for humanitarian operations in Liberia and Haiti (*Washington Post* 2005; BBC News 2006; *The Telegraph* 2007; Save the Children 2008). Female IDPs and refugees also encounter rape while collecting water or fuel. These encounters have been coined "firewood rape" by aid workers due to the endemic nature of sexual violence outside settlements and camps (UNFPA 2007b).

Displaced households that are disproportionately female headed are often forced to migrate to urban areas. They lose significant assets, as well as access to social networks, which contributes to their poverty and thus vulnerability to violence. They may end up living in squatter settlements or slums where access to resources such as water, sanitation, firewood, and food is minimal. Typically, the responsibility for procuring these basic needs is relegated to women and girls. Having to travel in unfamiliar territory beyond the confines of their community, they are especially vulnerable to sexual violence, including gang rape. Such violence has been documented by Amnesty International (2011b) in their report on women in the Solomon Islands. Approximately 25,000 people displaced by conflict and ethnic violence between Malaitan and Guadalcanese groups in the Solomon Islands from 1998 and 2003 now live in slums near Honiara, the capital. In those slums they do not have access to adequate sanitation, a reliable water supply, or safety. Solomon Islands women bear the burden of collecting water for their families. As many as two-thirds of women and girls have encountered gender-based and sexual violence while traveling to fetch water or use latrines (Amnesty International 2011b).

Although the sexual and gender-based violence experienced by IDPs is particularly rife, women and girls who stay in their homes and villages after conflict also experience increased violence. Women who have lost their assets, employment, and right to education during war struggle to survive and meet their family's basic needs. They typically have little choice but to engage in precarious forms of work where they are susceptible to abuse and violence. Begging and prostitution, for instance, "may be resorted to as a means of redressing poverty, creating further vulnerability to violence and trafficking" (Chinkin 2008, 11). In Rwanda, for example, the 70 percent of households headed by females fell into poverty at greater rates than male-headed households after the genocide because they lost their access to or ownership of land (Rombouts 2006, 205). Land was either transferred to a son or other male relative or sold for survival reasons.[8] Tilman Bruck and Marc Vothknecht (2011, 107–108), analyzing women's relative economic position before and after violent conflict, find that the interruption of schooling, especially secondary schooling, affects girls more than boys and has a long-term impact on their economic well-being.[9] Women's participation in the labor market sometimes increases for survival reasons after conflict. This is termed the "added worker effect" (see Menon and Van der Meulen Rodgers 2011). However, women face discrimination in seeking formal employment because of the preference for male employees and the reintegration of male combatants, as well as women's typically lower levels of skill and education than men in conflict-affected countries. Women's self-employment and informal sector business activities, such as prostitution and market trade, also increase after conflict, possibly in response to the lack of other employment opportunities. These precarious forms of work heighten the chances of experiencing abuse and violence.

Scholars of gender and postconflict argue that the return to normalcy after armed conflict marginalizes the potential for women's economic and political empowerment. As in previous experiences of the aftermath of war and revolution, contemporary conflict-affected societies expect that women will revert to traditional domestic roles subordinate to men (Handrahan 2004; Pankhurst 2008; Turshen 2000). Male combatants who return to civilian life frequently express a sense of entitlement to being the breadwinners, employees, managers, and owners. However, women combatants—often economically driven to join armed groups in the first place—suffer not only gender-based violence but also economic marginalization after conflict.[10]

Drawing on available studies, I have described heightened forms of gender-based violence in the aftermath of conflict. I have suggested that the failure to address equality in access to social and economic resources in postconflict societies accentuates women's economic poverty and material insecurity relative to men and, consequently, their vulnerability to violence. The next section examines the phenomenon of "peacekeeping economies" in order to begin to explain why and how sexual and gender-based violence increases despite the formal end to war or armed conflict.

Gendered Peacekeeping Economies

The UN-led peacekeeping and humanitarian intervention in Kosovo brought a large, comparatively wealthy, and primarily male international presence into the country. Their presence generated strong demand for sexual services, which in turn resulted in an increase in the number of women trafficked from both within and beyond Kosovo. Some research indicates that there was direct complicity between trafficking syndicates and UN Interim

Administration Mission in Kosovo (UNMIK) peacekeepers (UNDP 2010; Human Rights Watch 2002). The impoverished economic situation in Kosovo, especially among women and female-headed households, attracted or lured many women into the sex industry. Ironically, the creation of a thriving sex industry is one of the lasting legacies of the UN mission in Kosovo. Documented instances of trafficking in Bosnia, Liberia, and Iraq, which are discussed in Box 8.1, have also been linked to the demand generated by the "peacekeeping economy" (Human Rights Watch 2002; UNMIL 2007, cited in Jennings 2008).

Peacekeeping economies include all the economic activities in a postconflict society introduced by international peace operations involving military, police, and civilian personnel; public and private contractors; and those employed formally in professional and administration roles or informally where their livelihoods depend on the international operations (Rehn and Sirleaf 2002). These economies are gendered specifically because the presence of international actors, in particular, well-resourced men, leads to the expansion of sex industries largely employing women as sex workers, trafficked prostitutes, sex slaves in homes, in brothels, or on the streets. The expansion often involves "more open-ended unarticulated sexual exchanges that offer economic benefits" and sometimes a lesser degree of vulnerability to violence (Save the Children 2008; Jennings and Nikolić-Ristanović 2009; Higate and Henry 2004). For instance, a study commissioned by the Liberian

---

Box 8.1 POSTCONFLICT TRAFFICKING IN IRAQ

Rania was sixteen years old when officials raped her during Saddam Hussein's 1991 crackdown in Iraq's Shia South. "My brothers were sentenced to death, and the price to stop this was to offer my body," she says. "Iraq has a whole generation of women who are in their teens now, whose bodies have been turned into battlefields from criminal ideologies." Since the US invasion, the rise in religious extremism has been matched with increasing violence against women. Accurate statistics are hard to come by, but estimates are that between 2003 and 2006, nearly 3,500 Iraqi women went missing, many sold or traded for sex work. Though difficult to prove, UN news reports estimate that 25 percent were likely to be trafficked abroad with no knowledge of their own fate. Human Rights Watch (HRW) says the government has done little to combat the issue. "This is a phenomenon that wasn't prevalent in 2003," says HRW researcher Samer Muscati. "I admit that Iraqi government institutions are not mature enough to deal with this topic yet, as the departments are still in their growing phase" (quoted in Murray 2011).

National AIDS Control Program identified the category of "homegirls" typically not dependent on sexual transactions for survival but who use transactional sex or transactional relationships with "boyfriends" to maintain or improve their standard of living (Jennings and Nikolić-Ristanović 2009, 18). These women might be considered as informally benefiting from and/or depending on the peacekeeping economy. These under-the-radar transactions tend to be accepted as normal and unproblematic given the mutual, albeit unequal, needs of both parties, despite UN sexual conduct protocols proscribing them. In Haiti, the local and UN informants that Jennings and Nikolić-Ristanović (2009) talked to saw the prospect of UN personnel sexually abusing or exploiting Haitian women and girls as being no more or less than what could be expected "given their poverty, insecurity, lack of rights and protections." They perceived the sex industry to be part of the local culture rather than constructed by international actors in the postconflict setting.

Across all sectors—not only in incipient sex industries—peacekeeping economies are constructed on the basis of gender divisions of labor, reinforcing the inequalities between women and men with respect to income, education, and other resources. Women are disproportionately employed in the service, sex, and entertainment industries, attending to the demands of male expatriates, elites, and criminals with economic power. And within these sectors, the cases of Kosovo and Bosnia show that positions of power, ownership, and influence, especially those industries controlled by organized crime, tend to be occupied by men, with women's participation concentrated in the middle or lowest levels (Jennings and Nikolić-Ristanović 2009; UNODC 2009). Although perceived as only temporary, peacekeeping economies typically outlast the formal post-peacekeeping mission, shaping gendered economic and social power relations in the long term. For example, the infrastructure developed for prostitution during the peacekeeping period, the demand created by the large international presence, and organized crime involvement in illegal trafficking are all enduring in Bosnia and Kosovo (Hajdinjak 2002; Pallen 2003; Pugh 2004). People become used to earning money through jobs created by the sex industry. Ten years after the Bosnian conflict, government trafficking data show that women continue to be both imported and exported, with the number of foreign women decreasing and the number of Bosnian victims increasing significantly (Jennings and Nikolić-Ristanović 2009). These numbers reflect the economic desperation and lack of economic opportunities that many Bosnian (and other) women face. Box 8.2 discusses *The Whistleblower*, a film that uncovers the ongoing violence against women in Bosnia and the complicity of international actors.

Box 8.2 THE WHISTLEBLOWER

Based on a true story, this 2010 film was released in theaters around the world in late 2011. It tells the story of Kathryn Bolkovac, a Nebraska policewoman (played by Rachel Weisz) who went to Bosnia as a peacekeeper after the war ended there in 1999. The impact of the war still goes on for the young women who are trafficked into Bosnia because of the international presence, and sometimes by local police, international soldiers, contractors, and peacekeepers. The film depicts the fear and psychological torture the young women suffer, as well as the violence. Kathy, the heroine, risks her job and her own safety to uncover a wide-scale, child sex slave and human-trafficking scandal involving a US military contractor, Democra Corp (a pseudonym for the real-world DynCorp), and the United Nations. She is helped by Madeleine Rees, head of the Women's Rights and Gender Unit of the UN Commission on Human Rights (played by Vanessa Redgrave), who is now the executive director of the international NGO Women's League for International Peace and Freedom in Geneva. There is no happy ending to this movie. Seen to be a threat to UN operations in Bosnia, Kathy is fired by the private contractor she worked for (although she won a wrongful dismissal case in 2011), one of the young women dies a brutal death, and the trafficking continues. The film implies that it is hard for individuals to make a difference in the world when the public accountability of international actors is so limited and when a lone woman's voice—like Kathy's—is operating in a highly masculinized setting of police officers and peacekeepers.

Gender equality goals that were ostensibly "mainstreamed" and sometimes an explicit rationale of UN peace operations in postconflict countries are effectively undermined by the political economy of gender.[11]

As we saw in Chapter 7, UN policies to end sexual and gender-based violence against women during and after armed conflict demonstrate little self-reflection. Here they fail to understand the stake of the United Nations itself in the creation of illegal sex industries that perpetuate violence against women. The zero-tolerance policy on sexual relationships with locals and code of conduct for peacekeepers treat sexual misconduct as an exceptional occurrence rather than a systemic part of the United Nations' presence in postconflict societies. They deal with the issue of sexual exploitation and abuse only on "an individual level, with application and sanctions restricted to UN personnel" (Jennings and Nikolić-Ristanović 2009, 20). Administrative rules and regulations, even if they could be enforced, cannot eliminate the political economy of sex and the culture of violence against women that the United Nations has helped to flourish.

Institutional Failures and the Prioritization of Law and Order

To return to our key questions, how and why is sexual and gender-based violence often exacerbated in the postconflict period? Two key insights emerge from the analysis of peacekeeping economies and the illicit sex trade they foster. The first is that foreign interventions, whether by the United Nations, the United States, or any other state, are destabilizing forces that frequently accentuate and fail to challenge the harm against women and girls. The second insight is that peace-building processes often do little to create economic and decision-making opportunities for girls and women. Women remain a marginalized group in many postconflict economies and societies despite the reality that they have become heads of thousands of households as a result of both the death or disappearances of their spouses and the economic austerity policies after war. Displaced women may not be able to recover income-generating property because of the failure of governments and international actors responsible for peace building to anticipate the need for legal reform recognizing their legal rights to land. War crimes against women tend to go unpunished after conflict, as in the cases of Timor-Leste and Kosovo, encouraging a climate of impunity for gender-based violence. The neglect of land rights and reparations for wartime sexual and gender-based violence are both major obstacles limiting women's engagement in peace building and their capacity to benefit from economic and political reconstruction. Rather than focusing on securing social and economic livelihoods for women and men after conflict, however, the purpose of most UN peace-building missions is primarily to reestablish law and order.

Physical security and electoral machinery have been prioritized over social and economic security in recent postconflict experiences. Yet a political economy approach stresses that we cannot separate political stability and security from economic development. Ongoing sexual and gender-based violence "creates and perpetuates an atmosphere of insecurity that makes it harder for girls to safely attend school or for women to access water points, marketplaces and polling booths, thereby negatively affecting economic recovery and a return to normality" (UNIFEM 2010, 9). If women are unable to access housing, food, health, education, and basic services, their vulnerability to violence increases. Indeed, the key argument of this book is that women's access to productive resources affects their access to justice and physical security (CEDAW 2006, 29).

Analysts usually make the linkage between political economy and violence against women in terms of the underresearched impact of conflict-related sexual violence on food production and supply during reconstruction, given women's role as the major agricultural producers (UNIFEM 2010, 9). Rarely do international actors make policy that seeks to achieve core economic and social rights and resources as a major way to end the violence and foster peace (United Nations News Center 2009). But if key rights such as those to land and housing, to transact in one's own legal name, to equality in marriage, and to freedom of mobility are not secured early enough, then many women who are poor will be denied economic opportunities during the postconflict reconstruction period. Paradoxically, the emphasis on judicial and legal justice for female victims of violence may inadvertently marginalize their basic needs, as discussed with respect to the DRC in Chapter 7. For these women, recovery, protection, and future prevention of violence "is often tied to their ability to move on and generate incomes for themselves and children" (IRIN News 2009; Anderlini 2010, xiv).

But what if a military intervention takes place after a commitment to ensuring gender equality and women's empowerment in all peace and peacebuilding operations such as contained in UN Security Council Resolution 1325 of 2000? Both the cases of Timor-Leste and Kosovo involved a significant commitment to gender mainstreaming by UN administrations, the UN Transitional Administration in East Timor (UNTAET) and UNMIK, including support for institutional reform such as establishing a gender equality ministry; promoting women's representation in political parties, government, and the police and armed forces; supporting women's civil society groups; targeting programming to women's needs in development and health interventions such as maternal and infant health programs; assisting in the drafting of laws against gender-based and domestic violence; and mandating the inclusion of women in disarmament, demobilization, and reintegration (DDR) and security sector reform processes. Have these institutional reforms made a difference to the progress in women's rights and reduced violence against women during nation building?

Mary Caprioli and Kimberley Douglass (2008, 45) examined whether foreign interventions ostensibly to promote transition to democracy in six postconflict countries have advanced women's political, social, and economic rights[12] by increasing gender equality or lessening violence against women. Certainly many foreign interventions, including the recent US intervention in Afghanistan, are justified by states on the basis that they uphold human, and specifically women's, rights. But Caprioli and Douglass find no dramatic positive or negative effect of intervention on women's rights in any of the states, in neither the three that evidence democratic change (El Salvador, Mozambique, and Namibia) nor the three that do not (Cambodia, Haiti, and Somalia). Rather, their analysis shows that nation-building and democratization processes do not take into account women's unequal political, economic, or social status, nor do they address norms in the private and public spheres, both of which are crucial if violence against women is to be targeted and stopped.

Gender mainstreaming interventions try to address the culture of impunity for violence against women carrying over from war/conflict with support for domestic violence laws and policing, but they cannot address the often dire economic situation after conflict associated with corruption and criminality. Women who experience extreme income inequality working in the informal economy or most precarious employment positions in the labor market suffer the most from the legacy of poor investment in gender-equal economic and social development with respect to education, health, housing, food security, water, property, and land rights. In this way, women disproportionately experience the negative effects of the militarized model of peace-building intervention that is focused on establishing order through formal legal and political institutions rather than through social and economic development. As Kathleen Jennings and Vesna Nikolić-Ristanović (2009, 23) state, there is "a fundamental mismatch between the United Nations' goals of mainstreaming gender and promoting gender equality, and its participation in and perpetuation of a peacekeeping economy that has concrete and often negative impacts on the local women and men it encompasses." Gender equality strategies may increase the legitimacy of norms associated with the liberal peace, including electoral democracy, the market economy, humanitarian intervention, and regional economic integration, without actually achieving gender-equal outcomes (see Whitworth 2004).

Marginalization of Women's Economic and Social Rights

Regrettably, the disconnect between the security and the economic reconstruction agendas has serious, long-term consequences for the advancement of women's rights, particularly their economic rights and equality (UNDP 2010). UN Women's *Price of Peace* report discussed in Box 8.3 shows that attention to women's needs and gender equality are low priorities in the planning frameworks and budgets of twelve postconflict countries. Indeed, the least attention to gender issues is evident in spending on economic recovery and infrastructure. For instance, the United States committed $21 billion to the reconstruction in Iraq in 2003 and 2004. Only a portion of the $500 million allocated to support democracy was specifically aimed at the social and political development of Iraqi women (Caprioli and Douglass 2008: 51; US State Department 2005). This neglect on the part of international actors ensures that gender inequalities with respect to economic power are accentuated in postconflict peace building with implications for the continued scourge of violence faced by women at home and in public.

Echoing these findings with respect to Iraq, a UN Development Program (UNDP) report (2010) reviewing reconstruction aid to four postconflict countries (East Timor, Sierra Leone, Kosovo, and South Sudan) found there had been only very limited resources allocated to promote gender equality or address women's specific needs. In all contexts, critical gender gaps existed, including, for example, with respect to girls' access to education, women's

---

Box 8.3 THE PRICE OF PEACE: FINANCING FOR GENDER EQUALITY
IN POSTCONFLICT RECONSTRUCTION (2010)

The United Nations Development Programme (UNDP 2010) examined postconflict planning frameworks across twelve countries, including 6 Post-Conflict Needs Assessments, 5 Poverty Reduction Strategy Papers (PRSPs), 6 UN Development Assistance Frameworks, and over 394 project documents from Multi-Donor Trust Funds (MDTFs) and Joint Programs across six countries (UNIFEM 2010). The planning framework documents are important as they identify the problems and the actions that need to be taken to address them, and thus constitute the basis for funding by governments, the United Nations, and its partners. UNIFEM conducted a content analysis of the activities, indicators, and budgets and identified whether these address women's needs and issues. Estimated percentages of activities, indicators, or budget lines that address women's needs and issues out of the total number of activities, indicators, or total budget were calculated for every thematic area. The budget allocated to address women's needs and issues was then calculated using the weighted average of all percentages by area, with the total budget for the area as the weighing factor. The findings show that only 11 percent of the budget is allocated to activities addressing women's needs and issues, and only 7 percent is allocated to indicators. A direct budget analysis shows that even less, just 6 percent of the total budget, is explicitly allocated to gender issues. In the Post-Conflict Needs Assessments examined, less than 5 percent of activities and only 3 percent of budget lines mentioned women's needs. Low and diminishing levels of gender responsiveness were also evident in PRSPs: between 5 and 6 percent of the budget allocated to activities and indicators addressed gender needs, whereas the extent of inclusion of women's needs and issues was only 3 percent at the budget level. Further analysis in terms of major thematic areas revealed that the social protection and human rights, education, and health areas paid the most attention to women's issues. In contrast, though the budget for the area of economic recovery and infrastructure represents a significant portion of total funds, it showed the lowest degree of gender responsiveness.

---

reproductive health needs, access to water for domestic consumption, and women's access to agricultural inputs and to economic opportunities, as well as sexual and gender-based violence (UNDP 2010, 35). Donors focused their assistance on reconstruction and/or humanitarian assistance, expecting that later assistance would focus on development. Thus, significant postconflict resources were allocated to security sector reform, disarmament, demobilization and reintegration, and the law and justice sector more generally, as well as some humanitarian needs. In respect to the top priority area, security, at least 60 percent of the budgetary allocations go toward the salaries of arms-bearing military contractors. However, donors underwrite only 4 percent of security sector expenditures and thus have limited influence in this sector (UNDP 2010).

In 2009 in Southern Sudan, for example, 29 percent of the budget was allocated to security and 12 percent to roads, with basic education receiving just 7 percent, primary health care a mere 3 percent, water provision 2 percent, and production only 2 percent. These top six government-defined budget priorities remained consistent for the six years prior to the review. Yet in order to prevent violence, capacity development should not just focus on security-sector institutions; rather, funding for ending gender-based and sexual violence should be mainstreamed across planning and budgeting in all relevant sectors including security and roads but also agriculture, education, health, and economic reconstruction. For example, roads might be considered by many to have limited gender relevance. But access to roads and transport can either foster or hinder women's economic empowerment and there is no reason why women could not be employed in these sectors as well.

The case of Timor-Leste illustrates the tensions between liberal peace versus political economy approaches. In particular, it shows how prioritizing the establishment of political institutions over social and economic development can entrench violence against women despite the formal end to political violence (Coleman 2004; Handrahan 2004). Conceiving security and democratization as separate from socioeconomic needs and empowerment may advance the security and rights of some groups, but it cannot advance the majority of women's security and rights given the disproportionate poverty and discrimination they experience.

Timor-Leste: Domestic Violence Is a Security and a Development Issue

During the time of the UNTAET, domestic violence against women was pervasive across the whole society (Hall and True 2009). In 2000, 40 percent of all offenses committed against women were by male family members

(Charlesworth 2009, 22). Women suffered all types of violence during the Indonesian occupation including rape, forced sterilization, and sexual slavery, but there was no public truth, reconciliation, or justice process for the women victims. This culture of impunity toward acts of violence against women committed during conflict or occupation has a direct bearing on the crime, social tension, communal violence, and political instability after the new state, Timor-Leste, was formed. "Violence within the family became a way for men to reassert their domestic power" after the Indonesian withdrawal (Charlesworth 2009, 23; Fitzsimons 2007, 351, 353). The 80 percent unemployment rate in urban areas affected men's ability to function in their traditional roles as breadwinners. And as Chapter 3 argued, men's sense of powerlessness with respect to breadwinning is a major determinant of the prevalence of domestic violence. The situation in Timor is not atypical of other postconflict reconstruction processes. Women often become heads of households during conflict when men are absent fighting as soldiers or after disasters. Men may feel themselves powerless and unable to fulfill their duty to protect their families. This can arouse their resentment and violence against women family members, especially if they are traditionally the economic providers (UNFPA 2008, 7).

At the same time, without reparative justice including a public admission of the wrongs committed against women, the impunity toward conflict-related sexual and gender-based violence both sanctioned and rendered invisible endemic domestic violence. Not only did victims have no recourse, but also impunity and silence bred future impunity (Harris-Rimmer 2009). Rather than addressing these human rights violations in the private sphere or the social and economic deprivation that exacerbates this violence, international and Timorese elites turned their attention to establishing formal legal and political institutions.

Despite the lack of official international or governmental attention and the contradictory UN practice undermining women's local struggles for political rights, the local women's movement focused their activism on ending domestic violence.[13] After independence, Timorese women were able to talk about domestic violence rather than just the violence against women perpetrated by the Indonesian military (Hall and True 2009). Prior to this, former NGO Fokupers director Pereira had thought domestic violence was "normal" since it was "happening to everyone" (Hall and True 2009). In 2000, the National Women's Congress identified domestic violence as a critical problem that needed to be addressed. The congress provided the impetus for a national campaign for a law against domestic violence involving a strong coalition of local and international partners campaigning for such a law in

Timor (Congress of Women 2000). The United Nations Development Fund for Women (UNIFEM), the UN agency dedicated to gender equality, played a significant role in the formation of the East Timorese national campaign against domestic violence using funds allocated by the United Nations to strengthen Timorese civil society.[14] In the space of a few years, a vocal civil society movement emerged involving both men's and women's groups and key political leaders. This coalescing of East Timorese civil society against domestic violence was a dynamic, organic process facilitated but not directed by international donors. The domestic violence law was passed in 2010, although the Timorese government is struggling to develop the practical means and know-how to provide direct services to communities and victims, especially in rural villages. Australian and New Zealand police forces seconded to Timor have played a role in increasing community awareness of domestic violence and enforcing the new law. But international police are not always well equipped to intervene in culturally and gender-sensitive ways. They can bring with them militarized understandings of their role as part of a peacekeeping mission that does not include protecting and educating against domestic violence.

Opportunities or Setbacks for Women in Peace Building?

Some research suggests that postcrisis situations are opportunities for transforming gender relations and empowering women rather than setbacks for women's rights that exacerbate violence. The common case cited is Rwanda, where, following the genocidal killing of an estimated 800,000 people, the majority of whom were men, women's political representation in the national parliament in 2002 rose to 56 percent, the highest female proportion in the world (Holt 2003; Devlin and Elgie 2008). Women have seen other gains in that country as small landholders and entrepreneurs with newfound rights to land and property and equal inheritance. Girls have also shot ahead in the education system, where previously over 40 percent of women were illiterate (Rombouts 2006; Boseley 2010). Gendered hierarchies remain in Rwanda.[15] And the gender imbalance in power is manifest in the high incidence of rape of young girls and of domestic violence, with nine out of ten women reporting that their husbands had forced them to have sexual intercourse—considered rape in most countries—in the period 1998–2003 following the genocidal conflict (International Red Cross 2004). Heidi Rombout (2006, 205) stresses that "the weak structural position of women in society has had an impact on the degree and forms of violence women experience, such as sexual violence, both in times of peace and war." Moreover, she argues that violence has been used as a tool to oppose women's emancipation in postgenocide Rwandan society. Rwanda demonstrates that there are important opportunities for improving the political, economic, and social status of citizens, and women citizens particularly, during the rebuilding of societies after crises. However, many of those postconflict opportunities explicitly discriminate against women. Despite the UN Security Council resolutions promoting women's roles in peace, women have remained largely absent from the negotiating tables of warring parties. Participation by women in settlements and postconflict governance remains inconsistent and tokenistic. Huge volumes of policy statements and seminar reports on Resolution 1325 have been issued, but much of the action remains declarative rather than operational—and therefore does not translate into changes in practice and impacts for women on the ground (Care International 2010, 4).

A review by UNIFEM of 24 major peace processes conducted since 1992 found on average that women made up less than 8 percent of negotiating parties, and only 18 out of 300 peace agreements signed since the end of the Cold War mention sexual and gender-based violence (UNIFEM 2010). For example, in Kosovo, only one woman participated in the peace talks; in South Sudan, although six women were included in the Sudan People Liberation Movement (SPLM) delegation for the final round of peace talks, no women were on the negotiating teams or acted as mediators; and in Sierra Leone, despite women activists' pivotal role in bringing leaders to the pre-Lomé negotiating table, the women were not officially integrated into the peace process (UNDP 2010). Ines Alberdi, UNIFEM's former executive director, makes the consequence clear: "[Women's] striking absence at this stage means they lack voice in everything that follows" (UNIFEM 2010).

Beyond peace talks, women are likewise excluded from a wide range of public decision-making processes involved in peace building: constitutional reform processes, elections planning, postconflict needs assessments and priority setting, economic reconstruction programs, donor conferences, and many more (Bernard et al. 2008). For example, in Iraq, only three out of twenty-five members of the US-led Coalition Provisional Authority were women, there was only one woman in the interim cabinet, and there was not a single woman on the drafting committee of the interim constitution. Few women have held decision-making positions in reconstruction or state-building agencies in postconflict countries. Despite a UN directive in East Timor that women should be 30 percent of all national and district hiring within every classification/level of employment, this commitment was not realized.[16] Women were likewise excluded from the planning of economic reconstruction in Sierra Leone, Timor-Leste, Kosovo, and Southern Sudan (UNDP 2010). An evaluation by the UNDP found that where gender experts were included, they did not, generally, have the expertise to cover all sectors. For example, none of the countries had a gender and economic policy adviser with budget analysis skills. Donor conferences, with very few exceptions, were held externally (for example, this was the case for the first five donor conferences for Timor-Leste), which restricted the number and types of local participants, women or men. Where women did participate in either peace talks or donor-pledging conferences, they were not supported in preparing for or engaging in the processes. They were not provided access to all conference documentation or space on the agenda to present issues of concern, nor given decision-making responsibility or a formal seat at the negotiating table. No systematic processes existed in any of the case studies to ensure consultation with women's groups during mediation, during negotiation, or in the range of postconflict planning processes. There was rarely an explicit focus on integrating gender expertise consistently or equitably into postconflict planning and financing assessments.

Postconflict reconstruction may involve neoliberal restructuring of the economy, as well as the establishment of liberal political and legal systems. Naomi Klein (2007) coins this process "disaster capitalism." This restructuring may involve privatization of public services and infrastructure, which unintentionally regresses women's rights by placing a greater burden on their labor in the household and reducing public employment opportunities (Seguino 2008). In the early phases of state building, it is common to designate mass employment opportunities for men, such as road building and housing construction, which typically offer quick employment to large numbers of men. Not surprisingly, since few women have been involved in decisions about economic reconstruction, mass employment opportunities for women that are culturally acceptable have typically not been planned or implemented. For instance, in the first years of the Afghan reconstruction, external actors had a limited vision of women's economic activity, such as in the form of sewing projects (Bernard et al. 2008). Yet where economic programs are initiated, equitable inclusion of women and men is essential. Consultation with women prior to job allocation can help determine areas of cultural sensitivity. Anderlini (2010) explains that in Afghanistan, women would be ostracized if they engage in road building, but in Kenya it is acceptable. In Nepal, women have been traditionally involved in heavy construction work, so they should have equal opportunity to access construction jobs. Moreover, in many settings men and women grow different crops or have different responsibilities regarding animal husbandry. Without knowledge of these local practices or with assumptions based on preconflict times, humanitarian and development interventions may be ineffective. They may accentuate existing social and economic gender inequalities and in so doing, heighten women's vulnerability.

Postconflict Gender Discrimination Heightens Vulnerability to Violence

Violence is a barrier to women's participation in postconflict peace building, perpetuated by women's absence from decision making about political and economic reconstruction. The lack of political representation and participation of women is, in part, a consequence of the gender inequality in the enjoyment of economic and social rights and women's experience of violence in the public realm. Women's capacity to engage in peace building is closely linked to their economic security. Poverty prevents women from participating in public decision making and thus constrains their contributions to good governance and long-term recovery. However, when this gender imbalance in decision making is sanctioned by the international community, it reinforces local religious hostility toward women's public involvement and heightens women's vulnerability to violence. In Iraq, "most women candidates refused to campaign in public in the lead-up to the January 2005 elections because of fears of violence. Men feared violence too but the violence perpetrated against women had religious support" (Charlesworth 2009, 26). Women who defend human rights and make a public stand for peace not only risk violence from their own family, community, and government but also lack access to technical, financial, or moral assistance from multilateral agencies. State and nonstate armed actors often threaten women to stand down. They are subject to harassment, arrests, and murders (Anderlini 2010). Based on their own experience and research in the field, Care International argues that "without protection, [political] participation is unsustainable and may do more harm than good for the women themselves" (Care International 2010, 6).

Yet women's participation in the economy and in politics is crucial for the rebuilding of societies especially given the frequent death, absence, or migration of men due to conflict. But cultural and political forces may encourage a return to traditional identities to reestablish national or community sovereignty, defending it from perceived threats or outside powers. In this situation, gender roles, and women's status in particular, becomes contested. This contradiction can generate significant tension and violence against women in families, communities, and the public sphere. These cultural factors, as well as the political economy causes of violence, are often misunderstood (Merry 2006, 2009). International actors are often not attuned or equipped to address the sociocultural factors that contribute to gender-based inequality and tolerance of violence against women. Yet to tackle such violence, a local sociocultural framing, as well as a political economy approach, is essential.

Linking Justice, Cultural, and Political Economy Approaches

I have argued in this chapter that prioritizing legal justice and establishing political and electoral institutions after conflict overlooks the importance of economic and social reconstruction in preventing gender-based violence. This reconstruction includes economic measures such as vocational training for survivors of violence, use of temporary employment schemes (for example, food-for-work or cash-for-work schemes) to build safe houses for women, special vulnerable persons units for police stations, and reparations programs to provide monetary or in-kind redress for survivors. Gender-sensitive reconstruction may also include sociocultural measures such as engaging traditional (male) leaders to combat stigmatization of survivors and to condemn and control violent expressions of masculinity, education programs to combat stigmatization, and national recognition and support for victims. For instance, the apology by the president of Sierra Leone to survivors of sexual violence was crucial in sending a message to the broader society promoting the status and upholding the rights of survivors (UNIFEM 2010).

As well as practically attending to basic needs, the economic empowerment of women and girls is typically the catalyst for women's political empowerment. Care International (2010) has worked with women and their communities during and after conflict in several countries, supporting their self-organizing capacities. Care International's programs help women and girls to transition from basic life-saving assistance, such as food aid or emergency health projects, to small-scale income generation, agricultural livelihoods, and microcredit schemes. Over a period of five to ten years, Care International found that "women participating in groups associated with these projects gained in self-confidence and trust, and the capacity to participate in decision-making and advocacy at the local level" (Care International 2010, 5). But even more crucially, through action research in the field conducted over three years reviewing over 1,000 projects in more than thirty countries, Care International found that international agencies tend to focus on the short term and at microlevel, effectively "saving one woman at a time" without fostering linkages to wider economic, social, or political processes that could catalyze sustainable change. Box 8.4 describes Care International's Roco Kwo program that has taken the opportunity of the postconflict setting to establish women's material livelihoods in the hope that political empowerment will follow.

Approaches to Postconflict Prevention of Violence Against Women

How does a political economy approach to understanding the causes of violence against women in postconflict help us to devise better strategies to
prevent this violence? The argument of this book is that directly attending
to women's relative economic capacities, political voice, and social status
will significantly alter the structural conditions in which many women find

themselves, vulnerable and unable to protect themselves from violence. There are many local-level interventions that have been very successful at addressing short- to medium-term violence, for example, in IDP and refugee camps. For instance, the Women's Commission for Refugee Women and Children (WCRWC) offers a practical recommendation to provide cooking fuel or noncooking food to women in order to limit their risk to violence when traveling outside camps to collect firewood. In Darfur, the WCRWC advocated for the provision of "firewood patrols" to accompany and protect women. They have also advocated including women in the design and establishment of camps or urban settings. Deciding on where to place latrines, washing facilities, or other services women and girls use regularly can minimize their vulnerability to violence. While important in particular settings, these mitigating measures do not directly address the underlying drivers of violence against women and girls. In the final section of this chapter I wish to highlight two approaches to preventing violence that have the potential to transform the gendered inequalities that shape women's vulnerability to violence and in so doing contribute to eliminating that violence for good.

Putting Women in Charge of Security—Good Practice in Liberia

One approach to altering a culture of endemic violence after conflict and that is pervasive across social relations, especially between men and women, is to recruit and train women for decision-making positions across public and private sectors but crucially as those in charge of protection and security of citizens. From a political economy perspective, the singular focus on law and justice and instituting liberal democratic institutions typically overlooks the unequal power relations in the economy and society that fuel violence to start with. Yet reforming the security sector by putting women in charge can begin to unsettle those power relations by increasing the employment opportunities open to women and publically sanctioning their equal social status. Liberia is considered "good practice" by the United Nations because women without arms played a major role in negotiating the peace between warring parties and have subsequently, under the leadership of Africa's only woman president, Ellen Johnson Sirleaf, hosted the first UN female peace-keeping troops from India in 2007 and, until recently, the only woman UN envoy, UN Mission in Liberia (UNMIL) Special Representative to the Secretary-General (SRSG) Ellen Margrethe Løj (UN INSTRAW 2009, 10).[17] Women stood up—Christians and Muslims together—to confront warlords and government forces terrorizing Liberians, and as a result they brought down a dictator after a fourteen-year struggle (Aker and Freeman 2010).

Following an impasse in six-week-long peace talks in 2003 and violence perpetrated against civilians by all parties, women activists involved in the Women's Mass Action for Peace barricaded negotiating teams in the meeting rooms, demanding a complete solution within two weeks. They also demanded that no warlords be included in the transitional government. Their actions broke the deadlock and agreement was reached within two weeks.[18]

Since then, women have begun to assume formal positions in the security sector for protecting human rights. This change is starting to have an impact on the social and economic empowerment of all women across Liberian society (Cordell 2010; Willett 2010; Simic 2010). The presence of the all-female (Indian) police unit, which was deployed in Liberia in early 2007 (now replaced by a Ghanian unit seconded from the African Union), inspired Liberian women to join the local police force, with the number of women officers in Liberia's own police force rising to 15 percent.[19] There is increased reporting of gender-based violence because women who were targeted in the civil war or abuse in fighting forces are more comfortable reporting these crimes to women. Girls' enrolment in school has also increased, and observers have noted that girls have been inspired by the female faces they see in the police and security sector and see greater future employment opportunities available to them (Cordell 2009).[20] Moreover, decreasing rates of sexual abuse and exploitation are evident. Liberia still needs to attend to integrating women and girl fighters into national programs for disarmament, demobilization, reinsertion, and reintegration (Annan et al. 2010; McKay and Mazurana 2004; MDRP and UNIFEM 2005; Schroeder 2005; McKay et al. 2006). They can be marginalized, rejected from new security structures, and forced into sexually exploitative income generation work where the risk of ongoing violence is great. Yet female ex-combatants often have useful skills to bring to peace building and a commitment to the betterment of their communities.

Even while the outcomes are gradual in Liberia, they are altering the local political economy of violence against women by redressing the power imbalance between women and men. The United Nations expects to see a significant change in gendered peacekeeping economies including decreases in the cases of HIV/AIDS, in the number of brothels around peacekeeping bases, and in the number of babies fathered and abandoned by peacekeepers after their mission comes to an end (Simic 2010). A thorough longitudinal evaluation researching these effects will need to be conducted by the United Nations to fully understand the difference that putting women in charge of security makes.

The Role of Reparations in Postconflict Gender-Equal Development

A second approach to the prevention of recurring violence against women in postconflict settings is to explicitly devise reparations programs for gendered harms—notably sexual violence, perpetrated against individual women and women as a group during conflict—to develop the economic and political capacities and livelihoods of women and girls. By conceptualizing reparations for gross violence and mass violations of human rights in a development framework and not merely as a legal justice approach to righting previous wrongs to individuals or restoring the preharm situation, we can potentially affect the gendered inequalities in access to resources and status that are root causes of most forms of violence against women. Ruth Rubio-Marin (2006, 25) asks how, in their modest contribution to democracy building, reparations help to either reinforce or subvert some of the preexisting structural gender inequalities that are commonly built into the social tissue of civil society resulting in women's systematic discrimination.

Focusing on reparations shifts our attention away from the overwhelming attention given to criminal justice and what to do with the perpetrators toward the victims of violence and how to reclaim their lives and potentialities (Rubio-Marin 2006, 23–24). Shifting the focus from individual to collective reparations also helps us to think about violent social structures and the prevention of future violence. And finally, designing reparations programs that address community development in a future-oriented way is a crucial strategy for addressing gender dimensions of recovery and (recurring) violence, especially given women's increased socioeconomic activities at the community level after conflict when many have become the sole breadwinners for families.

In Timor-Leste, where 40 percent of the population lives in poverty, the Truth and Reconciliation Commission (known by its Portuguese acronym CAVR) framed reparations and its recommendations in broader recovery terms with key measures for women. Recognizing that many victims, especially of sexual violence, will not come forward publicly, CAVR defined beneficiaries as not only those who appeared before it but also those identified over a two-year period following the commission's end. About 25 percent of those who made statements to the commission were women. This is significantly more than can have been expected to speak up had CAVR not quite so consciously created a gender-sensitive space. To prevent gender bias, CAVR also instituted a quota system for reparations, ensuring that 30 percent of the total compensation was set aside for women victims, widows, children, and other family members harmed by the death or torture of their husbands, fathers, and brothers, taking into account both primary and secondary harms.[21] Social services, material support, and economic empowerment through livelihood activities, group counseling, and community education were all conceived as reparations programs. Women-friendly recommendations that emerged from the commission process included support to single mothers and victims of sexual violence and scholarships for their children; support for the disabled, widows, and torture victims; and support to the most affected communities. Specific measures were suggested to encourage women's participation. For example, scholarship fund programs were tied to provision of services to women, so that in coming forward for their children, the women would benefit, too. Public education programs addressing attitudes to violence and to women were recommended alongside victim counseling services and other measures (Wandita, Campbell-Nelson, and Pereira 2006).

Beyond the Timor example and others, securing women's land and property rights must be a major focus of postconflict recovery efforts and could be addressed through reparations, since there is good evidence presented in this book that these economic rights are a major deterrent to violence against women, leveling the playing field with men and allowing women to protect and depend on themselves. In instances where women's right to land is not addressed, they are more likely to be marginalized in the future as well. Moreover, in the case of war widows and their dependents, they are likely to be vulnerable to greater violence in the aftermath of conflict (UNIFEM 2005).

Conclusion

In this chapter we have seen how violence against women does not end after conflict. Rather, the culture of impunity carries over from armed conflict into private homes and the nooks and crannies of society. The breakdown of political, economic, and social structures, in which women are often the most marginalized and also paradoxically the most responsible for the survival of others, puts women in precarious situations where they are highly vulnerable to abuse and violence. Moreover, the invisibility of this violence against women during and after conflict marginalizes women in reconstruction and state-building processes despite the right of women to participate in these processes according to UN Security Council Resolution 1325.

The political economy approach advocated in this book identifies the social and economic inequalities between women and men and the culturally embedded notions of masculinity as the root causes of violence against women and women's marginalization in conflict and postconflict. Such an approach calls for a systematic human or community security response to recovery and peace building that must be backed by specifically targeted mandates, reparative resources, gender-specific training, and incentives to be effective. For instance, the interagency UN Action Against Sexual Violence in Conflict mandate discussed in Chapter 7 should be expanded to embrace the protection and promotion of women's human rights, including their economic and social rights in postconflict peace building.

To the extent that women's economic and social rights are neglected in postconflict processes, so too are their political and civil rights. To overcome the economic, social, and cultural obstacles to women's participation in post-conflict decision making, their representation must be deliberately sought, preferably through a quota system, targeted consultations, and the strengthening of local policy machinery focused on women's rights. Women's civil society representatives must also be involved in redefining and ensuring implementation of the new community security approach. Women's participation means more than including women as observers in decision-making settings and having a few women candidates standing in elections. To help address any resistance to increasing women's participation, their participation could be championed by local (male) leaders, other states, and regional organizations.

Reconceptualizing peace building through the frameworks of human security and women's human rights that address the underlying structures of socioeconomic inequality fueling violence against women would go far toward realizing the deed, not just the text, of Resolution 1325 and subsequent UN resolutions. If UN peacekeeping missions are to bring human and community security, rather than generating illicit peacekeeping economies, they must be explicitly tasked with changing aggressive constructions of masculinity in society, state, and military institutions and providing gender-equal economic opportunities and reconstruction programs to address the economic and social dimensions of women's empowerment. Some analysts might consider this United Nations "mission creep," but protecting physical security and ensuring sustainable peace are ultimately dependent on ensuring the economic and social aspects of security. Only the United Nations has the multidimensional capabilities in gender, security, human rights, and development work to realize this broader, long-lasting conception of community security. But this work must be done in partnership with local organizations, including women's civil society groups. As one UN official commented, "we can't develop our peacekeeping program without understanding the perpetrators and victims better" (notwithstanding those within their own ranks).[22]

CHAPTER 9 | # Who Suffers Most?
*Gendered Violence in Natural Disasters
and their Aftermath*

Introduction

The previous two chapters examined the direct and indirect impact of armed conflict and postconflict peace building on gender-based violence against women, revealing a pattern of heightened violence and vulnerability during and after conflict. This chapter investigates how global environmental forces in the form of natural disasters from floods, droughts, and famines to earthquakes, tsunamis, and hurricanes affect the life expectancies of women and men differently. For instance, the death rate of women after the 2004 Indian Ocean South Asian tsunami was at least three times higher than that of men in some communities. There is good, albeit disturbing, evidence that if women and girls survive disasters, in their aftermath they face a greater risk of experiencing gender-based and sexual violence. not surprising

But why are women so vulnerable to death and violence as a result of disaster compared with men? Consistent with the argument of this book, there is a political economy of gender inequality at work that explains pervasive violence against women: the major reason women are particularly vulnerable during a crisis and that violence against them increases is because of their economic and social status before disaster strikes. It is a familiar but no less troubling story. Women are generally poorer than men, they do not own land, they are less likely than men to have an education or access to health care, they are often less mobile due to cultural constraints, and they have less of a political voice in environmental planning and decision making. Yet women are not just victims; they are also survivors who can help countries recover more quickly from natural disasters and conflict. If they are included in disaster preparedness and planning decisions, women can find ways to prevent and protect all members of communities from the worst effects of future disasters. However, just as we saw with peace negotiations and reconstruction decisions, women are often excluded from policymaking on environmental and disaster issues. Gender-based violence and women's particular needs in the postdisaster phase, which if not addressed increase their risk of violence further, are frequently neglected by disaster recovery plans and humanitarian assistance.

This chapter is organized into four parts. The first part conceptualizes natural disasters as social disasters that magnify existing inequalities and oppressions within social structures and whose severity is largely a result of political and economic conditions that are humanly constructed. The second part takes the case of the South Asian tsunami disaster and investigates the immediate gendered impact of the disaster, particularly in Sri Lanka and Aceh, Indonesia, with respect to the disproportionate female mortalities, and whether gender-based violence against women increased or not as a result of the disaster. I also assess the impact of humanitarian relief, compensation schemes, and recovery programs after the tsunami and the agency of women compared with men in decisions about reconstruction and future disaster preparedness and planning. Did they accentuate or mitigate gendered inequalities and violence against women? Given the analysis of gendered violence during and after disasters, the third part of the chapter argues that gender-sensitive planning and deliberation involving women can prevent this violence and offers some lessons based on primary research of responses to the 2009–10 Christchurch earthquakes. The final part of the chapter draws implications from these natural disasters for climate change and its impact on gendered violence. Following the international NGO Women's Environment and Development Organization (WEDO 2008), I argue that involving women in climate change decision making and preparedness is crucial for the survival of communities and their ability to counter the impact of climate change. Heightened violence against women is likely to be a primary effect of climate change disaster, as well as a secondary effect due to the loss of livelihoods and the disproportionate displacement of women and children as refugees.

Natural Disasters Are Social Disasters

Social scientists contend that there is no such thing as a "natural" or inevitable disaster (see Squires and Hartman 2006), because past and present political decisions and economic interests shape every phase of a disaster.

They affect the preparedness and planning for disaster, the causes of disaster, and its impact on human survival and well-being, as well as government and humanitarian responses to disaster in the immediate and reconstruction phases. Political decisions and economic interests affect the magnitude of human loss in earthquakes and tsunamis, just as they may be deeply implicated in the causes of disasters, such as transport catastrophes or gradually rising temperatures and sea levels due to global warming that may result in the obliteration of human settlements and/or their means of sustenance.[1] Regardless of the time frame, whether a disaster's impact is sudden or unfolds gradually, studies of both developed and developing countries note that it is the most marginalized groups that tend to suffer the worst effects of disaster. At the same time, the World Bank reports that 95 percent of disaster-related deaths occur among the 66 percent of the world's population that live in the poorer countries (Enarson 2000, 3). Consider the loss of life and devastation caused by an earthquake of approximately the same magnitude a year apart in two countries: one in Haiti, an island country and one of the poorest in the world, and one in Christchurch, the third largest city in New Zealand, a wealthy OECD island country. In the former, people died and widespread violence was reported, including rape and sexual violence (Amnesty International 2011a). In the latter less than 200 people were killed, and despite cases of quake-related domestic violence, no cases of rape were reported. Despite the lesser loss of life, the insurance claims from the Christchurch quake are the largest the world has seen from a disaster precisely because of the wealth and development of that city.[2] Thus, from the perspective of understanding the human world, disasters provide us with unique insight into social structure, inequalities, and the prevailing norms shaping human behavior.

Disasters systematically discriminate against groups with lesser capabilities, resources, and opportunities (Neumayer and Plümper 2007). Their negative effects are multiplied for some groups and minimized for other, usually better-resourced, groups. Indeed, one's chances of surviving a disaster are largely dependent on his or her social location with respect to gender, race, ethnicity, and social class. These social hierarchies, which often lead to exploitation and violence, are typically deepened through disaster. In short, vulnerability to death and violence is highly differentiated; proximity to disaster and the ability to anticipate, cope with, protect oneself, and recover in a disaster's aftermath (with support for evacuation through to insurance for rebuilding) are ultimately socially determined. Given that gender inequalities exist between women and men in every country in the world, it is not surprising, then, to find that disasters have a greater effect on women's mortality compared with men's and that violence against women increases in the aftermath of disaster (Rivers 1982; Seager 2006).

Eric Neumayer and Thomas Plümper (2007) analyzed the gender differences in natural disasters based on a sample of 141 countries in which natural disasters occurred from 1981 to 2002 (the period for which data existed). They found that natural disasters lower the life expectancy of women drastically more than that of men, and as the disaster intensifies, so too does this effect. In their modeling, women and children are up to fourteen times more likely than men to die in a natural disaster. Where there is greater gender equality, the gap between men's and women's expected mortality is less. But as predisaster gender inequalities increase, so too does the number of women compared with men likely to be killed in a disaster. In Neumayer and Plümper's (2007, 551) words, it is "the socially-constructed gender-specific vulnerability of females built into everyday socio-economic patterns that leads to the relatively higher female disaster mortality rates compared to men." As we have seen with respect to other global forces such as trade and financial liberalization, war, and armed conflict, women's lack of economic and social resources relative to men also makes them disproportionately vulnerable to the effects of disasters, including death. And women are even more vulnerable to violence in the aftermath of disasters. But there is nothing natural or inevitable about these deaths and violations. A comparison of two similar historical shipping disasters with drastically different survival rates by gender proves the point.

Economists Frey, Savage, and Torgler (2010) studied the Titanic and Lusitania disasters based on a statistical analysis of passenger and survivor lists from both ships, taking into account gender, age, ticket class, nationality, and familial relationships with other passengers. Significant gender differences emerged after a close look at survival rates. In the 1912 Titanic sinking, 1,500 people died, but women had a 50 percent better chance of survival than men, whereas in the 1915 torpedo of the Lusitania by a German U-boat, 1,198 people died, and a far greater proportion were women. Frey et al. argue that the rapid sinking of the Lusitania led to a selfish, survival-of-the-fittest reaction, disregarding early twentieth-century social norms or the official protocol of protecting women and children first, which played out in an orderly fashion in the Titanic disaster since the boat took over four hours to descend. For the authors, time is the major determinant of human behavior and they assume that due to biology, men under pressure will always have greater survival rates in a disaster than women unless social norms, however misguided, intervene.

From a social constructivist perspective, however, the ability to survive is not biologically given but socially learned and determined, including whether one can swim or climb trees, where one is located in a disaster (close to an evacuation route or not), and so on. What we should take, therefore, from the comparison of the Titanic and the Lusitania is quite simply that disasters need not disproportionately kill or harm women. That outcome is a social and political choice. Gender equality in social and economic resources, *not timing*, is the key to women's survival in disasters in the twenty-first century. Moreover, planning and preparedness can influence appropriate behavior and effective responses equally in a sudden, slow-moving, or recurring disaster. In disasters there are checklists for good practice, just as in hospital care there are checklists for good practice in the emergency room, in the intensive care unit, and for preventative, primary care health. Often these processes are in place in developed countries, and as a result we see far fewer fatalities during and after disasters than in developing countries, which have more poorly resourced government administrative structures. But the gendered impacts of natural disasters are shaped and sometimes exacerbated by government responses in developed states as much as in developing states, as Box 9.1 shows. Hurricane Katrina in New Orleans and the Christchurch earthquakes increased both structural and physical violence against some women due to race, class, and gender inequalities predisaster. Governments in both cities responded differently to vulnerable groups of women, although because of the very recent nature of the Christchurch earthquakes, a full comparison cannot be made. In New Orleans, though, recovery and rebuilding programs have heightened social and political inequalities rather than diminished them.

Disasters are not one-off events. As Thomas Homer-Dixon (2006) argues, they are part of ongoing dynamic processes of global change shaped by demographic shifts, natural resource dependency, urbanization, and climate change all humanly constructed. The impact of a natural disaster depends on the overall human capabilities and resources of a society and magnifies a society's divisions and inequalities. But as crises disrupt normal incremental development, disasters are opportunities for progressing major social and political change in local communities and political-economic organization. We can learn from previous disasters and from the fissures in our societies that they tragically make visible. The South Asian tsunami that occurred on December 26, 2004, killing over 230,000 people in fourteen countries and displacing 1.7 million, one of the deadliest in recorded history, is one such disaster we can learn from (Rofi, Doocy, and Robinson 2006, 340).[3] To onshore waves of up to thirty meters caused by an undersea megathrust earthquake in the Indian Ocean, add pervasive gender inequalities in education, literacy, income, land, political representation, and employment in

Comparing the disasters of Hurricane Katrina in 2002 and the earthquakes in Christchurch, New Zealand, in September 2010 and February 2011 highlights the vulnerability of women in disaster situations. In the weeks immediately following the Christchurch earthquake, New Zealand police reported that domestic violence had increased by one-fifth, on top of increased incidents since the earthquake in September 2010 (*New Zealand Herald* 2011). Police have stated that reported cases of domestic abuse are only about 18 percent of the total (Stylianou 2011). Subsequent reports by women's refuge groups have confirmed the spike in domestic abuse. Christchurch Women's Refuge (CWR) notes the severity of incidents and the increase in young women entering safe houses (Tolerton 2011). The women going to shelters after Hurricane Katrina were also not necessarily the same women—there were new women, including from middle-class families and immigrants, seeking help (Jenkins and Phillips 2008, 62). Christchurch police cited the closure of the city center as a reason why more people were drinking at home, aggravating the risk of domestic violence (Stylianou 2011). Many women in Christchurch returned to abusive spouses or partners due to financial circumstances such as losing their job, an occurrence similarly noted in New Orleans (Jenkins and Phillips 2008, 57). There has been an increase in interest in safe houses since the June 2011 aftershock in Christchurch, which, for many women, catalyzed their decision to leave. The trend has been most pronounced in rural areas, where family violence increased 40 percent (Turner 2011).

After their offices were destroyed in the February quake, the CWR moved to a safe house, the location of which had to be kept secret. Crucially, the CWR maintained their twenty-four-hour telephone support and refuge services throughout the February earthquake (Christchurch Women's Refuge 2011). Unlike in New Orleans, where staff of domestic violence shelters were a part of the diaspora, the staff of the women's refuges in Christchurch were similarly "displaced" but continued their role throughout the post-disaster period. Consequently, the CWR was fully operational within a week (Christchurch Women's Refuge 2011; Turner 2011).

	BEFORE HURRICANE KATRINA	AFTER HURRICANE KATRINA
Women % of the population	54%	52%
Black women % of the population	47.2%	37.3%

Box 9.1 (*continued*)

	BEFORE HURRICANE KATRINA	AFTER HURRICANE KATRINA
% of women living below the federal poverty line (*NB: 13.3% national average*)	23%	15.1%
% of black women living below the federal poverty line	36.6%	23%
# of single mothers	45,183	26,819
# of black single mothers	33,675	15,118
# of single mothers in poverty	23,131	9,883
# of black single mothers in poverty	19,744	6,610

SOURCE: Institute for Women's Policy Research Factsheet. 2010, August. *Women in New Orleans: Race, Poverty and Hurricane Katrina*. Washington: IWPR.

Recent statistics for New Orleans after the city's reconstruction show a decrease in single mothers and women living below the poverty line, especially black women, as outlined in the previous table. However, rather than an improvement in the circumstances of women in New Orleans, these decreases reflect the fact that fewer black and poor women have returned to the city. The Institute for Women's Policy Research (2005) found that many former residents of public housing (poorer women) have not returned. The UN Special Rapporteur on Adequate Housing report (2011, 7–8) notes that the costs of the hurricane were "therefore intimately linked to pre-existing social, economic and land use patterns, directly related to housing and urban planning policies." In the aftermath of Katrina, discrimination against low-income renters was a serious obstacle to the poorer population's ability to return to their homes—a need more acute because of the lack of alternatives available due to lower household income (see Elliot and Pais 2006, 315). The bulk of the reconstruction funds went to rebuilding homeowner units rather than rental units, which the majority of women and poorer people relied on for housing. The race and gender discrimination on the basis of reconstruction planning fundamentally altered the socioeconomic composition of the city, a fact confirmed by the Institute for Women's Policy Research's (IWPR) statistics on reduced women in poverty.

decimated coastal regions of the Indian Ocean from South Asia to Africa, and you get disproportionate loss of female lives and heightened gender-based violence and vulnerability in the aftermath.

Gendered Violence and the South Asian Tsunami

There is abundant, albeit incomplete, evidence that many more women than men died in the South Asian tsunami. Aceh, Indonesia, was at the epicenter of the disaster and was particularly hard hit, as Box 9.2 shows. In Aceh, Sri Lanka, and Southern India, the death toll among women was three or four times higher than men, resulting in an unbalanced current sex ratio. While there were some surviving women-only households and many widowed heads of households, overall, male survivors outnumbered women in all the tsunami-hit areas (Oxfam International 2005, 2).[4] Women and girls were less likely to know how to swim, and their garments may have hindered

Box 9.2 DEATH STATISTICS				
ACEH BESAR DISTRICT VILLAGE	POPULATION PRETSUNAMI	SURVIVORS	SURVIVING FEMALES	SURVIVING MALES
Gampong Baru	242	123	39	84
Meunasah Masjid	1,110	159	45	114
Lamsenia	220	124	26	98
Dayeuh Mapplam	4,500	270	79	191
North Aceh District Village	Population Pretsunami	Total Dead	Female Fatalities	Male Fatalities
Sawang	Not available	93	70	23
Kuala Keureutou	Not available	85	68	17
Kuala Cangkoy	Not available	146	117	29
Matang Baroh	Not available	42	29	13

SOURCE: Oxfam International. 2005. "The Tsunami's Impact on Women." *Briefing Note*, March 4.

them from running or clambering onto roofs or up trees. Oxfam International (2005, 2) recorded the following first-hand account from Lampu'uk, Aceh:

> When the survivors had picked themselves up out of the mud of the tsunami, several appalling facts became clear. The first was that their town no longer existed. The second was that four out of five of its former inhabitants were dead. But it took a while to realise the strangest thing of all: that among those who made it to higher ground, or who kept their heads above the surging waters, so few were women.

Gender-based domestic and sexual violence increased significantly in the immediate aftermath of the tsunami (Fisher 2010, 902). Reports from NGOs and welfare centers (police reporting being unreliable given women's silence in highly unequal and discriminatory societies) included incidents of domestic violence, rape, harassment, and sexual violence (CATAW 2005). Young girls (and children) who were orphaned and women who were separated from family were most vulnerable (CATAW 2007, 15–16; Action Aid 2007, 20). Heightened violence against women continued in the weeks and months after the tsunami as the humanitarian and relief effort took over. Instead of addressing women's concerns, the relief effort served to increase discrimination against them.[5] Compensation was generally handed out to male members of the family who, in many cases, did not share it with the women or surviving women-only households (Fisher 2010, 14). There was a large increase in documented cases of physical abuse, rape, and forced and early marriage as a result (Felten-Biermann 2006, 82–86). Examples from Sri Lanka include women who were battered because they resisted their husbands' selling their jewelry or disputed their husbands' use of tsunami relief funds or and women who were blamed for the deaths of their children. Most egregious were those cases of "tsunami" early marriage, where poor families sold their daughters off or girls as young as thirteen years of age were coerced to provide for their own and their family's basic needs (Fisher 2010, 909). In Cuddalore, India, there is evidence of girls and women being married within their extended families, orphaned girls married off by extended family, and other forced marriage.[6] Some women and girls were ostracized in communities due to being unmarried and pregnant or widowed as a result of the tsunami (CATAW 2007, 15).

The lack of adequate housing and resulting violence women are subjected to have been found to be major problems in the aftermath of natural disasters. In the Asian tsunami camps and packed resettlement sites, reports were received of verbal and physical harassment and inappropriate behavior by men (while bathing, for example) and of women and girls' great fears of violence (Oxfam International 2005, 13; CATAW 2005). In Sri Lankan camps for the displaced, poor lighting around toilets and lack of private washing and sanitary facilities increased the incidence of sexual violence against women (Oxfam International 2005, 10). A woman living in one of the camps told Oxfam International (2005, 10) about her experiences there: "In the night we get scared because there are no lights. It's frightening for us, we know there are snakes and you can't see who is around the toilets and washing areas." In temporary housing areas some women were forced to have sex with their husbands, where they were in view of others, including their children, which was a source of shame for women, but refusal often resulted in harassment by husbands (CATAW 2007, 15). Overcrowding and the lack of adequate housing after the tsunami allowed some men to take advantage of the convenience and impunity of the situation to perpetrate violence against women. In her study of violence in the postemergency phase, Fisher (2010, 908) found that women respondents generally felt the increase in violence was more *visible* due to the communal living conditions. A study of the housing reconstruction aspects of the international response to the tsunami in Sri Lanka and Tamil Nadu revealed a disregard for women's and girls' rights (Housing and Land Rights Network, Habitat International Coalition 2005). The insecurity and inadequacy of posttsunami housing facilities and provisions demonstrated the lack of consultation with women and consideration of their needs (CATAW 2007, 13). Further, concern has been expressed by the UN Special Rapporteur on the Right to Adequate Housing that postdisaster reconstruction and redevelopment benefits some but can overlook vulnerabilities and inequalities affecting others' access to housing (Special Rapporteur on Adequate Housing 2011, 15).

Reports by the NGO the Coalition for Assisting Tsunami Affected Women (CATAW)—a group of Sri Lankan women's networks and organizations—about the high prevalence of gender-based violence and the special needs of women in the aftermath of the tsunami were initially dismissed (CATAW 2005). The evidence of this violence against all groups of women, usually perpetrated by men known to them, reveals the failure of governments and international actors to properly consider and implement gender-sensitive humanitarian aid and recovery, particularly with respect to adequate housing. Many women experienced further violence and harassment, primarily due to the lack of sensitivity of gendered differences in access to funds and available services (CATAW 2007, 19). There was widespread discrimination in aid distribution because it was linked to "ownership" and "head of household" status, both of which privileged men (Action

Aid 2007, 19; CATAW 2007, 19–20). CATAW also found that "the provision of relief aid distribution was a mechanism for relatives and separated husbands to harass and violate women by claiming the goods themselves, or by taking the goods away after the women had collected them" (CATAW 2007, 18). In Sri Lanka, the government's tsunami compensation scheme paid cash relief to the male head of household (CATAW 2007, 12). Ration cards and other government benefits were also registered in the husband's name (Oxfam International 2005, 10). Housing was given to the husband; single, divorced, or widowed women were not given housing entitlements (CATAW 2007, 12). Women were economically marginalized and more dependent on men for basic needs after the tsunami, thus increasing their vulnerability to violence (CATAW 2007, 19; Fisher 2010, 910). Aid given to husbands fueled alcohol consumption, domestic abuse, and sexual violence. Instances were reported of men offering impoverished tsunami-affected women money or goods for sex or engaging in relationships under a false pretence that marriage would follow. In the tsunami-affected coastal regions of southern India, the alcohol intake tripled, most likely because men were not going back to sea. That data, one doctor asserted, "should come as an eye-opener to the government that distributed cash without proper thought."[7]

In Sri Lanka, the government was slow and reluctant to acknowledge and respond to gendered abuse and violence against women, exacerbated by the lack of official reporting of incidents to the police and police unwillingness to interfere in "private" matters in camps or regular housing (Fisher 2010, 912). The social stigma associated with rape and the generally inferior social and economic position of women meant that the local authorities, mostly composed of men, were not sensitive to the heightened vulnerability of women in a postdisaster context (Felten-Biermann 2006, 83). As in conflict and postconflict settings discussed in Chapters 8 and 9, violence against women is often committed by "men in power," including police and paramilitaries positioned to provide "security" and humanitarian workers (Fisher 2010, 909–10). In some cases policemen and paramilitaries were the perpetrators of rape, a finding consistent with other disasters (Fisher 2010, 909; also Wiest, Mocellin, and Motsisi 1994). One informant in southern India reported: "I even have to deal with corrupt policemen who stop me on the road to demand a share of the relief-supplies" (*The Telegraph* 2005).

How can we explain the disproportionate mortality of women and girls and the increased gendered violence against them after the tsunami on December 26, 2004? Political economy analysis can help in two ways. First, the baseline economic and social status of women was low relative to men in the major countries affected by the tsunami (Oxfam International 2005, 10).[8] The posttsunami gendered imbalance in population placed greater pressure on women to procure basic needs for men and children. The loss of employment and family members, which also meant that they were faced with gendered household and caring tasks they would not have performed previously, fueled men's anger and resentment (Davis et al. 2005: Oxfam International 2005, 4–7). The disaster, therefore, only compounded preexisting gender inequalities and key determinants of violence, especially poverty and economic dependency, overconsumption of alcohol, and gendered violence associated with armed conflict. Box 9.3 shows how the tsunami exacerbated the numbers of displaced persons and the rate of violence against women, which were already high due to more than a decade of the armed conflict in both Sri Lanka and Aceh, Indonesia.

Second, the postdisaster violence against women, as well as the many more females killed in the tsunami, is the result of previous government and international inattention to gender-based violence in these areas carried over into the lack of gender-sensitive disaster preparedness and planning. The neglect of a critical gender perspective left women and girls vulnerable to the tsunami's most violent immediate and prolonged effects without adequate protection, assistance, or compensation. As the next section illustrates, the failure to consult women or consider women's social and economic rights in disaster policymaking and planning contributes to postdisaster gendered insecurities that heighten women's vulnerability to grave violence, including death.

Gender-Sensitive Disaster Planning: Preventing Violence Against Women

As the introduction to this chapter noted, women are not only victims in the aftermath of a disaster but also agents of change. Yet a common pattern is the exclusion of women from decision-making roles in pre- and postdisaster reconstruction and planning. In Aceh, for example, the authorities debating the "master plan" for the reconstruction of the province were almost exclusively male, and women's organizations struggled to take part in consultation systems (Oxfam International 2005, 13). Women were similarly excluded from posttsunami decision making in Sri Lanka, where their predisaster unequal status limited their consultation and involvement in local governance and reconstruction (CATAW 2005; Oxfam International 2005, 10). Fisher (2010, 911) argues that the "low participation of women in planning and decision making

Following the Asian tsunami, relief efforts in Sri Lanka and Aceh conducted by the international community focused on the seemingly apolitical natural disaster. Both Sri Lanka and Aceh are sites of separatist conflicts against the dominant governments, and both conflicts have persisted for over two decades. Sarah Fisher observed the deleterious effects of the 2004 tsunami on a population already exposed to a long-standing civil war and precarious humanitarian state of affairs (2010, 903–04). Women caught up in the conflict between the Liberation Tigers of Tamil Eelam (LTTE) and the Sinhalese-dominated government were subjected to sexual and physical abuse by armed forces on both sides. Moreover, among the estimated 800,000 displaced people, conditions in the internally displaced person (IDP) camps exacerbate domestic violence and create an environment conducive to sexual violence against women (Bourke-Martignoni 2002). The tsunami had the greatest impact in the northeastern region, also the region most affected by conflict. These conflict-related experiences of violence were especially relevant to national levels of violence against women and the incidence of postdisaster violence. In particular, a conflict or postconflict environment may serve to "normalize" the prevalence of violence against women. For example, Fisher notes that in the northern province of Jaffna, informants were less likely to feel that domestic abuse had increased (2010, 908). She explains that although the impact of the tsunami was significant, its effect had less impact than the civil war of the last twenty years, which had already given rise to humanitarian emergency and mass displacement (Fisher 2010, 908). High levels of violence in temporary accommodation centers were well known and expected. Similarly, Fisher reports that in the North and East, several respondents reported LTTE recruitment of child soldiers (male and female) taking place in camps (2010, 909). In Sri Lanka, fighting has severely hampered reconstruction efforts by redirecting government expenditure to the military and jeopardizing funding from international donors (Senanayake 2006). In short, Sri Lankan and Acehnese women's insecurity is compounded by the reinforcing effects of the tsunami, the conflict, poverty, and gender injustices. Yet, instead of embracing the challenges posed by this diversity, the dominant actors within these post-2004 reconstruction programs have largely conceded to the complex political and cultural sensitivities associated with operating in a closed, postconflict society. For women in these conflicts, it creates a double dilemma: not only does the conflict itself become marginalized, but also women's role in it is further silenced (Koo 2012).

at the local, district, and state levels was a considerable barrier to gender-sensitive disaster response and resulted in insufficient attention to post-disaster violence" in that country. In Muslim areas, there were virtually no women at all involved, and those who were involved were ostracized—one woman even had to flee her area (Fisher 2010, 911). In Aceh Darussalam, the posttsunami gender programming introduced as a condition of international aid failed to address the religious and cultural differences among women, privileging urban, middle-class, and Muslim women (Jauhola 2010). The absence of women from pre- and postdisaster policymaking is a problem in and of itself. Importantly, however, it leads to gender-blind programs, as we have seen with the compensation and housing programs following the Asian tsunami, which exacerbate violence against women. The lack of accurate data on the effects of the tsunami on women is indicative of the "invisibility" of women in disaster preparedness and impact assessment in tsunami-affected countries.

In Christchurch, New Zealand, the outcomes for women and gendered violence were significantly better than in the Asian tsunami-affected countries. Yet this was largely because of the more equal status of women relative to men in New Zealand and the informal, predisaster relationships established between police, civil defense, and women's refuges and battered women's shelters, for instance. As Box 9.4 explains, surprisingly, there was no systematic, gender-sensitive disaster planning in place in New Zealand, despite its high ranking on all gender equality indicators, and despite the fact that poor, single, battered women typically with children were extremely vulnerable to further marginalization and violence in the aftermath of the Christchurch earthquake. All indications from those involved in emergency and recovery support services in Christchurch suggest that a gender-sensitive disaster protocol integrated within civil defense and emergency services was sorely needed in the aftermath of the earthquake.

There are lessons to be learned—and practices to be made routine—from the informal, grassroots approaches in the Christchurch earthquake that turned out to be effective, as there are good practices to take stock of from the Asian tsunami response. For example, after the tsunami, the governments of Tamil Nadu and Kerala stationed women fire officers and police officers and women doctors in the camps and affected villages. This helped to deter violence against women and provided women survivors with a safer environment (Oxfam International 2005, 7). Oxfam International (2010, 5), working in tsunami-affected areas, opted to elect women representatives as community liaisons to share women's intimate knowledge of community needs (see also Enarson 2000). They also attended to gender concerns in Indonesia and Cuddalore (India) by consulting women in project planning, ensuring

In places like Haiti, the lack of disaster planning and governance creates
conditions that give rise to shocking examples of sexual and gender-based
violence (Institute for Justice & Democracy in Haiti et al. 2010; Amnesty
International 2011a). Research about the New Zealand disasters indicates that
domestic violence increases by 100 percent, sometimes 200 percent, following
a disaster event (Houghton 2010; *New Zealand Herald* 2011b). When the city of
Christchurch, New Zealand, was struck by a series of earthquakes and aftershocks beginning on September 4, 2010, the disaster was a crucible of how a
developed state such as New Zealand would attend to the vulnerable groups of
women in domestic violence shelters. The spike in domestic violence observed
after each earthquake is instructive insofar as it demonstrates that domestic
violence services are "frontline services" in the wake of disaster[9] (*New Zealand
Herald* 2011a). In 2006, New Zealand Ministry of Civil Defence indicated their
intention to involve women's refuges in regional and district disaster plans
pursuant to the advocacy and research of Dr. Rosalind Houghton (Collins
2006). This case study assesses the degree to which this has been achieved.

The New Zealand Ministry of Civil Defence sets broad guidelines for
regional authorities' (known as Civil Defence Emergency Management
[CDEM] groups) preparation of emergency response plans. For instance, in
its *Mass Evacuation Guidelines*, the ministry urges the CDEM groups to identify communities that may be vulnerable in an emergency in their planning
process (Ministry of Civil Defence and Emergency Management [MCDEM]
2008, 25). From a policy perspective, the impetus exists to include battered
women as a "vulnerable group" that must be proactively accounted for in
planning for contingencies. The guidelines go on to state the rationale for
such forward preparation: "there are likely to be several at-risk groups in any
particular area who may need special consideration in order to ensure that,
during an evacuation, they are successfully taken care of" (MCDEM 2008,
25) Curiously, vulnerable women do not feature in this list of groups to consider, which includes Maori communities, ethnic communities (non-English
speakers/English as a second language), remote/isolated communities, aged
and/or infirm people, people with disabilities, tourists, people in prisons or
residential institutions, and schools (MCDEM 2008, 25).

When questioned about the inclusion of battered women's shelters and
refuges in emergency plans and checklists, a representative of the Canterbury
Regional Civil Defence Emergency Management Group—which caters to
the Christchurch area—stated that such arrangements were the prerogative
of individual regional groups.[10] Canterbury CDEM has "response priorities"
that arise pursuant to a particular disaster; in this case it was "saving lives."
Where "vulnerable people" would factor into their response is in relation to
the second priority category, which is "reducing suffering." Battered women

(*continued*)

Box 9.4 (*continued*)

and the facilities they rely on do not constitute "vulnerable people" for the purposes of Canterbury CDEM's response procedures and are not included in databases listing other "vulnerable groups" such as aged care and children's facilities. According to the Canterbury CDEM, if a women's refuge had an urgent or imminent need and contacted Civil Defence, their request would be triaged along with all other requests for service, balanced against the competing factors of resources and urgency. However, all staff *are* made aware during training of the importance of information privacy, one of the reasons for which is the potential for domestic violence. It would seem that women's refuges are dealt with on an ad hoc basis, reactive to emergent issues rather than proactively checked on, secured, and communicated with.

This was the overwhelming experience of the several women's refuges in Christchurch. It was the combination of effective preexisting networks among the Christchurch refuges with police and with other refuges in Auckland and the fortunate eventuality that the refuges had enough staff able to continue working that these facilities remained functional throughout the disaster. The Christchurch Women's Refuge (CWR), through the quick thinking of their office manager, had the toll-free crisis line diverted to Auckland within 30 minutes of the February quake.[11] Their downtown head office was already damaged in the December 26, 2010, aftershock, so the organization was temporarily located at a safe house, without any women residents, at the time of the February quake. CWR called their own structural engineer to assess the state of the safe house and determine their ability to maintain operations at the premises. Likewise, the Battered Women's Trust worked exclusively with police, with whom they have strong preexisting cooperation, to move residents of their damaged safe house to another location.[12] Even so, they report that the phone lines were so badly affected that the only way they could gain police assistance to move residents from their affected safe house was to contact their national office in Wellington. The CEO there used her influence with police nationally to have the residents moved to a safe place since the refuge's vehicle was stuck in liquefaction.

Only those refuges renting properties from the government-run Housing New Zealand Corporation were contacted—and not by Civil Defence but by the Ministry of Social Development, which has primary responsibility for their properties in a disaster—as part of standard procedure.[13] After the February quake, the Battered Women's Trust report that they were invited to a meeting run by the Civil Defence Welfare Group, which asked for input on priorities and safety concerns. Clearly, Civil Defence can identify the potential needs and concerns of women's refuges but failed to incorporate them into their preexisting plans.

According to the Canterbury CDEM, one of the difficulties identified in including women's refuges in any disaster checklist or plan is the constant anonymity on which they rely. The Canterbury CDEM stated that the fact that few people know where the safe houses are "keeps them off the radar of civil defence."[14] A similar comment was made by a staff member at the Maori women's Otautahi Refuge. In actuality, this should not hinder the incorporation of checks on women's refuges in postdisaster plans. The whereabouts of all safe

Box 9.4 (*continued*)

houses in the city are known to police and are red-flagged on the police system, and a security assessment has been carried out on each of them.[15] Anonymity is about not releasing the addresses unnecessarily and maintaining the confidentiality of individual women and children and their families. In the event refuge facilities were damaged, Civil Defence (or nominated police) would need to coordinate transport to safe houses with refuge staff or arrange alternate safe houses.

When Rosalind Houghton asked a Civil Defence official in 2008 why they did not make contact with a refuge following flooding, the official responded: "No, because where would you draw the line? Would you then call the SPCA and ask them if they're ok. . . . [T]o be quite frank, ringing people to see if they're alright would be done in a couple months time. It would not happen" (Houghton 2010, 201).

Putting aside the unfortunate analogy drawn between battered women and abandoned pets, the "tyranny of the urgent" is a commonly cited inhibitor to including gender in considerations, not only in disasters but also in any pressure situation. Canterbury CDEM urged refuges to enhance their independence and resilience through preparedness and procedures, a part of the overall principle "Get Ready, Get Thru." Admittedly, self-readiness is an important factor and likely to greatly influence impacts and adaptive capacity. But when this principle was put to a long-standing manager of one of the refuges, she stated that it had not been advocated to refuges despite being the only alternative available to them in an emergency absent formal coordination. Better communication around such a plan is vital.[16] Economic security is a primary factor in social vulnerability (Enarson 2000, 1). Women in refuges literally do not have the economic resources *to* prepare; the economic impacts of a disaster intensify already tenuous livelihoods. Moreover, battered women cannot readily utilize the avenues of mitigation that other people can use, such as community shelters, because of the potential to be located by abusive partners and the likelihood that such conditions would aggravate their existing high levels of psychological distress.

Women's refuges throughout New Zealand have the unenviable task of being "essential services" without formal support from Civil Defence (whose mandate, remember, is to coordinate all "essential services"), whose services and resources are not merely temporarily strained, but strained for a sustained period of time following a disaster. According to the Battered Women's Trust, normal methods of dealing with domestic violence postdisaster simply "do not stand up." They thought that there exists a serious misconception that battered women, like other people, and like physical damage, will "return to normal." Government departments are enthusiastically trying to "build back better" and calling on refuges to "think strategically" about how the disaster is "a new opportunity" when, in fact, the refuges can hardly address the immediate needs of those families who require their services due to a lack of resources and capacity. Such naivety reveals an embarrassing dislocation of government from the realities of addressing domestic violence.

The Christchurch earthquakes belie any presumption that emergency planning in a developed state attends to "vulnerable people." The outcome of the

(*continued*)

Box 9.4 (continued)

Christchurch earthquake is a testament to the management and dedication of refuge staff in these situations, challenging the conventional notion of women as victims and illustrating their invaluable insight into what needs to happen postdisaster. In a country that is aware of a preexisting high baseline of domestic violence, of the likelihood that this will rise during and after a disaster, and of the worldwide trend that women are overrepresented in the impacts of disasters, why does gender-sensitive planning not exist? Perhaps more to the point, given this example, what can we learn? The Christchurch example shows what is "conspicuously missing" from disaster management. Disturbingly, the need to attend to "vulnerable women" in disasters is in an area where empirical evidence is available and ominous—"it seems to make perfect sense doesn't it? It just didn't happen."[17]

women's participation (at equal pay) in work programs, and building shelters in areas where women felt safe. In Kerala, the government agreed to register permanent houses owned by married couples in the names of both spouses so that one could not sell the house without the consent of the other, preventing one partner from leaving a spouse after a disaster without any entitlement to housing compensation (Oxfam International 2005, 7; Special Rapporteur on Adequate Housing 2011).

Building on these initiatives, gender-sensitive disaster planning must become a key government priority in order to prevent heightened violence against women. This planning would require the immediate collection of sex- and age-disaggregated data when disasters occur, direct allocation of compensation and aid to women, inclusion of women staff in disaster agencies such as civil defense, and collaboration with groups in the community including women's refuges and social services for victims of violence (Fisher 2010). In Box 9.5, Enarson (2000) suggests establishing gender and disaster working groups to initiate integrated planning and collect gendered data for disaster emergency response plans. These working groups could analyze baseline gender relations and seek proactive ways to bolster women's economic and political capacities. In the event of a disaster, women's specific physical and material vulnerabilities would then be anticipated and an operational response would be triggered.

Conclusion

Despite the human tragedy from natural disasters, the postdisaster period—like the postconflict phase discussed in Chapter 8—can create opportunities for transforming women's economic and social situations. There is some

Elaine Enarson (2000, ix), who founded the field of gender and disaster studies, states, "Disaster preparedness, mitigation, relief, and reconstruction initiatives must be inclusive and equitable; . . . the economic needs and resources of both women and men must be anticipated by planners and addressed proactively; and . . . reconstruction must foster conditions empowering women rather than undermining their capacities and increasing their vulnerability to subsequent disasters."

- *Address baseline gender relations*: Analyze gender-specific vulnerabilities with respect to:
  - Household structure
  - Demographic trends
  - Division of labor
  - Occupations
  - Working conditions
  - Control of economic resources
  - Women in need—sole, invalid, battered
- Transform the capacities of women with respect to the:
  - Work patterns of women
  - Work skills of women
  - Resources of women
- *Identify women with critical knowledge about vulnerabilities* who can be integral during a disaster, providing information on people, resources, local conditions, and idiosyncrasies
- *Identify barriers to women's involvement* in disaster recovery policymaking (Enarson 2000, 36)

evidence that the gendered population imbalance in the Asian tsunami-affected communities, for example, has forced a change in the conventional gender divisions of labor, empowering both women and men. Chhaya Datar, the head of the department of women's studies at the Tata Institute of Social Sciences, Mumbai, notes that for the southern Indian women affected by the tsunami, "the struggle for survival has triggered their innate urge to be emancipated." Husbands do not object either, Parandam, a village Panchayat elder, explained, since "the last six months have been such a struggle for survival that nobody cares if these roles overlap." Sunny Jose, the head of the tsunami relief and rehabilitation program at Action Aid India's Cuddalore Center, observed that "before the tsunami came, women couldn't think beyond fish vending, and neither were they allowed by their husbands to search for work outside their neighbourhoods." But now "NGOs working in the area are teaching these women such vocational crafts as tailoring, tile-making, shoe-making and the like, so that they can become economically independent" (*The Telegraph* 2005).

As this chapter stated at the beginning, there is no such thing as a natural disaster. At least, the impact and long-term effects of disasters on different groups including women and men are determined by the economic, political, and social structures and institutions in any given community. Gender-based violence, during and after disasters, can be eliminated in the future with gender-sensitive planning and deliberation. WEDO (the Women's Environment and Development Organization), for instance, took Neumayer and Plümper's (2007) statistical research on the disproportionate female mortalities after natural disasters, and the connection to women's lesser achievement of economic and social rights revealed by the research, and used that finding to lobby for greater attentiveness to gender inequalities in climate-change policymaking at the United Nations (WEDO 2008). With respect to climate change and its likely adverse effects, good planning can predict and prevent the gendered impacts that include heightened violence against vulnerable women and girls. However, too often the invisibility of violence against women both during and after disaster exacerbates gender inequalities and marginalizes women in key recovery and disaster preparedness decision-making processes (Wilson, Phillips, and Neal 1998). Such marginalization has occurred even at the United Nations and in the United Nations Framework Convention on Climate Change (UNFCCC) climate-change negotiations, as revealed in Box 9.6.

UN should be ashamed of themselves

Box 9.6 CLIMATE CHANGE: OVERCOMING THE TYRANNY
OF THE URGENT?

At the Copenhagen Conference of Parties to the UNFCCC, parties pledged to increase climate financing. However, following the appointment of a nineteen-person all-male High Level Advisory Group on Climate Change Financing by UN Secretary-General Ban Ki Moon, women's groups lambasted the decision to exclude women from a group centrally involved in financing, design, and implementation of climate change mitigation in developing countries (Rust 2010). Since women are disproportionately represented among the world's poorest people and those most vulnerable to the impacts of climate change, and climate change exacerbates existing structural inequalities between women and men, the decision was "incomprehensible" to NGOs (Rust 2010). In response, the secretary-general has moved to include more women on the panel, an omission caused by "time constraints" that precluded the consideration of appropriate gender balance.

As the deleterious impacts of climate change have begun to be experienced in some of the more impoverished and vulnerable parts of the world, we must overcome the "tyranny of the urgent" that, for expediency or other reasons, excludes women from key decision-making roles about climate-change preparations and perpetuates violence against women and girls.

Conclusion

Researching Violence against Women—
The Point is to End it . . .

WE HAVE COME TO the end of this book, and it is a cliché of course, but we have only just gotten started. While I grapple with the enormity of the problem of violence against women, its global scope, and its structural determinants, more rapes are committed, young women trafficked, women workers abused, and female protesters and partners beaten alike. To quote from the most famous political economist Karl Marx, as is inscribed on his grave, "Philosophers have interpreted the world in various ways, the point however is to change it." What does this book suggest might change violence against women with the ultimate aim of eliminating it?

Throughout the chapters of this book, I have consistently argued that relatively poor access to economic, social, and political resources for women and men is associated with being both perpetrators and victims of violence. Violence is all around us; It could happen to any of us at any time. Yet there are factors and processes that make that violence much more likely to happen. I have connected this vulnerability to violence to the relative disempowerment experienced by many women and some men. This book identifies the linkages between different forms of violence against women and macrostructural processes by focusing on strategic sites where political-economic processes can be seen to be maintaining or creating the structural gender inequalities that underpin violence against women. The fact that many women and men do not enjoy basic economic and social rights that would allow them to live a dignified life has to do in part with global processes including neoliberal economic restructuring, unregulated trade and financial flows, disasters that collide with unequal social structures, and war and militarism's draining of resources. Poor women, for instance, are more vulnerable to violence, and the experience of violence in turn exacerbates their poverty (Kishor and Johnson 2004).

I have also argued that the norms accepting the use of violence—whether in the private home, which is also a workplace and increasingly a globalized workplace, or in public, in conflict-affected areas, after crises, or in apparently peaceful settings—are integrally connected to gender norms and identities, in particular the masculinities I discussed in Chapter 3.

What can we do about violence against women given the gendered norms and global material processes that cause it? In Chapters 1 and 2, I observed that high-profile global initiatives to end violence against women have been largely disconnected from efforts to empower women, economically and politically. Yet, when women have access to productive resources and they enjoy social and economic rights, they are less vulnerable to violence across all societies. In particular, women are less vulnerable to violence when they have a good economic status, including access to full-time employment, land/property rights, access to credit/capital, and enjoyment of social and political rights, such as rights to education, housing, food, water, health and reproductive health, social security, justice, and political representation. However, this broader political economic order is often neglected in analyses of violence against women. Governments, nonstate actors, and international organizations need to work together to create enabling conditions for the enjoyment of economic and social rights. Doing so would represent a major step toward eliminating violence against women, its causes, its consequences, and its costs.

This book has sought to synthesize the theoretically informed empirical evidence that can provide a basis for future evidence-based practical interventions by national and global actors to eliminate violence against women that are more likely to be effective than present ones. The evidence collected in the chapters of this book furthermore suggests that all policies should be assessed from the vantage point of whether or not they are likely to exacerbate violence against women (see also True 2009a). Based on our knowledge of the structural determinants of violence, we can anticipate the gendered impacts of economic development policies, trade deals, budget austerity cuts, and monetary policies, for instance. In the case of liberal economic and monetary policies that facilitate the closure of plants and factories as companies move to foreign locations to lower their costs of production, we know that the large loss of employment will lead to increased levels of crime and domestic violence, and that women will be disproportionately affected. In the case of trade deals that leave little domestic policy space for upholding basic economic and social rights and fulfilling government obligations to international human rights treaties, we know that this will likely increase poverty, economic stress, and, inexorably, violence.

As for the austerity policies, as governments attempt to balance their budgets and attract investment anew after the financial crisis and the large-scale bailout of the financial industry, these have been already shown to affect women's job losses and the public services they need to a greater extent than men. For instance, in New Zealand, one of the first public services to be cut was post-trauma counseling for victims of sexual violence. Fortunately, after street protests and a huge amount of lobbying from those in the sexual violence sector who drew on the available research to show the crucial value of this counseling, funding was restored. But where were the women and men in government who opposed this cut in the first place? Policy change to end violence against women first and foremost must change societies' attitudes (and social movements, for their part, must change the minds of policymakers). We need to persuade our fellow citizens that saying no to violence involves more than a personal stand, although that is certainly a start; it involves changing political and economic agendas. Current global initiatives to end violence against women are unlikely to be successful while they remain disconnected from the larger struggle for social and economic equality. Nicole Kidman as a UNIFEM ambassador sends out personalized messages to opinion leaders on November 27, "End Violence Against Women Day." That is worthwhile. But individuals can be effective change agents only if they comprehend and then work to change the political and economic structural conditions that fuel and perpetuate violence against women.

In the remainder of this last chapter, I canvas the future research agendas and questions that I see emanating from this book. I then discuss the two key areas that, based on the research and analysis conducted here, look to be the most promising approaches likely to have the most traction in the medium to long term in achieving the goal of ending violence against women (VAW). Finally, although I am strictly not a policy scholar, I felt it important to say something about *how* we as anti-VAW advocates might move beyond saving one woman at a time to actually bringing about the policy changes that recognize and respond to the political economy of violence against women.

New Directions for Research

This book gives a broad overview of empirical evidence on VAW drawn from a variety of disciplines. The particularly striking thing about violence against women is how it cuts across so many areas of life—socially, economically, and politically. Thus, there are multiple sites where VAW can be researched and addressed, but as the book argues, efforts in one area—health or criminal justice, for instance—may be undermined by macro forces elsewhere, contributing to VAW simultaneously. One research agenda, therefore, is to explore cases of multi-agency cooperation to end VAW and to assess the potential for multidisciplinary collaboration on instances where the individual and the socioeconomic causes and consequences of VAW are most manifest, such as in the area of housing policy (see Centre on Housing Rights and Evictions [COHRE] 2010). Another area that is underresearched is the impact of gender inequalities, in its different dimensions, including gender norms of male superiority and ideas of manhood, on violence against women (World Health Organization 2010). For instance, existing research suggests that inequalities in employment matter more than in education in the prevalence of violence in any given society. We need large-scale studies that collect better data to be able to tease out this bigger picture of the conditions in which violence is accentuated or prevented. This macro-empirical research—to which this book contributes—should be able to inform the development of some key outcomes for women that could serve as *indicators for the prevention of violence*—indicators that could be rigorously monitored by advocates (see SRVAW 2008b).

As I said at the outset of the book, every chapter is the basis for a doctoral project or a book in its own right. The research questions are literally spilling off the pages. It has been hard not to go off on all of these tangents here. Among other key research agendas, I see a great need for research on violence after disasters and for institutional mechanisms to prevent disproportionate deaths and violence against women in disasters. Integrating security and political economy approaches to violence and human rights is particularly pressing given the scourge of sexual violence in conflict and postconflict settings. Researchers will need to investigate and evaluate socioeconomic responses to victims of sexual violence war crimes in weak institutional contexts where legal and criminal justice strategies are hardly effective. Much more effort needs to be made to bridge the disconnect between security and economic reconstruction agendas in peace-building contexts. Studies that map the successes of women decision makers postconflict and postcrisis in rebuilding key social and economic institutions and policies to prevent recurring violence should also be a top priority. Research on all postconflict countries is called for but especially Rwanda, Liberia, and East Timor, where we have already seen women securing a foothold in political institutions and making some progress toward greater societal awareness of violence against women and new policies to address it.

In all these interdisciplinary research endeavors, it will be critical to apply a feminist methodology that is attentive to all forms of power especially those more hidden aspects, to different types of knowledge, and to relationships with research participants who will often also be survivors of violence. As Brooke Ackerly and I have argued, practicing reflexivity is an essential feminist ethic and, in fact, what sets most feminist research apart (Ackerly and True 2008, 2010). In the field of violence against women, in difficult and challenging settings, it has never been more important to think through one's ethical practice as a researcher. There is increasing recognition of this among scholars and NGO researchers and in UN agencies, but there are not always good guides to ethical research on violence in local and international settings where power relations are hugely stilted and victims are socially marginalized. Feminist methodology is deeply concerned with such settings and with how to do research to bring about political and social transformation. I humbly recommend Brooke Ackerly and my book *Doing Feminist Research in Political and Social Science* as a place to start for VAW researchers.

Priorities for Preventing Violence

This book suggests that two approaches should be prioritized in local and international interventions to prevent violence: "empowering women economically" and "men changing men." Neither is a "new" solution, and it is true to say that both are increasingly being purported by key actors the world over, although often not specifying concretely what might actually be involved in accomplishing these. Let me, however, try to spell out what is involved in these most crucial approaches to ending violence against women.

Economic Empowerment

There is an emerging consensus that women's social, political, and economic empowerment is key to ending violence against women and the culture of impunity. The UN General Assembly, following the 2010 Commission on the Status of Women, passed a resolution on it (UN General Assembly Resolution 2010). Hillary Clinton in her speech during the sixteen days to End Violence Against Women in December 2011 also highlighted women's economic empowerment as her central message, noting in particular the costs to everyone, not just to women, from this violence (Clinton 2011). The United Nations' world survey on the role of women in development and the World Health Organization's (2010) analysis of VAW research suggest that women's economic empowerment is a critical part of violence prevention (United Nations Department of Economic and Social Affairs 2009). Many governments, nongovernmental organizations, and scholars agree.

But what do we mean by empowerment, and who defines it? For feminist scholars, it's not a term that we can take for granted, especially if we are to hang major strategies for political and policy change on it. We certainly know what disempowerment looks like. The African Development Forum (2008, 2) has called for attention "to underlying social and economic drivers of women's vulnerabilities and equitable access." They further stated that "weak economic power, subordinate social status and lack of voice define women's experience across the continent" and that "within this context there are indications that violations against women are increasing." Thus, we could interpret economic empowerment as simply meaning improving women's socioeconomic and legal status. This would include increasing women's awareness of their rights and establishing measures to ensure women's rights related to owning and disposing of property and assets. Enabling women and girls' access to secondary and tertiary education and to decent employment with good working conditions and remuneration should also be an integral part of antiviolence strategies. The achievement of these conditions will require governments to prioritize women's employment in any foreign investment, trade, and development partnerships and to require that multinational corporations sign on to the UN Global Compact Women's Empowerment Principles (WEPs). From the perspective of nongovernmental actors, mechanisms like the WEPs could become the basis for more rigorous monitoring of corporate practices to ensure that they are held accountable for practices that exacerbate violence against women in the communities from which they profit.

There is a key paradox, however, with women's economic empowerment that this book has only touched on but that is reflected in the body of feminist scholarship since the 1980s on women's increasing employment in the export processing zones of developing countries. Global economic processes can cause women to get jobs over men or migrate for them—which may be economically empowering for them on the one hand but which may involve workplace abuse and lead to heightened domestic violence on the other hand. This can happen because men simultaneously are disempowered by the same globalizing processes and express their disempowerment by reasserting masculine control over intimate partners and other women as described in Chapter 3. It can also happen because women's migration for economic empowerment heightens their vulnerability to violence and exploitation from strangers in the dislocated and underregulated communities around special economic zones and the like. The case of Ciudad Juarez discussed in Chapter 4 is part of this contradictory logic. How, then, does a feminist political economy perspective theorize the paradox of empowerment and exploitation? I argue that economic opportunities including through migration are crucial for women, and often to escape violent local contexts. But they must not come at the expense of basic human rights or allow local and national governments in sending countries to relieve themselves from the responsibility of providing meaningful employment and nondiscriminatory economic opportunities for women in their local environments. We must hold states and local governments accountable (through legal and policy mechanisms such as the United Nations CEDAW and Security Resolution 1325 and others) for creating economic development that improves local livelihoods and employment chances for women, as well as men.

Men Changing Men

A second approach to preventing violence against women involves the advocacy of men in addressing their own and their fellow men's behavior and masculine identities. There is a growing men's movement to end violence against women, described in Chapter 3. It is important, however, never to underestimate the resistance to social change and to understand from whence that resistance comes. Antiviolence advocates realize that this resistance comes very often from men who are threatened by the apparent losses they experience when women's economic and social status is rising. Thanks to Connell (1998), we know about "patriarchal dividends" and have seen several examples in this book where men's resistance to policy change, in governments and communities, deflects VAW as a private issue, not one for public policy. Women who oppose male hegemony, moreover, often experience an increase in domestic violence. Thus, those in the struggle to end violence against women recognize that partnering with feminist men (yes, men can be feminists, too!) is a crucial step. But men must be invited to join this struggle and, as I argued in Chapter 3, in ways that are motivating and sensitizing, allowing them to connect with other men in raising awareness of violence and gender inequalities.

Beyond Saving One Woman at a Time: Key Strategies for Policy Change

Finally, to the question of how, as anti-VAW advocates, we might move beyond short-term solutions that save one woman at a time to bringing about the policy changes that directly address the political economy of violence against women by ensuring that women are able to enjoy freedom from fear and from want: This book has challenged existing approaches to violence against women and set the agenda for political and policy change but up until this point has not focused on how to bring about such change. I cannot end this book without giving fellow advocates some strategies for making change from what I know of the scholarship on public policy and advocacy politics.

First of all, advocates must seize "windows of political opportunity" (see Keck and Sikkink 1998). They do not come labeled, though. Therefore, we must learn to take advantage of propitious timing and circumstance (see Kingdon 1995). Serious questioning of economic policy after the impact of the global financial crisis represents one such window of opportunity. The crisis symbolized the problems of male monopoly and provided a window of opportunity to change the gendered order of things. Initially, when men were the first ones to lose their jobs, it was women who were touted as the ones to bring the world to recovery. However, as we saw in Chapter 6, women are disproportionately affected by the recession. The crisis is perpetuating, even heightening the same gendered inequalities and violence against women as before. But now is not the time to give up. Rather, it is the time for campaigns to point out the connections between violence against women and economic policy: violence is an economic issue; economic policies engender violence.

As is often the case, advocates for ending VAW are poised to seize these chances (and are already lobbying for change), but much of the challenge is to convince policymakers to seize the opportunity also. Public policy research reminds us that focusing our advocacy efforts on problem definition and agenda setting is foremost—given that this is how issues are chosen to be given attention (Carpenter 2007). The more an issue finds purchase in public consciousness, the more politicians will pay attention. It is also crucial to present an argument for policy change in an appealing form, that is, not antimen but positive win/win, pointing out the benefits to others albeit not in a purely instrumental way. For instance, continual appeals for action against VAW on the basis of women's rights have made way for more economically based arguments that show the cost of not acting to end VAW, as well as arguments that show the economic gains of gender equality for society. For example, if governments raised women's employment to male levels, GDP would grow by 8 percent in the United Kingdom, 9 percent in the United States, and 16 percent in the European Union (Bennhold 2011).

Another important factor in bringing policy issues into the public domain is to disrupt the normalization of injustice and the proverbial status quo.

Ironically, VAW is an extremely tangible issue—too often it leaves irreparable physical damage and scars. Yet, its occurrence often in the private sphere and in violent and desensitized contexts such as that of war and disaster has hindered societal awareness. Once issues are exposed in the public realm, ignoring them becomes much harder. We saw this in the case of the publicity surrounding acid burnings in Chapter 3, and with respect to the publicity about UN peacekeepers' complicity in sex trafficking highlighted by the film *The Whistleblower* discussed in Chapter 8. In both cases action was led by prominent women officials and parliamentarians, as well as women's groups, who had to overcome serious obstacles to bring the issue to light. They found success and new protocols and legislation was passed. These policy or "norm entrepreneurs" undermined the image of VAW as a private issue, problematized it, and lobbied for change (Mintrom and Norman 2009; Finnemore and Sikkink 1998).

Violence against women is an issue that cuts across many public policy areas (criminal justice, human rights, public health, political economy) and that is exacerbated by many local and global factors and processes. Addressing it, as well as broader patterns of gender inequality, will require significant change to the status quo. Norm entrepreneurs distinguish themselves from other agents of policy change because they challenge our existing understanding of the problem and propose solutions to it. Central to success of any such individual leaders is the formation of local and transnational coalitions that can coordinate campaigns for change. Laurel Weldon's (2006) analysis of the violence against women movement reveals some of the key elements that have made transnational cooperation possible and the issues that have had to be overcome. Transnational policy networks have been shown to increase the likelihood of policy diffusion (True and Mintrom 2001), and coalitions can increase the likelihood that advocates will achieve policy change. But this is not to dismiss the importance of local and grassroots women's groups in promoting change. Although this book has argued that there are global patterns of violence against women, violence happens in local, often highly female-averse, contexts. Forging local coalitions is an important aspect of gaining momentum, especially coalitions with strategically situated people, including men.

Finally, in the struggle to end violence against women, we must lead by example. This is the impetus behind men's efforts to end VAW, exemplified by the White Ribbon Campaign discussed in Chapter 3. And it underscores the fact that policy change will never succeed without societal support. In many places a fundamental shift in ethics is required; in others the shift needs to be in ending silence. Many men and women know that violence is wrong—they even abhor it—but they will not intervene. Campaigns like the White Ribbon stress the importance of reporting and intervening to end violence against women. Leading by example is a central tenet of policy change because it will create and publicize nonviolent gender identities, alternative ways of being a man or a woman. There is no truer maxim than Mahatma Gandhi's challenge to us to "be the change you want to see in the world" or Václav Havel's (who died as I finished this book) to live nonviolently, as if the world were a better place already.

NOTES

Chapter 1

1. According to Karl Marx, the task of the social critic as scholar is to improve "self-understanding of the age concerning its struggles and wishes ([1843] 1967, 215).

2. Statement by Ron Redmond, chief spokesperson for the UN High Commissioner for Refugees, January 2009.

3. Clair Apodaca (1998) has developed the WESHR achievement index of statistical data that measures progress in women's economic and social rights in all countries that have ratified CEDAW across two time periods. She argues that aggregated data masks significant differences in the realization of economic and social rights between males and females: "Women lag behind men in every indicator of economic and social rights" (Apodaca 1998, 151).

4. Referred hereafter as the "SG's in-depth study."

5. Available at http://www.un.org/en/women/endviolence/pdf/VAW.pdf, p. 2.

6. For example, the Gender Development Index and the Gender Empowerment Index, 1995–2010, as well as the new 2011 Gender Inequality Index published in UN Development Program's annual Human Development reports.

7. See "CEDAW Committee Concerned by Impact of Financial Crisis on Rights of Women and Girls," Press Release, February 6, 2009. Also United Nations Commission on the Status of Women, Press Release WOM/1390, 2003, New York.

8. The 1993 declaration is repeated in the "United Nations Elimination of Violence Against Women (Resolution 2003/45)," where economic exploitation is added to the definition of violence against women.

9. CEDAW Committee, General Recommendation No. 19, 11th session, 1992.

10. Prevalence studies estimate the percentage of persons within a demographic group who are victimized within a specific time frame (usually one year, five years, or lifetime). Incidence studies measure violence by counting the number of separate victimizations or incidents of violence perpetrated against persons within a specific demographic group during a specific time frame (one year, five years, or lifetime). These are presented as a victimization rate.

11. In Managua, Nicaragua, 63 percent of children from families where women had suffered domestic violence had to repeat at least one school year and on average left school four years earlier than classmates who did not experience domestic violence (Hombrecher 2007, 42).

Chapter 2

1. Social Watch, Press Release, Gender Equity Index 2008. See http://www.socialwatch.org/node/9267.

2. See http://www.svri.org/emergencies.htm (accessed December 1, 2011).

3. Many scholars argue that both covenants assume "progressive realization, that is, the continuous improvement of rights" (Elson 2002, 80). They both impose positive duties on governments to eliminate discrimination and hold governments legally responsible for ending violations immediately and as far as possible (Rubenstein 2004). All human rights have an economic and material aspect; therefore, insufficient resources cannot be a defense against noncompliance with the International Covenant on Economic, Social and Cultural Rights (ICESCR; Chinkin 2008, 19). These rights, too, have minimal standards of compliance. Upholding economic and social rights in particular imposes an affirmative obligation on states to meet basic needs, and this requires the implementation of practical strategies and methods to ensure that this outcome is achieved (Rubenstein 2004). Moreover, states cannot, for example, introduce macro-economic reforms or trade liberalization policies that would undermine their compliance with obligations under the ICESCR (Chinkin 2008, 41).

4. Ethnography is the study of a located society or culture over a significant period of time through participant observation or immersion. See Ackerly and True (2010).

5. Laura Shepherd's (2008, 383) research on the neoliberal framing of UN Security Council Resolution 1325 is an exception, although the political economy analysis is deployed mainly as discursive critique. Important exceptions are Roberts (2012) and Jacobsen (2012).

6. This is a complex phenomenon, certain aspects of which were addressed in the Special Rapporteur on Violence Against Women's 2007 annual report (SRVAW 2007). See also AWID's (2008) study based on the responses of more than 1,600 women's rights activists globally.

Chapter 3

1. The United Nations Development Fund for Women discusses this relationship between masculinity and gender-based violence in "Masculinity and Gender-Based Violence UNIFEM Fact Sheet 5, 2001," available online.

2. The UK Equality and Human Rights Commission (2009) study found that the finance sector in the United Kingdom was characterized by greater occupational concentration than the economy as a whole.

Chapter 4

1. Number of trafficking cases worldwide are estimated to be twenty-seven million (Bernat and Zhilina 2010, 186). Data collected by the US Department of Justice (2010, 190) state that 99 percent of sex trafficking victims are female and 70 percent are young (under the age of twenty-five). Most trafficking offenders are male, but

about 20 percent of sex trafficking suspects/offenders are female (US Department of Justice 2009).

2. Women and girls are 77 percent of those trafficked; 12 percent are boys, and 9 percent are men (with 2 percent not identified by sex or age). Eighty-seven percent of all human trafficking is for sex, and 28 percent is for forced labor. The number of forced labor victims who were trafficked equals 2.45 million.

3. For instance, in the Asia-Pacific region the number of women in poverty relative to men has risen (Cameron and Newman 2008, 38).

4. See Bernhard, Landolt, and Goldring's (2006) study of Latin American women migrants to Canada, which accidentally found that in one in three cases the need to escape from violent husbands triggered the woman's decision to migrate.

5. Only three countries in the Asia-Pacific region have ratified the ICMR, and globally, no western receiving countries have ratified it (Iredale and Piper 2003).

6. See the recommendations and best practice measures undertaken by states to address violence against migrant women workers in 2007 (UN 2007) and the new ILO Convention 189 Decent Work for Domestic Workers ratified in 2010 and discussed later in the chapter.

7. Trafficking is discussed in the Beijing Platform for Action in five out of the twelve critical areas of concern—"women and health," "violence against women," "women and armed conflict," "the human rights of women," and "the girl child"— but, importantly, not in the area of "women and the economy."

8. The ILO Report (International Labour Organization 2010) estimates that domestic workers constitute between 4 and 10 percent of the total employment in developing countries and up to 2.5 percent in industrialized countries.

Chapter 5

1. The same can be said of men, however, with respect to other secondary manufacturing industries such as car production.

2. The femicide in Ciudad Juarez still continues today. According to Amnesty International, over 370 women have been found murdered between 1993 and 2005. See http://www.athenaresearchgroup.org/murdersinmexico.htm. See also Albuquerque and Vemala (2008).

3. Community surveys provided circumstantial evidence of the sex trade in Madang, Papua New Guinea (see Sullivan et al. "Tinpis Maror," 53. Observational evidence of a sex trade in Wewak (Papua New Guinea) (Sullivan et al., 2005, 109). In Papua New Guinea, seafarers and local women are a high-risk group for HIV/AIDS due to the sex industry in fisheries (Sullivan and Ram-Bidesi 2008, 44).

4. Herbert (2007, 3) cites an example: "One man from Malaysia took one small girl to the camp. He slept with her there. Her parents were included in this. This man from Malaysia abused her and gave her money, videos, clothes. This happened because her mother and father like the money. This man would like to take this girl overseas with him (to live) when it is time for his holidays. This girl is between 11 and 15 years of age-maybe 13?"

5. Decent work has been an overarching principle of the International Labour Organization (ILO) and their operations since 1999. See ILO, 2006, "Decent Work Pilot Programme," http://www.ilo.org/public/english/bureau/dwpp/ (accessed August 9, 2011).

Chapter 6

1. Specifically, the project intends to expand the cargo-handling capacity of Lae port by building a tidal basin and improving the facilities at the port.

2. For a recent report on the impacts of budget cuts on domestic violence funding in the United Kingdom, see Towers and Walby (2012).

3. At the time of writing, Switzerland, Germany, Denmark, and Sweden were seriously discussing adopting mandatory gender quotas for corporate boards.

Chapter 7

1. According to Ron Redmond, spokesperson from the United Nations Agency for Refugees (UNHCR). See True (2009a).

2. This is the working definition used by the International Criminal Court and the Criminal Tribunals for the former Yugoslavia and for Rwanda, and the Special Court of Sierra Leone.

3. See the United Nations ECOSOC draft resolution (E/2004/L.14).

4. Michael Van Rooyen, director of the Harvard Humanitarian Initiative, which sends doctors to Congo to treat rape victims, quoted in *The Atlantic*, June 2011.

5. The UN interagency initiative comprises all relevant UN agencies working on sexual violence in conflict. UNIFEM (UN Development Fund for Women), UN Action Against Sexual Violence in Conflict, and UNDPKO (UN Department of Peacekeeping Operations), *Addressing Conflict-Related Sexual Violence: An Analytical Inventory of Peacekeeping Practice* (New York: UNIFEM, UN Action Against Sexual Violence in Conflict, UNDPKO, 2010).

6. For example, Dolan argues that economically marginalized men in northern Uganda welcomed the chance to restore their traditional male identity by following warmongers and becoming soldiers. See also the film *Gender Against Men* (2009). The film was produced by the Refugee Law Project (RLP), University of Makerere, Kampala, Uganda, and documents sexual violence against men in the conflict of the Great Lakes region.

7. The study was a demographic and health survey partly funded by the US government. The authors used current population estimates, which put Congo's population at around 70 million, to extrapolate that as many as 1.8 million Congolese women had been raped, with up to 433,785 raped in the one-year period—which would mean almost a rape a minute.

8. Nicky Dahrendorf, UN Action to End Sexual Violence coordinator in the Congo, interviewed in Bechler (2008).

9. OHCHR Expert Workshop on the Elimination of Violence Against Women, United Nations, Geneva, November 24–25, 2010.

10. The study analyzed information collected from 4,311 female rape victims treated in Panzi Hospital in South Kivu province over a four-year period.

11. This cross-sectional, population-based, cluster survey of 998 adults aged eighteen years or older used structured interviews and questionnaires, conducted over a four-week period in March 2010. Rates of reported sexual violence were 39.7 percent among women and 23.6 percent among men at 95 percent confidence interval.

12. For guides and examples see http://www.palgrave.com/methodology/doing-feministresearch.

1. Ban Ki Moon (2009) told the council in a message to a day-long open session on women, peace, and security delivered by Deputy Secretary-General Asha-Rose Migiro: "Women are likely to put gender issues on the agenda, set different priorities and possibly bridge the political divide more effectively. Experience also suggests that women's contributions in post-conflict situations can make a critical difference to community survival and reconstruction."

2. Anne-Marie Goetz, chief governance and security advisor, UNIFEM, quoted in Kurtzleben (2009).

3. For instance, Ghobarah, Huth, and Russett (2003) show that the risk of death and disability from infectious diseases rises sharply in conflict-affected countries, and that women and children are the majority of long-term victims.

4. These findings are indicative, based on a 2003 random survey of 388 Liberian women in refugee camps (UNFPA 2006).

5. These findings are indicative, based on a survey of 410 IDPs in Cartagena, Colombia, in 2003 (UNFPA 2006).

6. The "Women's Priorities in the Peace Process and Reconstruction in Darfur" statement, December 30, 2005, Abuja, states: "Wealth includes human resources, human capital, land as well as surface and underground natural resources. For the women of Darfur, wealth is of vital importance because the women are a factor of production; they are involved in all areas of activity and constitute nearly 60 per cent of the labor force in the agricultural and animal resource sectors. Yet, women do not have anything to show for their immense contributions to the economic service sectors such as financing, training, savings for production and production protection, as well as social service sector and infrastructure."

7. For a gender-sensitive study of displaced households in Colombia, see Ibanez and Moya (2006).

8. See Patricia Justino and Philip Verwimp (2006), based on panel data on Rwanda following the same households before and after conflict. Bruck and Schindler (2009) and Bundervoet (2006) find similar results for Mozambique.

9. Bruck and Vothknecht (2011) use the UNCP/PRIO armed conflict dataset and existing, albeit limited, quantitative data and qualitative case studies.

10. Annan et al. (2010, 877) analyze the gender differences in the postconflict impacts of war and reintegration on Lord's Resistance Army (LRA) soldiers in Uganda with a quantitative dataset building on earlier qualitative studies. During conflict they found that "unlike males . . . females have few civilian opportunities and so they see little adverse economic impact of recruitment" into the armed group. Negative economic effects persist in the postconflict period for soldiers especially where opportunities for schooling and work experience have been lost. Males returning from the LRA were well behind their peers. But this is not the case for most females, however, who appear to have had few economic opportunities prior to and during the conflict if they were not abducted. See also Mazurana and Carlson (2008).

11. The United Nations' zero-tolerance policy bans UN staff and personnel from exchanging money, employment, goods, services, and other assistance for sex, and from having sex with minors. It also "strongly discourages" any sexual relationships

between UN personnel and local men or women older than the age of eighteen. See United Nations Secretary-General (2003) and United Nations General Assembly (2006). The United Nations increasingly prefers the term *transactional sex* to describe the activities prohibited by the zero-tolerance policy, although it is unclear what constitutes the dividing line between a "real" and a transactional relationship; see Jennings (2008).

12. The proxy variables for women's rights are (1) women's equality judged by average lower fertility rates, (2) the percentage of women in the labor force, and (3) the difference between women's and men's literacy and some descriptive of the trend for the percentage of women in parliament.

13. UNIFEM promoted electoral quotas for women representatives in Timor-Leste in conjunction with the local women's movement, while another UN agency in Timor, the Electoral Affairs Division, strongly opposed any such affirmative action. For a fuller background to this story see Hall and True (2009); True (2009).

14. In 2007, the prime minister, Xanana Gusmao, and the president, José Ramos Horta, even spoke out against domestic violence and featured it on campaign posters: *Hapara Violensia Kontra Feto* ("Stop Violence Against Women").

15. In postgenocide Rwanda, fertility increased, but the evidence points to a child replacement effect only for lost sons in the decade after (Bruck and Schindler 2011). Traditional gender divisions of labor within family households persist as well. Schindler (2010) finds that in areas where there is a shortage of male partners, young, unmarried women engage in traditional feminine activities conforming to gender stereotypes (although, interestingly, she finds less gendered allocation of labor among female-headed households).

16. Although 33 percent of UNTAET international civilian officials were women, only 11 percent of UNTAET East Timorese staff were women, with just 4 percent in the civilian police force and 2.4 percent in the peacekeeping force (Charlesworth 2009: 23–24).

17. A second woman UN envoy, Ameenah Haq, has since 2010 been appointed to oversee UN operations in East Timor.

18. See the 2008 film *Pray the Devil Back to Hell: Women, War and Peace in Liberia*: www.praythedevilbacktohell.com/.

19. Women make up just 9 percent of the 14,000 police officers and 2 percent of the 85,000 military personnel in UN peace operations. The United Nations has set the goal of 20 percent female participation in police/military personnel operations by 2014 (see Cordell 2009).

20. At the end of the civil war, women's employment in the government sector was very low, representing 0.8 percent in the judiciary, 5.3 percent in bureaus and agencies, and 10.3 percent in ministries. See also http://www.visionews.net/india's-female-peacekeepers-inspire-liberian-girls/.

21. Potential gender inequalities in reparations programs could readily be institutionalized if, for instance, the programs considered land ownership, the number of dependents (i.e., head-of-household status), and the loss of opportunity and income in ascertaining compensation given the gender discrimination in these rights and status prior to conflict (Rubio-Marin 2006).

22. Nicky Dahrendorf, UN Action to End Sexual Violence coordinator in the Congo, interviewed in Rosemary Bechler (2008).

Chapter 9

1. Some scholars working out of complexity/chaos theory even argue that natural disasters such as earthquakes and tsunamis are "manmade" in that they are created by interactions between crisis drivers and human activities.

2. For how a country's low level of economic development, poor quality of governance institutions, and high degree of inequality increases the death toll from earthquakes, see Anbarci, Escaleras, and Register (2005).

3. Indonesia's national disaster recording agency listed 128,645 people dead, 37,063 missing, and 532,898 displaced (USAID 2005). In Sri Lanka, the government reported 31,147 dead, 4,115 missing, and 519,063 displaced (USAID 2005).

4. Rofi, Doocy, and Robinson (2006, 347) carried out a survey of households displaced by the tsunami in Aceh province in 2005 and gathered data on the sex and age of household members who were victims of the tsunami. They found that two-thirds of those who died were female, and that it was primarily people nine years and younger and sixty years and older who were killed during the tsunami. Oxfam International (2005, 4) also gathered sex-disaggregated data in the tsunami-affected areas of Aceh, India, and Sri Lanka. The findings confirm about two-thirds of the dead were female. Oxfam International (2005, 6) also found that in the heaviest affected areas the death rates of females outnumbered males by four to one, and in one area of India the only people to die were women.

5. In her Sri Lankan field research, Sarah Fisher noted the apprehension of women in talking about their experiences, fearing it would threaten their safety further, and so limited her data collection to persons involved in tsunami-related gender-based violence initiatives (2010, 8).

6. Oxfam International (2005, 5) notes that women forced into marriage and childbearing at a younger age, with less of an interval between pregnancies, generally have poorer lifelong health, education, and access to productive resources.

7. Dr P. Manorama, a Chennai-based doctor, quoted in Manecksha (2005). See also CATAW (2007, 19).

8. For example, Sri Lanka has a Gender Inequality Index (GII) value of 0.419, ranking it 74 out of 146 countries in the 2011 index. This measure is based on gender-based inequalities in three dimensions: reproductive health, empowerment, and economic activity. Gender-based violence is very common in the most affected tsunami countries. See Hussein (2000); UNFPA Asia and Pacific Regional Office (2010, 69).

9. Personal communication with Lois Herbert, Battered Women's Trust, November 23, 2011.

10. Personal phone interview, Canterbury Civil Defence and Emergency Management Group, November 22, 2011.

11. Personal phone interview, Christchurch Women's Refuge, November 22, 2011.

12. Personal phone interview, Battered Women's Trust, November 23, 2011.

13. Personal phone interview, Otautahi Women's Refuge, November 22, 2011.

14. Personal communication with Lois Herbert, Battered Women's Trust, November 23, 2011.

15. Personal communication with Lois Herbert, Battered Women's Trust, November 23, 2011.

16. Personal communication with Lois Herbert, Battered Women's Trust, November 23, 2011.

17. Personal phone interview, Battered Women's Trust, November 23, 2011.

REFERENCES

Abirafeh, Lina. 2007. "Freedom Is Only Won from the Inside: Domestic Violence in Post Conflict Afghanistan." In *Change from Within: Diverse Perspectives on Domestic Violence in Muslim Communities*, ed. M. B. Alkhateeb and S. E. Abugideiri. Great Falls, VA: Peaceful Families Project.

Ackerly, Brooke. 2008. *Universal Human Rights in a World of Difference*. Cambridge: Cambridge University Press.

Ackerly, Brooke, and Jacqui True. 2008. "Reflexivity in Practice: Power and Ethics in Feminist Research on International Relations." *International Studies Review* 10: 581–600.

Ackerly, Brooke, and Jacqui True. 2010. *Doing Feminist Research in Political and Social Science*. New York: Palgrave.

Action Aid. 2007. *Violence Against Women in the Post-Tsunami Context: People's Report, India, Maldives, Puntland (Somalia), Sri Lanka, Thailand*. London: Action Aid, June 4.

African Development Forum (ADF VI). 2008. *Action on Gender Equality, Women's Empowerment and Ending Violence Against Women in Africa. Consensus Statement and Plan of Action*. UN Conference Centre, Addis Ababa, Ethiopia, November 21.

Agarwal, Bina. 1994. "Gender and Command Over Property: A Critical Gap in Economic Analysis and Policy in South Asia." *World Development* 22, no. 10: 1455–78.

Aker, Dee, and Jennifer Freeman. 2010. "For Real Global Security, Put Women in Their Place—at the Negotiating Table." *Christian Science Monitor*, December 3.

Albuquerque, P. H., and P. R. Vemala. 2008. "A Statistical Evaluation of Femicide Rates in Mexican Cities along the US-Mexico Border." *Canadian Law and Economics Association (CLEA), 2008 Meetings*, October 5.

Allen, Katie. 2009. "Could Crash Spell Doom for City's Boys' Club?: Years of Macho Culture Ended in Financial Implosion. Now MPs Are to Examine Sexism in the Square Mile, but Is It Ready to Change?" *The Observer*, July 26.

Amnesty International. 2004. *Rwanda: "Marked for Death," Rape Survivors Living With HIV/AIDS in Rwanda*. AFR 47/007/2004. April 5.

Amnesty International. 2011a. *Aftershocks: Women Speak out Against Sexual Violence in Haiti's Camps.* London: Amnesty International.

Amnesty International. 2011b. *"Where is the Dignity in That?" Women in Solomons Islands Slums Denied Sanitation and Safety.* London: Amnesty International, September.

Anbarci, Nejat, Monica Escaleras, and Charles A. Register. 2005. "Earthquake Fatalities: The Interaction of Nature and Political Economy." *Journal of Public Economics* 89, no. 9–10: 1907–33.

Anderlini, Sanam Naraghi. 2010. *WDR Gender Background Paper.* Background paper for the 2011 World Development Report.

Anderson, Bridget, and Julia O'Connell Davidson. 2003. *Is Trafficking in Human Beings Demand Driven? A Multi-Country Pilot Study 29–32.* IOM Migration Research Series No. 15. Geneva: International Organization for Migration.

Annan, Jeannie, Christopher Blattman, Dyan Mazurana, and Khristopher Carlson. 2011. "Civil War, Reintegration, and Gender in Northern Uganda." *Journal of Conflict Resolution* 55, no. 6: 877–908.

Apodaca, Clair. 1998. "Measuring Women's Economic and Social Rights Achievement." *Human Rights Quarterly* 20, no. 1: 139–72.

Arend, Elizabeth. 2011. *International Financial Institutions (IFIs) and Gender Based Violence (GBV): A Primer.* Washington, DC: Gender Action.

Arend, Elizabeth, and Julie Ajinkya. 2011. *The World Bank and Gender Based Violence Case Study: The Democratic Republic of Congo.* Washington, DC: Gender Action.

Armstrong, Jo, and Sylvia Walby. 2012. *Gender Quotas in Management Boards.* European Parliament FEMM/Women's Rights Committee.

Arnold, Christina, and Andrea M. Bertone. 2002. "Addressing the Sex Trade in Thailand: Some Lessons Learned from NGOs, Part I." *Gender Issues* (Winter): 26–52.

Arteaga, Ana Maria. 2010. *Andean Migrant Women: Context, Policies and Migration Management.* Abriendo Mundos: Oxfam.

Ascoly, Nina, and Chantal Finney (eds). 2005. *Made by Women: Gender, the Global Garment Industry and the Movement for Women Workers' Rights.* Amsterdam: Clean Clothes Campaign.

Asian Development Bank. 2007. Papua New Guinea: Lae Port Development Project. Report and Recommendation of the President to the Board of Directors. Manila: ADB Office of Pacific Operations.

Askin, K. D. 2006. "Prosecuting Gender Crimes Committed in Darfur: Holding Leaders Accountable for Sexual Violence." In *Genocide in Darfur: Investigating the Atrocities in the Sudan,* ed. S. Totten and E. Markusen. New York: Routledge.

Asis, Maruja M. B. 2008. "Human Trafficking in East and South-East Asia: Searching for Structural Factors." In *Trafficking in Humans: Social, Cultural and Political Dimensions,* ed. Sally Cameron and Edward Newman. New York: United Nations University Press.

AWID. 2008. *Religious Fundamentalisms Exposed: Ten Myths Revealed About Religious Fundamentalisms.* Toronto: AWID.

Bachelet, Michelle. 2011. "UN Women's Bachelet Outlines New Peacebuilding Initiative." March 3. http://www.unwomen.org/2011/03/un-womens-bachelet-outlines-new-peacebuilding-initiative/.

Bacheva, Fidanka, Manana Kochladze, and Suzanna Dennis. 2006. *Boom Time Blues: Big Oil's Gender Impacts in Azerbaijan, Georgia and Sakhalin.* Praha and Washington, DC: CEE Bankwatch Network and Gender Action.

Bales, Kevin. 1999. *Disposable People: New Slavery in the Global Economy.* Berkeley: University of California Press.

Balakrishnan, Radhika. 2005. *Why MES with human rights? Integrating Macroeconomic strategies with human rights.* Marymount Manhattan College

Banister, Judith. 2004. "Shortage of Girls in China Today." *Journal of Population Research* 21, no. 2: 19–45.

Basile, Kathleen C. 2009. "Advancing the Study of Violence Against Women: Response to Jordan." *Violence Against Women* 15, no. 4: 428–33.

Bastick, Megan, Karin Grimm, and Rahel Kunz. 2007. *Sexual Violence in Armed Conflict: Global Overview and Implications for the Security Sector.* Geneva: Geneva Centre for the Democratic Control of Armed Forces.

BBC News. 2004. "Chinese Given Perks to Have Girls." August 12.

BBC News. 2006. "Children Have Been subjected to Rape and Prostitution by United Nations Peacekeepers in Haiti and Liberia, a BBC Investigation Has Found." November 30.

BBC News. 2011. "Bangladesh Wife-Mauling Suspect Sumon Found Dead." December 5.

Bechler, Rosemary. 2008 "Sexual Violence: Not Just a Gender Issue." June 5. www.opendemocracy.net/blog/rosemary-bechler/2008/06/05/sexual-violence-not-just-a-gender-issue.

Bennhold, Katrin. 2011. "Recession Seen Taking Toll on Gender Equality." *New York Times*, April 26.

Berik, G. 2004. "Mature Export-Led Growth and Gender Wage Inequality in Taiwan." *Feminist Economics* 6, no. 3: 1–26.

Berman, J. 2003. "(Un) popular Strangers and Crises (Un) bounded: Discourses of Sex Trafficking, the European Political Community and the Panicked State of the Modern State." *European Journal of International Relations* 9, no. 1: 37–86.

Bernard, Cheryl, Seth G. Jones, Olga Oliker, Cathryn Quantic Thurston, Brooke K. Stearns, and Kristen Cordell. 2008. *Women and Nation-Building.* Santa Monica, CA: RAND Corporation.

Bernard, J., S. G. Jones, O. Oliker, C. Quantic Thurston, B. K. Stearns, K. Cordell, 2008. *Women and Nation-Building.* Stanford: RAND.

Bernat, Francis P., and Tatyana Zhilina. 2010. "Human Trafficking: The Local Becomes the Global." *Women and Criminal Justice* 20, no. 1–2: 2–9.

Bernhard, J., P. Landolt, and L. Goldring. 2006. "Transnational, Multi-Local Motherhood: Experiences of Separation and Reunification Among Latin American Families in Canada." *CERIS, Policy Matters*, no. 24 (January).

Bindel, Julie. 2010. "Iceland: The World's Most Feminist Country." *The Guardian*, March 25. http://www.guardian.co.uk/lifeandstyle/2010/mar/25/iceland-most-feminist-country.

Biroscak, B. J., P. K. Smith, H. Roznowski, J. Tucker, and G. Carlson. 2006. "Intimate Partner Violence Against Women: Findings from One State's ED Surveillance System." *Journal of Emergency Nursing* 32: 12–16.

Bishop, R., and L. Robinson. 1998. *Night Market, Sexual Cultures and the Thai Economic Miracle.* New York: Routledge.

Blanchard, Eric. 2003. "Gender, International Relations, and the Development of Feminist Security Theory." *Signs: Journal of Women, Culture and Society* 28, no. 4: 1281–99.

Bock, Gisela. 1983. "Racism and Sexism in Nazi Germany: Motherhood, Compulsory Sterilization, and the State." *Signs* 8, no. 3: 400–21.

Bollineni, Keerthi. 2010. *Gender Based Violence in Public Places: Acid Throwing.* New Delhi: CEQUIN.

Boonzaier, Florence. 2005. "Woman Abuse in South Africa: A Brief Contextual Analysis." *Feminism and Psychology* 15, no. 1: 99–103.

Boseley, Sarah. 2010. "A Revolution in Rights for Women." *The Guardian,* May 28.

Bott, Sarah, Andrew Morrison, and Mary Ellsberg. 2005. "Preventing and Responding to Gender-Based Violence in Middle and Low-Income Countries: A Global Review and Analysis." *World Bank Policy Research Working Paper.*

Bourke-Martignoni, Joanna. 2002. *Violence Against Women in Sri Lanka: Report Prepared for the Committee on the Elimination of Discrimination Against Women.* Geneva: World Organisation Against Torture.

Branigan, Tania. 2011. "China's Village of the Bachelors: No Wives in Sight in Remote Settlement." *The Guardian,* September 2.

Braun, Yvonne A. 2010. "Gender, Development, and Sex Work in Lesotho." *Equality, Diversity and Inclusion,* 29, no. 1: 78–96

Brothers for Life. 2011a. "Introduction." http://www.brothersforlife.org/.

Brothers for Life. 2011b. "Springboks Say No to Gender-Based Violence." News and Media. http://www.brothersforlife.org/.

Brothers for Life. 2011c. "Brothers for Life Gender-Based Violence Campaign: Men Can Change." News and Media. http://www.brothersforlife.org/.

Brown, J., J. Sorrell, and M. Raffaelli. 2005. "An Exploratory Study of Constructions of Masculinity, Sexuality and HIV/AIDS in Namibia, Southern Africa." *Culture, Health & Sexuality* 7, no. 6: 585–98.

Bruck, Tilman, and Kate Schindler. 2009. "Small Landholder Access in Post-War Northern Mozambique." *World Development* 37: 1379–89.

Bruck, Tilman, and Marc Vothknecht. 2011. "Impact of Violent Conflicts on Women's Economic Opportunities." In *Women and War: Power and Protection in the 21st Century,* ed. Kathleen Kuehnast, Chantal de Jonge Outdraat, and Helga Hernes, 85–114. Washington, DC: US Institute of Peace.

Buchanan, Ruth. 1995. "Border Crossings: NAFTA, Regulatory Restructuring, and the Politics of Place." *Indiana Journal of Global Legal Studies* 2, no. 2: 371–93.

Bundervoet, T. 2007. "Estimating Poverty in Burundi." *HiCN Working Paper 20.* University of Sussex, Falmer-Brighton.

Bureau of Justice Statistics. 2007. *Intimate Partner Violence in the United States.* Washington, DC: US Department of Justice.

Buvinic, Mayra/World Bank. 2009. "The Global Financial Crisis: Assessing Vulnerability for Women and Children, Identifying Policy Responses." Written statement to the Interactive Expert Panel on Emerging Issues: The Gender Perspectives on the Financial Crisis, held at the Commission on the Status of Women, 53rd Session, New York, March 2–13.

Cabrera, Patricia Muñoz. 2010. *Intersecting Violences: A Review of Feminist Theories and Debates on Violence against Women and Poverty in Latin America.* London: Central America Women's Network.

Camacho, A. S. 2005. "Ciudadana X, Gender Violence and the Denationalization of Women's Rights in Ciudad Juarez, Mexico." *New Centennial Review* 5, no. 1: 259.

Cameron, Sally. 2008. "Trafficking of Women for Prostitution." In *Trafficking in Human$: Social, Cultural and Political Dimensions*, ed. Sally Cameron and Edward Newman. New York: United Nations University Press.

Cameron, Sally, and Edward Newman. 2008. "Trafficking in Humans: Structural Factors." In *Trafficking in Human$: Social, Cultural and Political Dimensions*, ed. Sally Cameron and Edward Newman. New York: United Nations University Press.

Cammaert, Major General Patrick. 2008. "Women Targeted or Affected by Armed Conflict: What Role for Military Peacekeepers?" Conference Summary. Wilton Park, Sussex, United Kingdom, May 27–29.

Capie, David. 2011. "Small Arms, Violence and Gender in Papua New Guinea: Towards a Research Agenda." *Asia Pacific Viewpoint* 52, no. 1: 42–55.

Caprioli, Mary, and Kimberly Douglass. 2008. "Nation Building and Women: The Effect of Intervention on Women's Agency." *Foreign Policy Analysis* 4, no. 1: 45–65.

Care International. 2010. *From Resolution to Reality: Lessons Learned From Afghanistan, Nepal and Uganda on Women's Participation in Peacebuilding and Post-Conflict Governance*. London: Care International.

Carpenter, Charli. 2007. "Setting the Advocacy Agenda: Theorizing Issue Emergence and Non-Emergence in Transnational Advocacy Networks." *International Studies Quarterly* 51: 99–120.

Carr, Jill. 2011. "Recession Is Blamed as UK Domestic Violence Soars By 35% in a Year." *Forbes Solicitors UK*, July 20.

Casey, E., and T. Smith. 2010. "'How Can I Not?': Men's Pathways to Involvement in Anti-Violence Against Women Work." *Violence Against Women*, 16, no. 8: 953–73.

CATAW. 2005. "Briefing Note for UNIFEM Consultation in Colombo." New York, May 13.

CATAW. 2007. *After the Wave: Moving On, Women's Voices in Sri Lanka*. Colombo: CATAW.

Causa, Adriana, and J. Ojam. 2008. *Compiladoras: Mujeres Piqueteras: Trayectorias, Identidades, participación y redes*. Buenos Aires: Ediciones Baobab.

CEDAW. 2005. "Report on Mexico Produced by the Committee on the Elimination of Discrimination Against Women Under Article 8 of the Optional Protocol to the Convention, and Reply From the Government of Mexico." CEDAW/C/2005/OP.8/MEXICO, United Nations, January 27.

CEDAW. 2006. "Concluding Comments on the Philippines Report, With Reference to Women in the Mindanao Province's Limited Access to Justice." CEDAW/C/PHI/5–6, United Nations, August 25.

Centre on Housing Rights and Evictions (COHRE). 2010. *A Place in the World: The Right to Adequate Housing as an Essential Element of a Life Free from Domestic Violence—the Cases of Argentina, Brazil and Columbia*. Geneva: COHRE.

Chan, E. K. L., X. Li, J. X. Gao, and T. Liu. 2008. "Sexual Violence Against Women and Children in China." *Collection of Women's Studies* 87, no. 4: 76–82.

Chant, Sylvia. 2001. "Men in Crisis? Reflections on Masculinities, Work and Family in Northwest Costa Rica." In *Men at Work: Labour, Masculinities, Development*, ed. Cecile Jackson. London: Frank Cass.

Chappell, Louise. 2008. "The International Criminal Court: A New Arena for Transforming Gender Justice." In *Global Governance: Feminist Perspectives*, ed. Shirin M. Rai and Georgina Waylen. Basingstoke: Macmillan Palgrave.

Charlesworth, Hilary. 2009. "Worlding Women in International Law." In *Gender and Global Politics in Asia-Pacific*, ed. Bina D'Costa and Katrina Lee Koo. New York: Palgrave.

Chávez, Franz. 2011. "Andean Migrant Women Create Opportunities." *IPS News*, December 1.

China National Bureau of Statistics (CNBS). 2004. *Women and Men in China: Facts and Figures*. Beijing: Department of Population, Social Science and Technology and the National Bureau of Statistics, August.

Chin, Christine. 1998. *In Service and Servitude: Foreign Female Domestic Servants in Malaysia*. New York: Columbia University Press.

Chinkin, Christine. 2008. *The Protection of Economic, Social and Cultural Rights Post-Conflict*. Geneva: United Nations Commission on Human Rights Gender Unit.

Christchurch Women's Refuge. 2011. "Media Release." March 2.

Chuang, Janie. 2006. "Beyond a Snapshot: Preventing Human Trafficking in the Global Economy." *Indiana Journal of Global Legal Studies* 13, no. 1 (Winter): 137–63.

Clark, K. A., A. K. Biddle, and S. L. Martin. 2002. "A Cost-Benefit Analysis of the Violence Against Women Act of 1994." *Violence Against Women* 8, no. 4: 417–28.

Clinton, Hillary. 2011. "It's Time to Get Tough on Violence Against Women." *The Guardian*, December 10.

Cockburn, Cynthia. 2010. "Gender Relations as Causal in Militarization and War." *International Journal of Politics* 12, no. 2: 139–57.

Cockburn, Cynthia. 2012. *Antimilitarism: Politics and Gender Dynamics of Movements to End War and Redefine Peace*. Basingstoke: Palgrave.

Cockburn, Cynthia, and Anne Oakley. 2011. "The Culture of Masculinity Costs All Too Much to Ignore." *The Guardian*, November 25.

Coleman, Isobel. 2004. "The Payoff from Women's Rights." *Foreign Affairs* 83, no. 3: 80–95.

Collins, Simon. 2006. "Civil Defence Adds Dealing with Family Violence to Disaster Planning." *New Zealand Herald*, January 19.

Congress of Women. 2000. "First Congress of Women of Timor Loro Sa'e." Plan of Action, June.

Connell, R. W. 1998. "Masculinities and Globalization." *Men and Masculinities* 1, no. 3: 3–23.

Coomaraswamy, Radhika. 2003. "Fishing in the Stream of Migration: Modern Forms of Trafficking and Women's Freedom of Movement." International Association of Refugee Law Judges 5th Conference, Wellington, New Zealand, October 22.

Cordell, Kristen. 2009. "Liberia Women Peacekeepers and Human Security." Op-Ed. *Open Democracy*, August.

Cordell, Kristen. 2010. *Best Practices for Gender Mainstreaming at the United Nations Mission in Liberia (UNMIL) From 2003 to 2008*. New York: United Nations Best Practices Unit.

Couldrey, M., and T. Morris (eds.). 2007. "Sexual Violence Weapon of War, Impediment to Peace." *Forced Migration Review* 27 (Oxford Refugee Studies Centre).

Covert, Bryce. 2011. "Local Governments Slash Funding for Domestic Violence Survivors." *The Nation*, October 19.

D'Almeida, Kanya. 2011a. "To Women's Rights, Financial Institutions Pay Lip Service Only." *IPS News*, November 30.

D'Almeida, Kanya. 2011b. "For Big Financial Institutions, Profits Trumps Women's Rights." *IPS News*, November 30.

Davidson, Karl. 2011. "White Ribbon Day Is Effective for Combating Family Violence." Families Commission, Wellington, November 24.

Davis, Ian, Kala Periris De Costa, Khurshid Alam, Madhavi Malalgoda Ariyabandu, Mihir R. Bhatt, Rita Schneider-Sliwa, and Satchit Balsari. 2005. *Tsunami, Gender, and Recovery*. Special Issue for International Day for Disaster Risk Reduction, Ahmedabad. October 12. http://www.southasiadisasters.net.

Day, T. 1995. *The Health-related Costs of Violence Against Women in Canada: The Tip of the Iceberg*. London, Ontario: Centre for Research on Violence Against Women and Children.

De Cicco, Gabriel. 2009. "Ciudad Juarez: Finally Steps Towards Justice." *AWID Issues and Analysis*, December 18.

Derks, Annuska. 2000. *Combatting Trafficking in South-East Asia: A Review of Policy and Programme Responses*. Geneva: IOM Research Series.

Desyllas, Moshula Capous. 2007. "A Critique of the Global Trafficking Discourse and U.S. Policy." *Journal of Sociology & Social Welfare* 34, no. 4: 57–79.

Devlin, Claire, and Robert Elgie. 2008. "The Effect of Increased Women's Representation in Parliament: The Case of Rwanda." *Parliamentary Affairs* 62, no. 2: 237–54.

Diep, Hanh. 2004. "We Pay—The Economic Manipulation of International and Domestic Laws to Sustain Sex Trafficking." *Loyola University Chicago International Law Review* 2, no. 2: 309–31.

Dinan, Kinsey Alden. 2008. "Globalization and National sovereignty: From Migration to Trafficking." In *Trafficking in Human$: Social, Cultural and Political Dimensions*, ed. Sally Cameron and Edward Newman. New York: United Nations University Press.

Dolan, Chris. 2002. "Collapsing Masculinities and Weak States: A Case Study of Northern Uganda." In *Masculinities Matter: Men, Gender, and Development*, ed. Frances Cleaver. London: Zed Books.

Ebrahim, Zofeen. 2010. "Pakistan—Women Advocate for Law Against Acid Attacks." *IPS News*, May 31.

The Economist. 2004. "The New Face of AIDS." November 25.

The Economist. 2006. "Women in the Workforce: The Importance of Sex: Forget China, India and the Internet: Economic Growth Is Driven by Women." April 12.

Eetgerink, Tisha. 2006. "Zuma's AIDS Remark 'Hugely Damaging.'" *Mail and Guardian*, April 5.

Ehrenreich, Barbara, and Arlie Russell Hochschild. 2004. *Global Woman: Nannies, Maids, and Sex Workers in the New Economy*. New York: Henry Holt/Macmillan.

Ehrhardt, Anke A., Diane di Mauro, Raymond Smith, and MAFLI. 2011. *HIV Prevention, Gender, and Leadership: The M·A·C AIDS Fund Fellowship in South Africa*. HIV Center Grand Rounds Series, March 17.

El Jack, A. 2003. *Gender and Armed Conflict: Overview Report.* Bridge Development—Gender, Institute of Development Studies, August.

Elias, Juanita. 2008. "Struggles Over the Rights of Foreign Domestic Workers in Malaysia: The Possibilities and Limitation of 'Rights Talk.'" *Economy and Society* 37, no. 2: 282–303.

Elliot, James R., and Jeremy Pais. 2006. "Race, Class and Hurricane Katrina: Social Differences in Human Responses to Disaster." *Social Science Research* 35: 295–321.

Ellsberg, Mary, and Lori Heise. 2005. *Researching Violence Against Women: A Practical Guide for Researchers and Activists.* Geneva: World Health Organization and PATH.

Elson, Diane. 2002. "Gender Justice, Human Rights, and Neoliberal Economic Policies." In *Gender Justice, Development, and Rights,* ed. Maxine Molyneux and Shahra Razavi. New York: Oxford University Press.

Enarson, Elaine. 2000. *Gender and Natural Disasters: Working Paper 1.* Geneva: ILO Recovery and Reconstruction Department.

End Child Prostitution and Trafficking USA (ECPAT-USA). 2010. *The State Department's 2010 Trafficking in Persons Report Is Out,* June 20.

Enloe, Cynthia. 1989. *Bananas, Beaches and Bases: Making Feminist Sense of International Politics.* London: Pandora.

Enloe, Cynthia. 2004. *Maneuvers: The International Politics of Militarizing Women's Lives.* Berkeley: University of California Press.

Enloe, Cynthia. 2010. *Nimo's War, Emma's War: Making Feminist Sense of the Iraq War.* Berkeley: University of California Press.

Equality and Human Rights Commission. 2009. *Financial Services Inquiry.* London, United Kingdom: EOHRC.

Eriksson Baaz, Maria, and Maria Stern. 2009. "Why Do Soldiers Rape? Masculinity, Violence and sexuality in the Armed Forces in the Congo (DRC)." *International Studies Quarterly* 53: 495–518.

Eriksson Baaz, Maria, & Maria Stern. 2010. *The Complexity of Violence: A Critical Analysis of Sexual Violence in the Democratic Republic of Congo (DRC).* Working paper on Gender-Based Violence, Nordic Africa Institute and SIDA, May.

European Commission. 2010. *More Women in Senior Positions: Key to Economic Stability and Growth.* Brussels: European Communities Directorate-General Employment, Social Affairs and Equal Opportunity.

Fawcett Society. 2011. *A Life Raft for Women's Equality.* London: Fawcett Society.

Felten-Biermann, Claudia. 2006. "Gender and Natural Disaster: Sexualised Violence and the Tsunami." *Development* 49, no. 3: 82–86.

Fernández-Kelly, Maria Patricia. 1983. *For We Are Sold, I and My People: Women and Industry in Mexico's Frontier.* Albany: State University of New York Press.

Fernández-Kelly, Maria Patricia. 1993. "New Alternatives for Latin American Development: Women in the Maquiladora Industries." In *New Research: Latin American Women's Studies,* ed. Silvia Arrom, Mary Ellen Brown, and Darlene J. Sadlier. Indiana: Women's Studies Program.

Fiji Law Reform Commission. 2004. FLRC media release. "Violence Against Women in Fiji." Suva: Fiji Law Reform Commission.

Finnemore, Martha, and Kathryn Sikkink. 1998. "International Norm Dynamics and Political Change." *International Organization* 54, no. 2: 887–917.

Fisher, Sarah. 2010. "Violence Against Women and Natural Disasters: Findings From Post-Tsunami Sri Lanka." *Violence Against Women* 16, no. 8: 902–18.

Fitzsimons, Tracy. 2007. Engendering Justice and Security After War. In *Constructing Justice and Security After War*, ed. Charles V. Call. Washington, DC: US Institute for Peace.

Flood, Michael. 2010. *Where Men Stand: Men's Roles in Ending Violence Against Women.* White Ribbon Prevention Research Series, No. 2. Sydney: White Ribbon.

Floro, Maria, and G. Dymski. 2000. "Financial Crisis, Gender, and Power: An Analytical Framework." *World Development* 28, no. 7: 1369–83.

Foreign Policy. 2011. *Special Report: The FP Top 100 Global Thinkers*, Washington, DC: Foreign Policy, December.

Fraser, Ian. 1997. "The Struggle for Control of Solomon Island Forests." *The Contemporary Pacific* 9, no. 1: 39–72.

Fraser, Nancy. 2009. "Feminism, Capitalism and the Cunning of History." *New Left Review* 56 (March/April): 97–117.

Frey, Bruno, David A. Savage, and Benno Torgler. 2010. "Interaction of Natural Survival Instincts and Internalized Social Norms Exploring the *Titanic* and *Lusitania* Disasters." *Proceedings of the National Academy of Sciences of the USA* 107, no. 11 (March 16): 4862–65.

Garcia-Moreno, Claudia, H. A. F. M. Jansen, M. Ellsberg, L. Heise, and C. Watts. 2005. *WHO Multi-Country Study on Women's Health and Domestic Violence: Initial Results on Prevalence, Health Outcomes and Women's Responses.* Geneva: World Health Organization.

Gender Action. 2011. *Gender Action Link: IFIs and Gender Based Violence.* Washington, DC: Gender Action.

Gender Action and Friends of the Earth International. 2011. *Broken Promises: Gender Impacts of the World Bank-Financed West-African and Chad-Cameroon Pipelines.* Washington and Amsterdam: Gender Action and Friends of the Earth International.

Geneva Centre for the Democratic Control of Armed Forces (DCAF). 2005. Women in an Insecure World, eds. Marie Vlachovà and Lea Biason. Geneva: DCAF.

Gentleman, Amelia. 2009. "Growth in Violence Against Women Feared as Recession Hits." *The Guardian*, March 4.

Gerome, Rebecca. 2011. "Limit Arms Exports to Reduce Violence Against Women." *Atlantic-Community.org*, April 14.

Gettleman, Jeffrey. 2011. "Congo Study Sets Estimate for Rapes Much Higher." *New York Times*, May 12.

Ghobarah, Hazem Adam, Paul Huth, and Bruce Russett. 2003. "Civil Wars Kill and Maim People – Long After the Shooting Stops." *American Political Science Review*, no. 2 Vol. 97: pp. 189-202.

Ghosh, Bimal. 2010. *The Global Economic Crisis and Migration: Where Do We Go From Here?* Geneva: International Organization for Migration.

Glaberson, William. 2009. "The Recession Begins Flooding Into the Courts." *New York Times*, December 27. http://www.nytimes.com/2009/12/28/nyregion/28caseload.html?pagewanted=all.

Guilmoto, Christophe Z. 2007. "Characteristics of Sex-Ratio Imbalance in India and Future Scenarios." UNFPA Fourth Asia Pacific Conference on Reproductive and Sexual Health and Rights, Hyderabad, India, October 29–31, 2007.

Gupta, Ruchira. 2010. *Address to the Seminar on a Human Rights Approach to Combating Human Trafficking: Challenges and Opportunities; Implementing the Recommended Principles and Guidelines on Human Rights and Human Trafficking.* Geneva: United Nations Office of the High Commissioner for Human Rights, May 27–28. http://www.facebook.com/note.php?note_id=10150197447835018

Hajdinjak, Marco. 2002. *Smuggling in Southeast Europe: The Yugoslav Wars and the Development of Regional Criminal Networks in the Balkans.* Sofia: Centre for the Study of Democracy.

Hall, Nina. 2009. "East Timorese Women Challenge Domestic Violence." *Australian Journal of Political Science* 44, no. 2: 309–25.

Hall, N., and J. True. 2009. "Gender Mainstreaming in a Post-Conflict State: Toward Democratic Peace in Timor Leste." In *Gender and Global Politics in Asia-Pacific,* ed. K. Lee Koo and B. Da Costa. Basingstoke: Palgrave Macmillan.

Hampton, Tracy. 2005. "Agencies Speak out on Rape in Darfur." *Journal of the American Medical Association* 294, no. 5: 542–44.

Hancock, Peter, Sharon Middleton, and Jaime Moore. 2010. "Export Processing Zones (EPZs), Globalisation, Feminised Labour Markets and Working Conditions: A Study of Sri Lankan EPZ Workers." *Labour and Management in Development* 10: 1–22.

Handrahan, Lori. 2004. "Conflict, Gender, Ethnicity and Post-Conflict Reconstruction." *Security Dialogue: Special Issue: Gender and Security* 35, no. 4: 429–45.

Hansen, Lene. 2000. "The Little Mermaid's Silent Security Dilemma and the Absence of Gender in the Copenhagen School." *Millennium: Journal of International Studies* 29, no. 2: 285–305.

Harikrishnan, K. S. 2010. "India: Lay-Offs From Recession-Hit Gulf Lead to New Lives at Home." *IPS News,* February 9.

Harney, Claire. 2011. "The Impact of the Recession on Domestic Violence Against Women and Support Services in Ireland: An Exploratory Study." *Critical Social Thinking: Policy and Practice* 3: 26–39.

Harris-Rimmer, Susan. 2009. "After the Guns Fall Silent: Sexual and Gender-Based Violence in Timor-Leste." Issue Brief: Timor-Leste Area Violence Assessment No. 5, November.

Harvard Humanitarian Initiative. 2010. *Now, the World Is Without Me: Report on Rape in Congo.* New York Oxfam USA.

Hausmann, Richard, Laura Tyson, and Saadia Zahidi. 2010. *Global Gender Gap Report 2010.* World Economic Forum, Geneva, December.

Heise, Lori, and C. Garcia-Moreno. 2002. "Violence by Intimate Partners." In *World Report on Violence and Health,* ed. Etienne G. Krug, Linda L. Dahlberg, James A. Mercy, Anthony B. Zwi, and Rafael Lozano. Geneva: World Health Organization.

Herbert, T. 2007. *Commercial Sexual Exploitation of Children in the Solomon Islands: A Report Focussing on the Presence of the Logging Industry in a Remote Region.* Solomon Islands: Church of Melanesia.

Higate, Paul, and Marsha Henry. 2004. "Engendering (In)security in Peace Support Operations." *Security Dialogue* 34, no. 4: 481–98.

Hill, Amelia. 2011. "Women's Equality: Clock Is Turning Back as Cuts Bite, Says Fawcett Society." *The Guardian,* November 4.

Holmes, Gillian. 2010. "An Analytical Framing of 'Conflict-Related Sexual Violence' in Response to Security Council Resolution 1888." OHCHR Expert Workshop on the Elimination of Violence Against Women, United Nations, Geneva, November 24–25.

Holt, Maria. 2003. "Palestinian Women, Violence, and the Peace Process." *Development in Practice* 13, no. 2–3: 2623–38.

Hombrecher, Unal. 2007. *Overcoming Domestic Violence: A Global Challenge, Experiences and Recommendations from an International Project.* Frankfurt: Social Service Agency of the Protestant Church in Germany and Bread for the World.

Homer-Dixon, Thomas. 2006. *Upside of Down: Catastrophe, Creativity and the Renewal of Civilization.* Washington, DC: Island Press.

Hooper, C. 1998. "Masculinist Practices and Gender Politics: The Operation of Multiple Masculinities in International Relations." In *The "Man" Question in International Relations,* ed. M. Zalewski and J. Parpart. Boulder, CO: Westview Press.

Horn, Denise. 2010. "Moldova: Bringing Women into the Democratization Process." Radio Free Europe, January 12.

Hoskyns, Catherine, and Shirin M. Rai. 2008. "Recasting the Global Political Economy: Counting Women's Unpaid Work." *New Political Economy* 12, no. 3: 297–317.

Houghton, Rosalind M. E. 2010. *"We Had to Cope With What We Had": Agency Perspectives on Domestic Violence and Disasters in New Zealand.* Unpublished doctoral thesis submitted to Victoria University of Wellington.

Housing and Land Rights Network, Habitat International Coalition. 2005. *Post-Tsunami Relief and Rehabilitation: A Violation of Human Rights.* Report of a Fact-Finding Mission to Tsunami Affected Areas of Tamil-Nadu, India, and Sri Lanka. South Asia Regional Programme, August.

Hudson, Natalie Florea. 2009. "Securitizing Women's Human Rights." *Journal of Human Rights* 8, no. 1: 53–70.

The Huffington Post. 2011. "Rumana Monzur, UBC Student Attacked In Bangladesh, Returns to Vancouver." July 5.

Human Rights Documentation Unit and Burmese Women's Union. 2000. *Cycle of Suffering.* Bangkok: Human Rights Documentation Unit and Burmese Women's Union.

Human Rights Watch. 1997. *The Scars of Death: Children Abducted by the Lord's Resistance Army in Uganda.* New York: Human Rights Watch.

Human Rights Watch. 1998. *Too Little, Too Late: State Response to Violence Against Women. Report on Russia.* New York: Human Rights Watch.

Human Rights Watch. 2002. *The War Within the War: Sexual Violence Against Women & Girls in Eastern Congo,* June. New York: Human Rights Watch.

Human Rights Watch. 2008a. *Five Years On, No Justice for Sexual Violence in Darfur.* New York: Human Rights Watch.

Human Rights Watch. 2008b. "Protect Domestic Workers from Violence." News Release, November 24. http://www.hrw.org/news/2008/11/24/protect-domestic-workers-violence.

Hussein, A. 2000. *Sometimes There Is No Blood: Domestic Violence and Rape in Rural Sri Lanka.* Colombo: International Centre for Ethnic Studies.

IANSA Women's Network. 2010. "Renewed Energy for the Control Arms Campaign." *Bulletin No. 22,* April.

Ibanez, A. M., and A. Moya. 2006. "The Impact of Intra-State Conflict on Economic Welfare and Consumption Smoothing: Empirical Evidence for the Displaced Population in Colombia." *HiCN Working Paper 23.* University of Sussex, Falmer-Brighton.

Inman, Philip. 2010. "Iceland Exits Recession." *The Guardian*, December 7.

Institute for Justice and Democracy in Haiti (IJDH), Bureau des Avocats Internationaux, Lawyers' Earthquake Response Network, MADRE, TransAfrica Forum, University of Minnesota Law School Human Rights Litigation and Advocacy Clinic, University of Virginia School of Law International Human Rights Law Clinic and Human Rights Program. 2010. *Our Bodies Are Still Trembling: Haitian Women's Fight Against Rape*. Boston: Virginia School of Law, July.

Institute for Women's Policy Research. 2005. *The Women of New Orleans and the Gulf Coast: Multiple Disadvantages and Key Assets for Recovery Part I. Poverty, Race, Gender and Class*. Washington, DC: IWPR, October.

INSTRAW. 2007. "Gender, Remittances and Development: The Feminization of Migration." *Working Paper 1*.

International Helsinki Federation for Human Rights (IHF). 2000. *Women 2000*. Austria: IHF.

International Labour Office. 2003. *Governing Body: Committee on Employment and Social Policy. Third Item on the Agenda. Employment and Social Policy in Respect of Export Processing Zones (EPZs)*. GB 286/ESP/3 286th Session, Geneva, March.

International Labour Organization. 2010. *Decent Work for Domestic Workers: Fourth Item on the Agenda, Report IV(1)*. 99th Session of the International Labour Conference, Geneva, June.

International Labour Organization. 2011. *Making the Crisis Recovery Work for Women! International Women's Day 2011*. Geneva: Bureau for Gender Equality.

International Red Cross. 2004. *IRC Report on Violence against Women from 1998–2003*. Kigala: Ministry of Gender and Family Promotion.

Iredale, Robyn, and Nicola Piper. 2003. *Identification of the Obstacles to the Signing and Ratification of the UN Convention on the Protection of the Rights of All Migrant Workers: The Asia-Pacific Perspective*. UNESCO.

IRIN News. 2009. "DRC: Sexual Violence Prevention and re-integration funding 'falls through cracks,'" November 4.

IRIN News. 2011. "Congo—New Laws Have Minor Impact on Sexual Violence." June 7.

Jacobsen, Ruth. 2012. "Women and After War." In *Women and Wars*, ed. Carol Cohn. London: Polity Press.

Jauhola, Marjaana. 2010. "Building Back Better: Negotiating Normative Boundaries of Gender Mainstreaming and Post-Tsunami Reconstruction in Nanggroe Aceh Darussalam, Indonesia." *Review of International Studies* 36, no. 1: 29–50.

Jeffrey, Leslie A. 2002. *Sex and Borders: Gender, National Identity and Prostitution Policy in Thailand*. Vancouver: UBC Press.

Jenkins, Pam, and Brenda Phillips. 2008. "Battered Women, Catastrophe and the Context of Safety After Hurricane Katrina." *National Women's Studies Association Journal* 20, no. 3: 49–68.

Jennings, Kathleen M. 2008. *Protecting Whom? Approaches to sexual exploitation and abuse in UN peacekeeping operations*. Oslo: Fafo.

Jennings, Kathleen M., and Vesna Nikolić-Ristanović. 2009. "UN Peacekeeping Economies and Local Sex Industries: Connections and Implications." *MICROCON (Micro Level Analysis of Violent Conflict) Research Working Paper 176*, September, Institute of Development Studies at the University of Sussex.

Jewkes, Rachel. 2002. "Intimate Partner Violence: Causes and Prevention." *The Lancet* 359: 1423–29.

Jewkes, Rachel, and N. Abrahams. 2002. "The Epidemiology of Rape and Sexual Coercion in South Africa: An Overview." *Social Science and Medicine* 55: 1231–44.

Jewkes, Rachel, and Robert Morrell. 2010. "Gender and Sexuality: Emerging Perspectives From the Heterosexual Epidemic in South Africa and Implications for HIV Risk and Prevention." *Journal of the International AIDS Society* 13, no. 6: 1–11.

John's Hopkins University Center for Communication Programs (JHUCCP). 2011. "Brothers for Life Goes International." Press Release, June 16.

Johnson, H., N. Ollus, and S. Nevala. 2008. *Violence Against Women: An International Perspective*. New York: Springer.

Johnson, Janet Elise. 2007. "Domestic Violence Politics in Post-Soviet States." *Social Politics* 14, no. 3: 380–405.

Johnson, Kirsten, Jennifer Scott, Bigy Rughita, Michael Kisielewski, Jana Asher, Ricardo Ong, and Lynn Lawry. 2010. "Association of Sexual Violence and Human Rights Violations With Physical and Mental Health in Territories of the Eastern Democratic Republic of the Congo." *Journal of the American Medical Association* 304, no. 5: 553–62.

Jolly, David. 2010. "Iceland Emerged From Recession in Third Quarter." *New York Times*, December 7.

Jones, Adam. 2010. "Genocide and Mass Violence." In *Gender Matters in Global Politics*, ed. Laura J. Shepherd. New York: Routledge.

Jordan, Carol E. 2009. "Advancing the Study of Violence Against Women: Evolving Research Agendas Into Science." *Violence Against Women* 15: 393–419.

Justino, Patricia, and Philip Verwimp. 2006. *Poverty Dynamics, Violent Conflict and Convergence in Rwanda*. Brighton: Households in Conflict Network.

Kabutaulaka, T. T. 1997. *Logging in Solomon Islands*. Canberra: ANU.

KAFA. 2010. "The 2010 White Ribbon Campaign in Universities." Press Release, Beirut, Lebanon.

Karega, Regina G. M. 2002. *Violence Against Women in the Workplace in Kenya: Assessment of Workplace Sexual Harassment in the Commercial Agriculture and Textile Manufacturing Sectors in Kenya*. Washington, DC: International Labor Rights Fund.

Katz, Marisa, and Peg Hacskaylo. 2009. "No Recession for Domestic Violence." *Washington Post*, August 5.

Kaufman, Michael. 2001. "The White Ribbon Campaign: Involving Men and Boys in Ending Global Violence Against Women." In *A Man's World?: Changing Men's Practices in a Globalized World*, ed. Bob Pease and Keith Pringle. London: Zed Books.

Kaufman, Michelle, and Mary Crawford. 2011. "Research and Activism Review: Sex Trafficking in Nepal: A Review of Intervention and Prevention Programs." *Violence Against Women* 17, no. 5: 651–65.

Keck, Margaret, and Kathryn Sikkink. 1998. *Activists Beyond Borders: Advocacy Networks in International Politics*. Ithaca, NY: Cornell University Press.

Kelleher Associates and M. O'Connor. 1995. *Making the Links*. Dublin: Women's Aid.

Kelly, L. 2000. "Wars Against Women: Sexual Violence, Sexual Politics and the Militarized State." In *States of Conflict: Gender, Violence and Resistance*, ed. S. Jacobs, R. Jacobson, and J. Marchbank. London: Zed Books.

Kersten, Joachim. 1996. "Culture, Masculinities and Violence Against Women." *British Journal of Criminology 36*, no. 3: 381–95.

Khan, Irene. 2008. "Neither Violence Against Women Nor Poverty Are Inevitable." Statement by Irene Khan, Executive Director, Amnesty International, November 25.

Khan, Irene. 2009. *The Unheard Truth: Poverty and Human Rights.* New York: W.W. Norton & Company.

Khan, Sumera. 2011. "Women-Specific Bills Passed: Fourteen-Year Jail Term for Acid-Throwers." *Express Tribune*, December 13.

Kingdon, John W. 1995. *Agendas, Alternatives, and Public Policies.* 2nd ed. Boston: Little, Brown.

Kishor, S., and K. Johnson. 2004. *Profiling Domestic Violence: A Multi-Country Study.* Calverton, MD: ORC Macro.

Klein, Naomi. 2007. *The Shock Doctrine: The Rise of Disaster Capitalism.* New York: Metropolitan Books.

Kofman, Eleonore, and Parvati Raghuram. 2007. *The Implications of Migration for Gender and Care Regimes in the South.* Stockholm: UNRISD.

Kongar, Ebru. 2008. "Importing Equality or Exporting Jobs? Competition and Gender Wage and Employment Differentials in US Manufacturing." In *Feminist Economics of Trade*, ed. I. Van Staveren, D. Elson, C. Grown, and N. Cagatay. London: Routledge.

Koo, Katrina Lee. 2012. "Gender at the Crossroad of Conflict, Tsunami, and Peace in Post-2005 Aceh." *Feminist Review,* forthcoming.

Kristof, Nicholas, and Sheryl WuDunn. 2009. *Half the Sky: Turning Oppression Into Opportunity for Women Worldwide.* New York: Random House.

Krug, Etienne G., Linda L. Dahlberg, James A. Mercy, Anthony B. Zwi, and Rafael Lozano (eds.). 2002. *World Report on Violence and Health.* Geneva: World Health Organization.

Kruttschnitt, Candace, Brenda McLaughlin, and Carol Petrie. 2002. *Advancing the Federal Research Agenda on VAW.* Steering Committee for the Workshop on Issues in Research on VAW. Washington, DC: National Research Council on VAW, US Committee on Law and Justice; National Academies Press.

Kumar K. C. B., G. Subedi, Y. B. Gurung, and K. P. Adhikani. 2001. *Nepal Trafficking in Girls With Special Reference to Prostitution: A Rapid Assessment.* Geneva: ILO.

Kurtzleben, Danielle. 2009. "Sexual Violence in War Hauled Out of the Shadows." *IPS News,* June 16.

La Strada International. 2008. *Violation of Women's Rights: A Cause and Consequence of Trafficking in Women.* Amsterdam: La Strada International.

Lansink, A. 2001. "Human Rights Focus on Trafficked Women: An International Law and Feminist Perspective." *Agenda* (South Africa).

Larrain, S. 1999. "Curbing Domestic Violence: Two Decades of Action." In *Too Close to Home: Domestic Violence in the Americas*, ed. A. Morrison and M. Loreto Biehleds. Washington, DC: Inter-American Development Bank.

Levinson, David. 1989. *Family Violence in Cross-Cultural Perspective: Frontiers of Anthropology.* Thousand Oaks, CA: Sage Publications.

Lewis, Stephen. 2008. "Mass Rape Proceeds Apace in the Congo and Zimbabwe While the World Watches." Inaugural Julia Taft Lecture, hosted by the Women's Commission for Refugee Women and Children in New York, December 8.

Li, Q., and M. Wen. 2005. "The Immediate and Lingering Effects of Armed Conflict on Adult Mortality: A Time-Series Cross-National Analysis." *Journal of Peace Research* 42: 471–92.

Li, Shuzhuo. 2007. "Imbalanced Sex Ratio at Birth and Comprehensive Intervention in China." UNFPA Fourth Asia Pacific Conference on Reproductive and Sexual Health and Rights, Hyderabad, India, October 29–31.

Lievore, D. 2003. *Non Reporting and Hidden Recording of Sexual Assault in Australia.* Canberra: Australian Institute of Criminology.

Lievore, D. 2005. *No Longer Silent: A Study of Women's Help Seeking Decisions and Service Responses to Sexual Assault.* A report prepared by the Australian Institute of Criminology for the Australian Government's Office for Women. Canberra: Australian Institute of Criminology.

Lim, L. L. 1998. *The Sex Sector: The Economic and Social Bases of Prostitution in South East Asia.* Geneva: International Labour Office.

Lindegger, Graham, and Michael Quayle. 2010. "Masculinity and HIV/AIDS." In *HIV/AIDS in South Africa 25 years on: Psychosocial Perspectives,* ed. P. Rohleder et al., pp. 41–54, New York: Springer.

Lindsay, Bethany. 2011. "Damage to UBC Student's Eye Deemed 'Catastrophic.'" *CTV News,* July 14.

Livingstone, Jennifer. 2004. "Murder in Juarez." *Frontiers* 25, no. 1: 60.

Lobasz, Jennifer, and Laura Sjoberg. 2012. "Introduction. Critical Perspectives on Gender and Politics. The State of Feminist Security Studies: A Conversation." *Politics & Gender* 7, no. 4: 573–6.

Lobasz, Jennifer. 2010. "Beyond Border Security: Feminist approaches to human trafficking." In Gender and International Security ed. Laura Sjoberg. New York: Routledge: 214-234.

Luft, Rachel E. 2008. "Looking for Common Ground: Relief Work in Post-Katrina New Orleans as an American Parable of Race and Gender Violence." *National Women's Studies Association Journal* 20, no. 3 (Fall): 5–31.

Mackenzie, Megan. 2009. "Securitization and Desecuritization: Female Soldiers and the Reconstruction of Women in Post-Conflict Sierra Leone." *Security Studies* 18, no. 2: 241–61.

Manecksha, Freny. 2005. "Restructuring Society Post-Tsunami." *India Today,* June 3.

Manz, Beatriz. 2008. "The Continuum of Violence in Post-War Guatemala." *Social Analysis,* 52, no. 2 (Summer): 151–64.

Marchand, M., and A. S. Runyan. 2000. *Gender and Global Restructuring.* New York: Routledge.

Márquez, Humberto. 2011. "Armed Societies, Another Tragedy for Women," *IPS News,* December 9.

Marx, Karl. [1843] 1967. "Letter to A. Rugs, September 1843." In *Writings of the Young Marx on Philosophy and Society,* ed. and trans. Lloyd D. Easton and Kurt H. Guddats, 211–15. New York: Doubleday Anchor.

Mary Kay Inc. 2011. *Truth About Abuse.* Dallas: Mary Kay Inc.

Mazurana, Dyan, and Khristopher Carlson. 2008. "War Slavery—The Role of Children and Youth in Fighting Forces in Sustaining Armed Conflicts and War Economies in Africa." In *Gender, Violent Conflict, and Development,* ed. Dubravka Zarkov. New Delhi: Zubaan Press.

McKay, Susan, and Dyan Mazurana. 2004. *Where Are the Girls? Girls Fighting Forces in Northern Uganda, Sierra Leone and Mozambique: Their Lives During and After War*. Montréal and Québec: Rights and Democracy (International Centre for Human Rights and Democratic Development).

McKay, Susan, Malia Robinson, Maria Gonsalves, and Miranda Worthen. 2006. "Girls Formerly Asso- ciated with Fighting Forces and their Children: Returned and Neglected." In *Coalition to Stop the Use of Child Soldiers*. London, UK.

McKinley, Jesse. 2009. "Cuts Ravage California Domestic Abuse Program." *New York Times*, September 25.

MDRP and UNIFEM. 2005. *Workshop Report: Taking a Gender Perspective to Strengthen the Multi-Country Demobilization and Reintegration Program (MDRP) in the Great Lakes Region*, October 31–November 2, Kigali, Rwanda.

Meger, Sara. 2010. "Rape in the Congo: Understanding Sexual Violence in the Conflict in the Democratic Republic of Congo." *Journal of Contemporary African Studies* 28, no. 2: 119–35.

Menon, Nidhiya, and Yana van der Meulen Rodgers. 2011. "War and Women's Work: Evidence from Nepal." *Households in Conflict Network Working Paper*. Brighton: University of Sussex.

Merry, Sally Engle. 2006. *Human Rights & Gender Violence: Translating International Law Into Local Justice*. Chicago: University of Chicago Press.

Merry, Sally Engle. 2009. *Gender Violence: A Cultural Perspective*. Chichester: Wiley-Blackwell.

Ministry of Civil Defence and Emergency Management (MCDEM). 2008. *Mass Evacuation Planning, Director's Guidelines for Civil Defence Emergency Management Groups [DGL 07/08]*. Wellington, New Zealand: Ministry of Civil Defence and Emergency Management.

Mintrom, Michael, and Phillipa Norman. 2009. "Policy Entrepreneurship and Policy Change." *Policy Studies Journal* 37, no. 4: 649–67.

"Montreal Principles on Women's Economic, Social and Cultural Rights." 2004. *Human Rights Quarterly* 26, no. 3: 3–7.

Mooney, E. 2005. "The Concept of Internal Displacement and the Case for Internally Displaced Persons as a Category of Concern." *Refugee Survey Quarterly* 24, no. 3: 9–26.

Morrison, A. R., and M. B. Orlando. 1999. "Social and Economic Costs of Domestic Violence: Chile and Nicaragua." In *Too Close to Home: Domestic Violence in Latin America*, ed. A. Morrison and L. Biehl. Washington, DC: Inter-American Development Bank.

Moser, C., and F. Clark. 2001. *Victims, Perpetrators or Actors? Gender, Armed Conflict and Political Violence*. London: Zed Books.

Murray, Rebecca. 2011. "Female Trafficking Soars in Iraq." *IRIN News*, August 27.

National Council to Reduce Violence Against Women and their Children. 2009. *The Cost of Violence Against Women and their Children*. Canberra: Australian Department of Families, Housing, Community Services and Indigenous Affairs (FaHCSIA), March.

National Institute of Justice (NIJ). 2004. *When Violence Hits Home: How Economics and Neighborhood Play a Role*. Washington, DC: US Department of Justice, Office of Justice Programs.

National Network to End Domestic Violence (NNEDV). 2011. "Congress Approves Vital Funding for VAWA." Press Release, December 6.

Neumayer, Eric, and Thomas Plümper. 2007. "The Gendered Nature of Natural Disasters: The Impact of Catastrophic Events on the Gender Gap in Life Expectancy, 1981–2002." *Annals of the Association of American Geographers* 97, no. 3: 551–66.

New Zealand Herald. 2011a. "Christchurch Latest Updates." February 28.

New Zealand Herald. 2011b. "Domestic Violence Increases." March 5.

Nikolov, Paul. 2010. "Proportionately Greater Amount of Icelandic Women Report Rapes and Domestic Violence." *The Reikjavíic Grapevine*, March 30.

Nussbaum, Martha. 2005. "Women's Bodies: Violence, Security, Capabilities." *Journal of Human Development* 6, no. 2: 167–83.

OHCHR. 2011. *Report of the Panel on Remedies and Reparation for Victims of Sexual Violence in the Democratic Republic of Congo to the High Commissioner for Human Rights*. Geneva: Office of the High Commissioner on Human Rights, March.

O'Connor, Sarah. 2008. "Icelandic Women to Clean up 'Male Mess.'" *Financial Times*, October 13.

O'Hara, Ailish. 2010. "Surge in Domestic Violence Blamed on the Recession." *Irish Independent News*, June 3.

Okin, S. M. 1989. *Justice, Gender and the Family*. New York: Basic Books.

Ormhaug, Christin Marsh, Patrick Meier, and Helga Hernes. 2009. *Armed Conflict Deaths Disaggregated by Gender*. PRIO paper. Oslo: Prio.

Oxfam International. 2005. "The Tsunami's Impact on Women." Briefing Note, March.

Paci, Pierella. 2002. *Gender in Transition*. Washington, DC: World Bank, Eastern Europe and Central Asia Region, May 21.

Pacific Islands Forum Secretariat. 2008. *Gender Issues in Tuna Fisheries: Case Studies in Papua New Guinea, Fiji, and Kiribati*. Fishtech Consultants. Suva: SPC.

Pacific Network on Globalization (PANG). 2008. *Social Impact Assessment of the Economic Partnership Agreement (EPA) Being Negotiated between the European Community and Pacific ACP States*. Suva: PANG.

Pallen, D. 2003. "Sexual Slavery in Bosnia: an Externality of the Market." *Journal of International Affairs* 13, no. 1: 27–43.

Pankhurst, Donna. 2008. "Gendered Peace." In *Whose Peace?: Critical Perspectives on the Political Economy of Peacebuilding*, ed. M. Pugh, N. Cooper, and M. Turner, 30–46. Basingstoke: Palgrave.

Parbring, Boss. 2010. "Major Problem of Male Violence Against Women in the West Nordic Region." *NIKK: Nordic Gender Institute*, September 10.

Parrenas, R. S. 2001. *Servants of Globalization*. Stanford, CA: Stanford University Press.

Pascall, Gillian, and Nick Manning. 2000. "Gender and Social Policy: Comparing Welfare States in Central and Eastern Europe and the Former Soviet Union." *Journal of European Social Policy* 10: 240–66.

Patel, Reena. 2010. *Working the Night Shift: Women in India's Call Center Industry*. Palo Alto, CA: Stanford University Press.

Peterman, Amber, Tia Palermo, and Karen Bredenkamp. 2011. "Estimates and Determinants of Sexual Violence Against Women in the Democratic Republic of Congo." *America Journal of Public Health* 101, no. 6: 1060–67.

Peterson, V. S. 2003. *A Critical Rewriting of Global Political Economy*. New York: Routledge.

Pettifor, A. E., D. M. Maesham, H. V. Rees, and N. S. Padian. 2004. "Sexual Power and HIV Risk, South Africa." *Emerging Infectious Diseases* 10: 1996–2004.

Phongpaichit, P. 1997. "Trafficking in People in Thailand." *Trans-National Organized Crime* 3, no. 4: 14–104.

Physicians for Human Rights. 2002. *War-Related Sexual Violence in Sierra Leone: A Population-Based Assessment.* New York: Physicians for Human Rights, June.

Piper, Nicola. 2003. "Feminization of Labor Migration as Violence Against Women: International, Regional, and Local Nongovernmental Organization Responses in Asia." *Violence Against Women* 9, no. 6: 723–45.

PlusNews. 2008. "Kenya: Sex for Jobs in Export Processing Zones," November 24.

Poulin, Richard. 2003. "Globalization and the Sex Trade: Trafficking and the Commodification of Women and Children." *Canadian Women's Studies* 22, no. 3 and 4: 38–43.

Programme on Women's Economic, Social and Cultural Rights (PWSCR). 2010. *Concept Paper,* March 4. http://www.pwescr.org.

Prupis, Nadia. 2010. "White House Steps Up Efforts to Battle Domestic Violence." *Truth Out Report,* October 30. http://archive.truthout.org/white-house-steps-up-efforts-battle-domestic-violence64677.

Prugl, Elisabeth. 2012. "If Lehman Brothers Had Been Lehman Sisters . . .: Gender and Myth in the Aftermath of the Financial Crisis." *International Political Sociology* 6, no. 1: 21–35.

Pugh, Michael. 2004. "Peacekeeping and Critical Theory." *International Peacekeeping* 11, no. 1: 39–58.

Rabin, Roni Caryn. 2011. "Nearly 1 in 5 Women in U.S. Survey Say They Have Been Sexually Assaulted." *New York Times,* December 14.

Radio Australia. 2008. "Solomon Official Accuses Foreign Logging Companies of Exploitation." September 19.

Rake, Katherine. 2009. *Are Women Bearing the Burden of the Recession?* London: Fawcett Society.

Ramírez, Carlota, Mar García Domínguez, and Julia Míguez Morais. 2005. *Crossing Borders: Gender, Remittances and Development.* Santo Domingo: INSTRAW.

Rao, Arati. 1995. "The Politics of Gender and Culture in International Human Rights Discourse." In *Women's Rights, Human Rights: International Feminist Perspectives,* ed. Julie Peters and Andrea Wolper. New York: Routledge.

Rao, V., and M. Bloch. 1993. *Wife-Beating, Its Causes and Its Implications for Nutrition Allocation to Children: An Economic and Anthropological Case Study of a Rural South-Indian Community.* Research Report, No. 93–298. Ann Arbor: University of Michigan, Population Studies Center.

Raworth, Kate. 2004. *Trading Away Our Rights: Women Working in Global Supply Chains.* Oxford: Oxfam International.

Red Mesa de Mujeres de Ciudad Juarez A. C. and Comite de America Latina y el Caribe para la Defensa de los Derechos de la Mujer (CLADEM). 2010. *Cotton Field: Proposals for Analysis and Monitoring of the "Cotton Field" Case Sentence, Regarding Human Rights Violations Committed by the Mexican State.* Mexico City: CLADEM.

Reed, Elizabeth, Anita Raj, Elizabeth Miller, and Jay G. Silverman. 2010. "Gender-Based Violence: The Missteps of Research on Dating and Intimate Partner Violence." *Violence Against Women* 16, no. 3: 348–54.

Rehn, Elisabeth, and Ellen Johnson Sirleaf. 2002. *Women, War and Peace: The Independent Experts' Assessment on the Impact of Armed Conflict on Women and Women's Role in Peace-building*. New York: UNIFEM.

Reinelt, Claire. 1995. "Moving Onto the Terrain of the State: The Battered Women's Movement and the Politics of Engagement." In *Feminist Organizations: Harvest of the New Women's Movement*, ed. Mayra Marx Feree and Patricia Yancey Martin. Philadelphia: Temple University Press.

Remenyi, Maria A. 2007. *The Multiple Faces of the Intersections between HIV and Violence against Women: Development Connections*. Washington, DC: Development Connections, UNIFEM, Pan American Health Organization, Inter-American Commission of Women, and the Latin American and Caribbean Women's Health Network.

Renzetti, Claire M. 2009 "Economic Stress and Domestic Violence." *National Resource Center on Violence Against Women*, September: 1–15.

Republic of South Africa (RSA). 2010. *Country Progress Report on the Declaration of Commitment on HIV/AIDS: 2010 Report*. UNAIDS. http://www.unaids.org/. . ./monitoringcountryprogress/.

Richburg, Keith B. 2009. "China/Burma Border Town Is New Front Line in Human Trafficking." *Washington Post*, December 26.

Rivers, J. P. W. 1982. "Women and Children Last: An Essay on Sex Discrimination in Disasters." *Disasters* 6, no. 4: 256–67.

Roberts, Angela Raven. 2012. "Political Economy of War." In *Women and Wars*, ed. Carol Cohn. London: Polity Press.

Rofi, Abdur, Shannon Doocy, and Courtland Robinson. 2006. "Tsunami Mortality and Displacement in Aceh Province, Indonesia." *Disasters* 30, no. 3: 340–50.

Romany, C. 1994. "State Responsibility Goes Private: A Feminist Critique of the Public/Private Distinction." In *Human Rights of Women—National and International Perspectives*, ed. R. J Cook. Philadelphia: University of Pennsylvania Press.

Rombouts, Heidi. 2006. "Women and Reparations in Rwanda: A Long Path to Travel." In *What Happened to the Women? Gender and Reparations for Human Rights Violations*, ed. Ruth Rubio-Marin. New York: Social Science Research Council.

Roth, Francoise. 2010. *OHCHR Expert Workshop on the Elimination of Violence Against Women*, United Nations, Geneva, November 24–25.

Roth, Francoise, Tamy Guberek, and Amelia Hoover Green. 2011. *Using Quantitative Data to Assess Conflict-Related Sexual Violence in Colombia*. Benetech and Corporacion Puntodevista, March 22.

Rubenstein, L. S. 2004. "How International Human Rights Organizations Can Advance Economic, Social and Cultural Rights: A Response to Kenneth Roth." *Human Rights Quarterly* 26, no. 4: 845–65.

Rubio-Marin, Ruth (ed.). 2006. *What Happened to the Women? Gender and Reparations for Human Rights Violations*. New York: Social Science Research Council.

Rust, Selina. 2010. "Climate Change: UN Boys Club." *IPS News*, March 18.

SANAC Women's Sector. 2010. *Report on Progress with the UNGASS Goals on Sexual and Reproductive Health, Phase II-2009/10*, January.

Sanday, P. R. 1981. "The Socio-Cultural Context of Rape: A Cross-Cultural Study." *Journal of Social Issues* 37: 5–27.

Sarson, J., and L. MacDonald. 2009. "Torturing by Non-State Actors Invisibilized, A Patriarchal Divide and Spillover Violence from the Military Sphere into the Domestic Sphere." *Peace Studies Journal* 2, no. 2: 16–38.

Sassen, Saskia. 2008. "Strategic Instantiations of Gendering in the Global Economy: The Feminizing of Survival." Unpublished paper prepared for the Expert Consultation on Political Economy and Women's Rights, convened by the Special Rapporteur of the United Nations Human Rights Council on Violence Against Women, Its Causes and Consequences, Istanbul, May 8–9.

Save the Children Fund. 2008. *No One to Turn To—The Under-Reporting of Child Sexual Exploitation and Abuse by Aid Workers and Peacekeepers*. London: Save the Children Fund, May.

Schafer, S. D., L. L. Drach, K. Hedberg, and M. A. Kohn. 2008. "Using Diagnostic Codes to Screen for Intimate Partner Violence in Oregon Emergency Departments and Hospitals." *Public Health Reports* 123: 628–35.

Scheper-Hughes, Nancy. 1995. "Primacy of the Ethical: Propositions for a Militant Anthropology." *Current Anthropology* 36, no. 6: 409–20.

Scheper-Hughes, Nancy, and Philippe I. Bourgois (eds.). 2004. *Violence in War and Peace: An Anthology*. London: Blackwell.

Schindler, K. 2010. "Who Does What in a Household After Genocide? Evidence from Rwanda." *DIW Discussion Paper 1072* (also appeared as *HiCN Working Paper 90*). http://ideas.repec.org/p/diw/diwwpp/dp1072.html.

Schroeder, Emily. 2005. "Multi-country Demobilization and Reintegration Program (MDRP) Gender Desk Study." Washington DC: World Bank.

Schuler, S. R., S. M. Hashemi, and S. H. Badal. 1998. "Men's Violence Against Women in Bangladesh: Undermined or Exacerbated by Microcredit Programmes?" *Development in Practice* 8, no. 2: 148–57.

Seager, J. 2006. "Noticing Gender (or Not) in Disasters." *Geoforum* 37, no. 1: 2–3.

Seager, Joni. 2008. *The Penguin Atlas of Women in the World*, 4th ed. New York: Penguin Books.

Segrave, Marie, Sanja Milivojevic, and Sharon Pickering. 2009. *Sex Trafficking: International Context and Response*. Portland: Willan Publishing.

Seguino, Stephanie. 2000. "Accounting for Gender in Asian Economic Growth." *Feminist Economics* 6, no. 3: 27–58.

Seguino, Stephanie. 2008. "The Road to Gender Equality: Global Trends and the Way Forward." In *Social Justice and Gender Equality: Rethinking Development Strategies and Macroeconomic Policies*, ed. G. Berik, Y. Rodgers, and A. Zammit, 44–69. New York: Routledge.

Seguino, Stephanie. 2009. "The Global Economic Crisis and Its Gender Implications." Written statement to the Interactive Expert Panel on Emerging Issues: The Gender Perspectives on the Financial Crisis, held at the Commission on the Status of Women, 53rd Session, New York, March 2–13.

Senanayake, Shimali. 2006. "An Ethnic War Slows Tsunami Recovery in Sri Lanka." *New York Times*, October 18.

Sharma, Manasi. 2009. "Recession-Related Domestic Violence on the Rise." *Global Envision*, April 10.

Shepherd, Laura. 2008. "Power and Authority in the Production of United Nations Security Council Resolution 1325." *International Studies Quarterly* 52, no. 2: 383–404.

Shisana, O., T. Rehle, L. C. Simbayi, W. Parker, K. Zuma, A. Bhana, C. Connolly, S. Jooste, and V. Pillay. 2005. *South African National HIV Prevalence, HIV Incidence, Behavior and Communication Survey*. Cape Town: HSRC Press.

Simic, Olivera. 2010. "Does the Presence of Women Really Matter? Towards Combating Male Sexual Violence in Peacekeeping Operations." *International Peacekeeping* 17, no. 2: 188–99.

Singh, J. P and Shilpa A. Hart. 2007 "Sex Workers and Cultural Policy: Mapping the Issues and Actors in Thailand" *Review of Policy Research* 24, 2: 155–173.

Sjoberg, Laura (ed.). 2010. *Gender and International Security: Feminist Perspectives*. New York: Routledge.

Snider, Laureen. 1998. "Towards Safer Societies: Punishment, Masculinities and Violence Against Women." *British Journal of Criminology* 38, no. 1: 2–39.

Sonke Gender Justice Network Website. 2011. "Fatherhood." http://www.men-care.org/prospectus.

Special Rapporteur on Adequate Housing. 2011. *Report of the Special Rapporteur on Adequate Housing as a Component of the Right to an Adequate Standard of Living*, A/66/270, August 5.

Squires, Gregory, and Chester Hartman (eds.). 2006. *There Is No Such Thing as a Natural Disaster: Race, Class and Katrina*. New York: Routledge.

SRVAW. 2000. *Report of the Special Rapporteur on Violence Against Women, Its Causes and Consequences, Radhika Coomaraswamy to the Human Rights Council. Submitted in Accordance With Commission on Human Rights Resolution 1997/44: Trafficking in Women, Women's Migration and Violence Against Women. E/CN.4/2000/68*. Geneva: United Nations, February 29.

SRVAW. 2001. *Report of the Special Rapporteur on Violence Against Women, Its Causes and Consequences, Radhika Coomaraswamy to the Human Rights Council: Violence Against Women Perpetrated and/or Condoned by the State During Times of Armed Conflict. E/CN.4/2001/73*. Geneva: United Nations, January 23.

SRVAW. 2004. *Report of the Special Rapporteur on Violence Against Women, Its Causes and Consequences, Yakin Ertürk to the Human Rights Council: Mission to El Salvador. E/CN.4/2005/72/Add.2*. Geneva: United Nations, December 20.

SRVAW. 2005a. *Report of the Special Rapporteur on Violence Against Women, Its Causes and Consequences, Yakin Ertürk to the Human Rights Council: Mission to Occupied Palestinian Territory. E/CN.4/2005/72/Add.4*. Geneva: United Nations, February 2.

SRVAW. 2005b. *Report of the Special Rapporteur on Violence Against Women, Its Causes and Consequences, Yakin Ertürk to the Human Rights Council: Mission to Guatemala. E/CN.4/2005/72/Add.3*. Geneva: United Nations, February 10.

SRVAW. 2006a. *Report of the Special Rapporteur on Violence Against Women, Its Causes and Consequences, Yakin Ertürk to the Human Rights Council: Mission to Afghanistan. E/CN.4/2006/61/Add.5*. Geneva: United Nations, February 15.

SRVAW. 2006b. *Report of the Special Rapporteur on Violence Against Women, Its Causes and Consequences, Yakin Ertürk to the Human Rights Council: Mission to Mexico. E/CN.4/2006/61/Add.4*. Geneva: United Nations, January 13.

SRVAW. 2006c. *Report of the Special Rapporteur on Violence Against Women, Its Causes and Consequences, Yakin Ertürk to the Human Rights Council: Mission to the Russian Federation. E/CN.4/2006/61/Add.2*. Geneva: United Nations, January 26.

SRVAW. 2006d. *Report of the Special Rapporteur on Violence Against Women, Its Causes and Consequences, Yakin Erturk to the Human Rights Council: The Due Diligence as a Tool for the Elimination of Violence Against Women*. E/CN.4/2006/61. Geneva: United Nations, January 20.

SRVAW. 2007. *Report of the Special Rapporteur on Violence Against Women, Its Causes and Consequences, Yakin Erturk to the Human Rights Council: Intersections Between Culture and Violence Against Women*. A/HRC/4/34. Geneva: United Nations, January 17.

SRVAW. 2008a. *Report of the Special Rapporteur on Violence Against Women, Its Causes and Consequences, Yakin Ertürk to the Human Rights Council: Mission to Democratic Republic of Congo*. A/HRC/7/6/Add.4. Geneva: United Nations, February 28.

SRVAW. 2008b. *Report of the Special Rapporteur on Violence Against Women, Its Causes and Consequences, Yakin Ertürk, to the Human Rights Council: Indicators on Violence Against Women and State Responses*. A/HRC/7/6. Geneva: United Nations, June.

SRVAW. 2011. *Report of the United Nations Special Rapporteur on Violence Against Women, Its Causes and Consequences, Rashida Manjoo: Addendum: Mission to the United States of America*. A/HRC/17/26/Add.5. Geneva, United Nations, June 6.

Stack, Sarah. 2011. "Recession Blamed for Massive Increase in Domestic Violence." *Irish Independent*, August 29.

Stanko, Elizabeth A. 2006. "Theorizing About Violence: Observations from the Economic and Social Research Council's Violence Research Program." *Violence Against Women* 12: 543–55.

Staudt, Kathleen. 2009. *Violence and Activism at the Border: Gender, Fear, And Everyday Life In Ciudad Juarez*. Austin: University of Texas Press.

Stylianou, Georgina. 2011. "Drinking at Home Fans Rise in Domestic Abuse." *Dominion Post*, May 19.

Sullivan, B. 2003. "Trafficking in Women: Feminism and New International Law." *International Feminist Journal of Politics* 5, no. 1: 67–91.

Sullivan, N., and V. Ram-Bidesi. 2008. "Gender Issues in Tuna Fisheries, Case Studies in PNG, Fiji and Kiribati." *Pacific Islands Forum Secretariat Report*.

Sullivan, Nancy. 2005. "Fishy Business: The Social Impact of the South Seas Tuna Company in Wewak ESP." Wewak: Help Resources.

Sulzberger, A. G. 2011. "Facing Cuts, a City Repeals Its Domestic Violence Law." *New York Times*, October 11.

Sutton, Barbara. 2010. *Bodies in Crisis: Culture, Violence, and Women's Resistance in Neoliberal Argentina*. Rutgers, NJ: Rutgers University Press.

Sweetman, Caroline. 2008. "Feminist Economics." In *From Poverty to Power: How Active Citizens and Effective States Can Change the World*. London: Oxfam International.

Sydney Morning Herald. 2011. "French Rivals Reject DSK 'Set-Up Plot.'" November 29.

Taylor, Ian, and Ruth Jamieson. 1999. "Sex Trafficking and the Mainstream of Market Culture." *Crime, Law and Social Change* 32: 257–78.

The Telegraph. 2005. "Women on Top." Calcutta India, July 31.

The Telegraph. 2007. "UN Staff Accused of Raping Children in Sudan." January 4.

Tetrault, M-A., 2003. "Kuwait: Sex, Violence and the Politics of Economic Restructuring", in *Women and globalization in the Arab Middle East: gender, economy and society*, Boulder: Lynne Rienner Publishers.

Theidon, Kimberly. 2011 (2004). *Intimate Enemies: Violence and Reconciliation in Peru.* Stanford, CA: Stanford University Press.

Tickner, J. Ann. 1992. *Gender in International Relations: Feminist Perspectives on Achieving Global Security.* New York: Columbia University Press.

Tickner, J. Ann. 1995. "Introducing Feminist Perspectives Into Peace and World Security Courses." *Women's Studies Quarterly* 23, no. 3–4: 48–57.

Tjaden, P., and N. Thoennes. 2000. *Extent, Nature and Consequences of Intimate Partner Violence: Findings From the National Violence Against Women Survey.* Washington, DC: National Institute of Justice, Centers for Disease Control and Prevention.

Tolerton, Nick. 2011. "Quake Stress Takes Its Toll." *The Star*, August 8.

Toope, Stephen J. 2011. "Update: UBC Responds to Rumana Monzur Attack." Vancouver: Office of President of the University of British Colombia, June 21.

Toosi, Nahal. 2010. "Pakistan—Proposed Domestic Violence Law Divisive." *Associated Press*, April 8.

Towers, Jude, and Sylvia Walby. 2012. *Measuring the Impact of Cuts in Public Expenditure on the Provision of Services to Prevent Violence Against Women and Girls.* London: Trust for London and Northern Rock Foundation.

True, Jacqui. 2003. *Gender, Globalization and Post-socialism.* New York: Columbia University Press.

True, Jacqui. 2009a. "The Political Economy of Women's Human Rights." In *Special Rapporteur on Violence Against Women, Its Causes and Consequences Annual Report to Human Rights Council. A/HRC/11/6/Add.6.* Geneva: United Nations, May 26.

True, Jacqui. 2009b. "Gender Mainstreaming in International Institutions." In *Gender Matters in Global Politics*, ed. Laura. J. Shepherd. New York: Routledge.

True, Jacqui. 2010. "The Political Economy of Violence Against Women." *The Australian Feminist Law Journal* 32 (June): 39–59.

True, Jacqui, and Michael Mintrom. 2001. "Transnational Networks and Policy Diffusion: The Case of Gender Mainstreaming." *International Studies Quarterly* 45, no. 1: 27–57.

Truong, T. D. 1990. *Sex, Money and Morality: Prostitution and Tourism in Southeast Asia.* London: Zed Books.

Truong, T. D. 2001a. "A Feminist Perspective on the Asian Miracle and Crisis: Enlarging the Conceptual Map of Human Development." *Journal of Human Development* 1, no. 1: 159–64.

Truong, T. D. 2001b. "Organised Crime and Human Trafficking." In *Transnational Organized Crime: Myths, Power and Profit*, ed. E. Viano, J. Magallanes, and Laurent Brid. Durham, NC: Carolina Academic Press.

Turner, Anna. 2011 "5 Minutes With: Nicola Woodward: CEO of Christchurch Women's Refuge." *The Star*, July 17.

Turshen, M. 2000. "The Political Economy of Violence Against Women During Armed Conflict in Uganda." *Social Research* 63, no. 3 (Fall): 803–25.

UN Global Compact/UNIFEM. 2010. *Women's Empowerment Principles: Equality Means Business.* http://www.unifem.org.au/LiteratureRetrieve.aspx?ID=69759.

UN INSTRAW. 2009. *Women, Peace & Security in Liberia: Supporting the Implementation of Resolution 1325 in Liberia.* Background Paper. March 10.

UNAIDS. 2009. *South Africa: Country Situation 2009*. Geneva: UNAIDS.

UNDP. 2010. *Power, Voice, and Rights: A Turning Point for Gender Equality in Asia and the Pacific*. New Delhi: McMillan Publishers India Ltd.

UNESCAP (United Nations Economic and Social Commission for Asia-Pacific). 2006. *Commercial Sexual Exploitation of Children (CSEC) and Child Sexual Abuse (CSA) in the Pacific: A Regional Report*. Bangkok: UNESCAP.

UNESCAP. 2009. *Pacific Perspectives on the Sexual Exploitation of Children and Youth*. Bangkok: UNESCAP.

United Nations Population Fund. 2006. *The State of the World's Population: The Good, The Bad, The Promising: Migration in the 21st Century*. New York: UNFPA.

United Nations Population Fund. 2007a. "Asian Son Preference Will Have Severe Social Consequences, New Studies Warn." Website Press Release, October 29. http://asiapacific.unfpa.org/public/site/global/lang/en/pid/301.

United Nations Population Fund. 2007b. *Dispatches from Darfur: Caring for the Ones Who Care for Others*. New York: UNFPA.

United Nations Population Fund. 2008. *The State of the World Population 2008: Culture, Gender, and Human Rights*. New York: UNFPA.

United Nations Population Fund Asia and Pacific Regional Office. 2010. *Health Sector Response to Gender Based Violence: Case Studies of the Asia Pacific Region*. Bangkok: UNFPA.

UNICEF. 1989. *The Invisible Adjustment: Poor Women and Economic Crisis*. Santiago: UNICEF, The Americas and Caribbean Regional Office.

UNICEF. 1999. *Women in Transition, Regional Monitoring Report, No. 6*. Florence: UNICEF International Child Development Centre.

UNICEF. 2000. "Domestic Violence Against Women and Girls." In *Innocenti Digest 6*. Florence: UNICEF Innocenti Research Centre.

UNIFEM. 2005. *The World's Women: Progress in Statistics*. New York: United Nations.

UNIFEM. 2010. *Women's Participation in Peace Negotiations: Connections Between Presence and Influence*. New York.

United Nations. 2007. *Violence against women migrant workers: Report of the Secretary-General*, Sixty-Second Session, A/62/177. New York.

United Nations Department of Economic and Social Affairs. 2009. *World Survey on the Role of Women in Development*. New York: United Nations.

United Nations Development Programme. 2010. *The Price of Peace: Financing for Gender Equality in Postconflict Reconstruction*. New York: United Nations.

United Nations Economic and Social Council. 2010. *Commission on the Status of Women Fifty-Fourth Session*, March 1–12, Agenda item 3 (c) Women's Economic Empowerment, E/CN.6/2010/L.5.

United Nations General Assembly. 2006. *Ensuring the Accountability of United Nations Staff and Experts on Mission with Respect to Criminal Acts Committed in Peacekeeping Operations*. UN Doc. A/60/980, August 16.

United Nations Global Compact. 2010. "Companies Leading the Way: Putting the Principles Into Practices." http://www.unglobalcompact.org/docs/issues_doc/human_rights/Resources/Companies_Leading_the_Way.pdf.

United Nations News Center. 2009. "Women Must Play Full Part in Peace-Building, Security Council Declares." News Release, October 5.

United Nations Secretary-General. 2003. Secretary-General's Bulletin: Special Measures for Protection From Sexual Exploitation and Sexual Abuse. UN Doc. ST/SGB/2003/13, October 9.

United Nations Secretary-General. 2006. *United Nations Secretary-General's (SG) In-Depth Study on Violence Against Women. A/61/122/Add.1.* New York: United Nations.

United Nations Secretary-General. 2009. *Opening Statement to the Security Council SG/SM/12517/SC/9760/Wom/1760.* New York: United Nations.

UNODC (Office for Drugs and Crime). 2009. *UN Global Report on Trafficking in Persons 2009.* New York: United Nations.

US Department of Justice. 2009. "More Than 1,200 Alleged Incidents of Human Trafficking Reported in the U.S.," January 15. http://bjs.ojp.usdoj.gov/index.cfm?ty=pbdetail&;iid=364.

US State Department, Office of Senior Coordinator for International Women's Issues. 2005. "U.S. Commitment to Women in Iraq." http://www.state.gov/g/wi/rls/48464.htm.

US State Department. 2005 CRS Report for Congress. Women in Iraq: Background and Issues for U.S. Policy. (Aaron D. Pina (Analyst in Middle East Religion and Cultural Affairs Foreign Affairs, Defense, and Trade Division). Washington DC, June 23.

USAID. 2005. *Fact Sheet 39 Indian Ocean—Earthquakes and Tsunamis.* July 7.

Varia, N. 2007. "Globalization Comes Home: Protecting Migrant Domestic Workers' Rights." In *Human Rights Watch World Report 2007.* New York: Human Rights Watch.

Violence Policy Center. 2010. *When Men Murder Women: An Analysis of 2008 Homicide Data.* Washington, DC: Violence Policy Center, September.

Vunisea, A. 2005. "Women's Changing Roles in the Subsistence Fishing Sector in Fiji." In *Pacific Voices: Equity and Sustainability in Pacific Island Fisheries,* ed. I. Novaczek, J. Mitchell, and J. Veitayaki, pp. 88–104. Suva, Fiji: Institute of Pacific Studies, University of South Pacific.

Walby, Sylvia, and Jonathan Allen. 2004. *Domestic Violence, Sexual Assault and Stalking: Findings from the British Crime Survey.* Home Office Research Study 276. London: Home Office.

Walker, Liz. 2005. "Men Behaving Differently: South African Men Since 1994." *Culture, Health and Sexuality* 7, no. 3: 225–38.

Wandita, Gulah, Karen Campbell-Nelson, and Manuela Leong Pereira. 2006. "Learning to Engender Reparations in Timor-Leste: Reaching out to Female Victims." In *What Happened to the Women? Gender and Reparations for Human Rights Violations,* ed. R. Rubio-Marin, 284–335. New York: Social Science Research Council.

Wardrop, Murray. 2008. "Recession Will Prompt Rise in Domestic Violence." *The Telegraph,* December 20.

Warner, Judith. 2010. "What the Great Recession Has Done to Family Life." *New York Times,* August 6.

Washington Post. 2005. "UN Faces More Accusations of Sexual Misconduct: Officials Acknowledge 'Swamp' of Problems and Pledge Fixes Amid New Allegations in Africa, Haiti." March 13, p. A22.

Watts, C., and C. Zimmerman. 2002. "Violence Against Women: Global Scope and Magnitude." *The Lancet* 359, no. 9313: 1232–37.

WEDO. 2008. *Gender, Climate Change and Human Security: Lessons from Baghdad, Ghana and Senegal.* New York: Women's Environment and Development Organization, May.

Weiler, Jonathan. 2004. *Human Rights in Russia: A Darker Side of Reform.* Boulder, CO: Lynne Rienner Publishers.

Weiss, Cora. 2011. Speech at the Novel Women's Initiative conference on ending sexual violence in conflict, Ottawa, May 24. http://www.opendemocracy.net.

Weissman, Deborah. 2004–2005. "The Political Economy of Violence: Toward an Understanding of the Gender-Based Murders of Ciudad Juarez." *North Carolina Journal of International Law and Commercial Regulation* 30 (Summer): 796–867.

Weissman, Deborah. 2007. "The Personal Is Political—and Economic: Rethinking Domestic Violence." *Brigham Young University Law Review* 2007: 387–450.

Weldon, Laurel. 2006. "Inclusion, Solidarity and Social Movement: The Global Movement Against Gender Violence." *Perspectives on Politics* 4, no. 1: 55–74.

White Ribbon Ride. 2011. *North Island Itinerary.* http://www.whiteribbon.org.nz.

Whitworth, Sandra. 2004. *Men, Militarism and UN Peacekeeping: A Gendered Analysis.* Boulder, CO: Lynne Rienner.

WHO Regional Office for Europe and Instituto Superiore di Sanita. 2001. *Violence Against Women in Situations of Armed Conflict.* Workshop Report, Naples, Italy, October 12–13.

Whyte, D. 2009. "Naked Labour: Putting Agamben to Work." *Australian Feminist Law Journal* 31: 57–76.

Wiest, R. E., J. S. P. Mocellin, and D. T. Motsisi. 1994. *The Needs of Women in Disasters and Emergencies.* Report prepared for the United Nations Development Program, Disaster Management Training Program, and the Office of the United Nations Disaster Relief Coordinator, University of Manitoba Disaster Research Institute, Winnipeg, Canada.

Willett, Susan. 2010. "Introduction: Security Council Resolution 1325: Assessing the Impact on Women, Peace and Security." *International Peacekeeping* 17, no. 2: 142–58.

Wilson, J. B. Phillips, and D. Neal. 1998. "Domestic Violence After Disaster." In *The Gendered Terrain of Disaster: Through Women's Eyes*, ed. E. Enarson and B. H. Morrow, 115–23. Westport, CT: Praeger.

Women, Health and Development Program and Pan American Health Organization. 2004. *Trafficking of Women and Children for Sexual Exploitation in the Americas.* Washington, DC: Women, Health and Development Program and Pan American Health Organization.

Women Without Borders. 2010. "Pakistan—Acid Attacks are Increasing—Burning Gender Injustice." May 4. http://www.humanrights.asia/news/forwarded-news/AHRC-FPR-023-2010.

Women's Aid. 2009. *Recession Traps Women in Abusive Relationships.* Dublin: Women's Aid.

Women's Aid. 2011. *Submission to the Department of Environment, Community and Local Government.* Dublin: Women's Aid, August 5.

Women's Grid. 2011. "Recession Blamed for Domestic Violence Increase." August 1, http://womensgrid.freecharity.org.uk/?p=7882.

Women's International League for Peace and Freedom (WILPF). 2007. "Discrimination and Violence Against Workers in the Cavite Export Processing Zone in the Philippines," Geneva: WILPF, December 13.

Women's Initiatives for Gender Justice (ICC) and Nobel Women's Initiative. 2010. *International Gender Justice Dialogue*, Puerto Vallarta, Mexico, April 20–21.

Women's Refugee Commission. 2007. *Room to Maneuver: Lessons from Gender Mainstreaming in the UN Department of Peacekeeping Operations*. A study by the Women's Commission for Refugee Women and Children, January, New York.

World Bank. 2003. *Breaking the Conflict Trap: Civil War and Development Policy. Policy Research Report*. Washington, DC: World Bank and Oxford University Press.

World Bank. 2006. *Gender Equality as Smart Economics: A World Bank Group Gender Action Plan (Fiscal Years 2007–2010)*. Washington, DC: World Bank, September.

World Bank. 2007. *Global Monitoring Report: Promoting Gender Equality and Women's Empowerment*. Washington, DC: World Bank.

World Bank. 2011. *World Development Report 2011: Conflict, Security and Development*. Washington, DC: World Bank.

WHO. (2005). *Multi-Country Study on Women's Health and Domestic Violence against Women*, Geneva. Available at: http://www.who.int/gender/violence/who_multi-country_study/Cover.pdf

World Health Organization. 2007. *Engaging Men and Boys in Changing Gender-Based Inequity in Health: Evidence from Programme Interventions*. Geneva: World Health Organization.

World Health Organization. 2010. *Preventing Violence Against Women and Eliminating Sexual Violence*. Geneva: World Health Organization.

World Health Organization. 2010. *Promoting Gender Equality to Prevent Violence Against Women*. Geneva: World Health Organization.

World Health Organization, OHCHR, UNFPA, UNICEF, UN Women. 2011. *Preventing Gender-Biased Sex Selection: An Inter-Agency Statement*. Geneva: World Health Organization.

Young, Brigitte. 2003. "Financial Crises and Social Reproduction: Asia, Argentina and Brazil." In *Power, Production and Reproduction*, ed. I. Bakker and S. Gill, 103–23. New York: Palgrave.

Young, Brigitte and Helene Schuberth. 2010. The Global Financial Meltdown And The Impact Of Financial Governance On Gender. Garnet Policy Brief, No. 10, January.

Younnis, Jumanah. 2011. "Egypt's Revolution Means Nothing If Its Women Are Not Free." *The Guardian*, March 9.

Zuckerman, Elaine, Elise Young, and Lisa Vitale. 2010. *World Bank and Inter-American Development Bank: Haiti Post-Earthquake Track Record on Gender, Agriculture and Rural Development*. Washington, DC: Gender Action.

CPSIA information can be obtained at www.ICGtesting.com
Printed in the USA
BVOW07s1420041214

377714BV00001B/5/P